MW01436095

Reaching Out To Joy
Jesus Over You

by
Father John Amsberry

Bloomington, IN   Milton Keynes, UK
authorHOUSE®

AuthorHouse™
1663 Liberty Drive, Suite 200
Bloomington, IN 47403
www.authorhouse.com
Phone: 1-800-839-8640

AuthorHouse™ UK Ltd.
500 Avebury Boulevard
Central Milton Keynes, MK9 2BE
www.authorhouse.co.uk
Phone: 08001974150

© 2007 Father John Amsberry. All rights reserved.

No part of this book may be reproduced, stored in a retrieval system, or transmitted by any means without the written permission of the author.

First published by AuthorHouse 3/14/2007

ISBN: 978-1-4259-9350-4 (sc)
ISBN: 978-1-4259-9417-4 (hc)

Printed in the United States of America
Bloomington, Indiana

This book is printed on acid-free paper.

Photography copyrighted Jeanne Hatch, no photos in this book may be reproduced in any form without written permission of the photographer.

Dedication

This book is dedicated to my Mom and Dad, Lorraine and Mel Amsberry, who raised eight boys and have been married over fifty-six years. The surest sign of God's love to me is how Mom and Dad have loved and forgave and stayed faithful to each other in the sacrament of marriage all these years in raising all of us boys. To see them holding each others hands and loving each other more now than ever is a most beautiful sight. I love you, Mom and Dad!

Thanksgiving

I thank God who, through the power of the Holy Spirit, gives us every loving and wise word we think, say and write. I have prayed that the words in this book are The Holy Spirit's. A mountain of thanks to Theresa Rivelli who has put countless hours into this book from finding my publisher, to collating, typing, and editing all the material. This book would not be in your hands without all her effort. Thanks to Eileen Pettycrew and Cheryl Ellis who gave me very helpful feedback in terms of how to present the material. For all the beautiful artwork, I thank Jeanne Hatch.

Contents

Dedication	v
Thanksgiving	vii
Introduction	1
JOY – Jesus Over You	5
Blessed	7
Reaching Out	9
You are Loved!	11
You Are the Pearl of Great Price	13
Say "No" to Wrath	14
Surrender	15
Only God is Good – All the Time	17
Money, Sports and Peace	18
Who Are Your John the Baptist's?	19
Give Without Counting the Cost	21
R U on the Right Road?	23
Do Not be Afraid -- Come Out of Hiding	25
So John Gave In	27
Go With the Flow?	29
Be A Sacrament	31
Our Faith is in the Facts, Not Feelings	32
Offended by Jesus?	34
The Battle of the Mind	36
Nothing Short of Sainthood	38
Be Stirred 24 -- 7	39
Light	41
Get Your Laws on my Body	42
Expect Perfection From God	45
Set Out and Bring Jesus	46
The Most High Becomes Most Low	48
Mercy, Within Mercy, Within Mercy	49
Change Up Your Diet	50
You've Got Mail	51
Go First Class!	53
Sentenced to Joy	55
The Greatest Leaders are the Best Followers	56
Turn to Each Other and God	57

Daily Bread	59
True Mirrors	61
Promises	62
God's Plan for You	63
You Are Loved – Be That Love	65
House of Love or Fear?	67
Jesus Loves Sinners	69
How We Suffer	71
B Forgiving	72
No Orphans	75
Who Will Save the Day?	77
Why Reject Abundant Life?	78
Zealously Knocking on Your Door	80
Gossip	82
Be Quiet	83
Humility is the Truth of Who We Are in God	85
You Can't Earn or Lose God's Love and Acceptance	87
U Love U?	89
Miracles	91
Pursue Like the Hound of Heaven	93
Why Just for Lent?	95
Reverence	97
Do You Want to be Well?	99
Your Mother and God	101
Taken, Blessed, Broken and Given	103
Finite or Infinite Eyes?	105
Two Beams and Keeping the Sabbath Holy	106
Sexuality and Lust	108
GAP – God Answers Prayer	111
Small Stuff, Big Deal	113
Extravagant Love	115
The Longest Distance	117
Whatever is not Transformed is Transmitted	119
His Heart Beats for You	121
Pray Together	122
Properly Positioned?	125
What is a Mountain For?	127
First Love	128
A.S.K.	129

Self-Esteem	130
Practice Choosing Life	131
FROG	133
NEWS	134
No Fear	135
The Master's Plan	136
God Suffers With Us	137
Fasting From God	138
It's an Inside Job	139
Faithfulness, Not Success	141
Make Jesus Big	143
Praise	145
Perfectly Loved in the Eucharist – Real Communion	147
Speaking Up	148
Ask the Inventor	149
I Was Hungry	150
Tempted? Be Accountable	151
Running Freely in God's Love	152
Praise Him	153
Love All	154
LAW – Love Always Wins	155
Heaven on Earth	157
Eucharist – Infinite Merciful Covenant	159
What Founds You?	161
Be What You Should Be – Set the World Ablaze	162
Shepherds With Staffs	164
The Eucharist is Not Fast Food	165
What Masters Master You?	167
Follow Unreservedly	169
God Sightings	171
Listen to Each Other	173
Me-on Trial?	174
Whose Telling Who?	175
No More Hiding	177
Honor	179
Cell Phones and Calling God	181
Pointing Fingers	182
Close to the Brokenhearted	184
Sexuality, Marriage, and The Eucharist	185

What Goes in Your Cup?	187
Word of Eternal Life	188
Disciples and Discipline	189
St. Patrick – Keeper of the Covenant	191
Eat Dinner Together	192
Fear or God?	194
The Lamb of God Become the Eucharist	195
Foot Washer	197
In Vain?	198
The Power of the Tongue	200
Who You Are	203
The Really Real	204
No Shame	206
Status	207
Behind the Veil	209
Our Possessions Possess Us	210
Submission – To be Sent Under a Mission	211
No Strings Attached	213
Silent No More	214
Your Word, O Lord	215
God is Good – All the Time	216
Hosting Jesus	217
Called to be a Prophet	218
Hypocrisy, Belief and the Church	219
Just Five Words	221
Share Your Heart	223
Be Least	225
An Angel of the Lord	226
Present to Presence	227
Don't Compare	228
Sacrifice	229
Arise, My Beloved and Beautiful One, and Come	231
Good News Messengers	233
Run to God	234
Naming	235
Outside the Box	237
Be Holy	238
PIG – Peace in God	239
Prayers	240

Introduction

You are familiar St. Paul's writings, correct? Sometimes one line can become very long and convoluted and even turn almost a whole chapter of a book. He would not get an "A" for grammar. But, in some ways I say, "So what? Big deal. He does not have to be perfect." Some say he wrote in the imperfect manner that he did because he was so full of grace that it was uncontainable and spilling out all over the place. Welling up with grace and words and light and life, St. Paul just filled the page as God rushed forth! And that is the way I would like you to look at this book. It is not perfect but neither am I. This book is about a perfectly loving God coming to save a sinner like me and you. It is about God rushing in with his grace and words and light and life to create this book, however imperfect it might be. So, I pray that God will be uncontainable in you and you will not worry so much about having perfect presentation and grammar in your life. You do not have to have your house in order for God to come in. Rather, invite God into your messy house and he will put it into order. Just, without ever stopping, keep letting God in and out. Let God and his JOY write straight with crooked lines. When people see you, may they see JOY!

Now I would just like to share with you how God fills imperfect me with joy as I try to serve him as a priest. Here is a day in my life.

Some might just ask, "What does a priest really do?" The answer is not much. (Joke!) I usually have about four Masses a weekend – three of c our regular weekend Masses and then a wedding or funeral or youth Mass or sometimes a Mass with the Sisters or in the jail. Other than my Masses on the weekend, I sit around most of the week and play video games on the computer and, weather permitting, try to get in as many rounds of golf as possible. Just kidding. Not interested in video games and I really can't stand to play golf – so hard to drive that ball well.

Actually, I thought I would give you a snap shot of a day in my life as a priest just to share what it can be like between Sundays. So, here we go… I woke up yesterday about 5am (a little earlier than normal) thinking about Caitlin. A senior in high school, very involved in life, joyful, on the dance team, dealt with various congenital physical problems throughout her life, from a strong Catholic family close to God, the Church and Catholic school education. The day before I got a call about 5:30pm telling me that Caitlin had died. No, God! Why? What about her mom and dad, family? Friends, community, church? My heart breaks. I go over to the school for a prayer service. About 200 kids and staff and teachers there. Shocked. Dazed. Dumbfounded. Praying. Crying. Telling stories. Hugging. Laughing. Sorrow. Questioning. Celebrating Caitlin's life. Guilt at not loving more and remembering what is really important in this life.

Then I go over to the family's house. Mom and dad are devastated. Mom's clothes are drenched in tears at the loss of the one she bore in her own womb. She weeps in my arms. Mother Mary – pray! Console. You know. You were there with your beloved Son. Pray saints and angels, family of God. Mom and dad have lost their precious daughter. Through her sobbing, mom says to me, "We need more 'You Are Loved' buttons." Yes, we need more love in this world. That is the only thing that really matters. All else pales.

When to have the funeral for Caitlin? She is set to graduate from high school within a month and her older sister will be graduating from college at about the same time. There were supposed to be two joyful graduations but now one has turned into a funeral. How does a family face this? Too big for the human heart. God is greater than the human heart. Come their way, Lord. Come their way.

I am also thinking about the four other funerals I have from Wednesday to Saturday. I had a funeral Wednesday and I have one Thursday and two on Saturday. I always try my best to do the funeral when the family wants it. I need to pray- and I do. I pray for all those who have died and their families. I need to prepare for each of those funerals. Meeting with the families, ministering, preparing the homilies, making sure the liturgy is set. Lots to do. I need to pray. Prepare. I am also preparing for the weekend homily at St. Joseph the Worker. This morning I have the school Mass at Holy Family at 8:25am. What should I do for a homily here, Lord? Holy Spirit? God answers. Get a marker and tell the kids that God writes their vocation on their hearts when they are conceived in their mother's womb. Have kids repeat, "God has a plan for my life. And I need to pray and pray and pray to find out what that plan is for me." There is more but that is the heart of it. Thank you Lord, for that inspiration –as always! I love you, Lord. You are faithful to me and all who call upon your name. So, this Thursday morning I have been praying, thinking, reflecting, and preparing homilies for a little over two hours. Time to shower, eat and do my 10 minute perusal through the paper. Then off to Mass at Holy Family.

Mass is great – Jesus is powerful in word and sacrament. Thank you, Lord. Off to LaSalle. It is the day after Caitlin has died. Many adults and administrators there in the halls helping all the shocked and mourning kids and each other. I listen, hug, pray, cry. I just keep thinking about Caitlin's family – her mom and dad drenched in tears.

I must leave after an hour for I have a Mass at St. Mary's Academy. I celebrate Masses at most of the Catholic high schools in Portland and I am basically the chaplain at St. Mary's haven't had tons of time to prepare for this homily. I am thinking it is going to be a small chapel Mass with around 70 people. Wrong. All school. About 650-700 people. That is a much different dynamic. Need energy, words, something to grab hearts and minds for Jesus. Come Holy Spirit. Inspire. I talk about Caitlin and how pretty much what we often think is so important is not. Love is what matters. I talk about Wisdom – how to live our lives here on earth. We get Wisdom from God and so learn how to live a life of love. I talk about how we must get this part right – i.e. life on earth, so that we can get eternity right. God moves in power. Thank you, Lord for working so powerfully on the dime. I do not like being unprepared. Girl comes up to me after Mass and says, "Fr. John, I have lots of questions about relationships and stuff." I ask her to email me because I have a memorial service to get to. Then that makes me think of all the emails and messages I must answer. But I have to go now because I have a memorial service at 3pm in Gresham. I have that homily prepared. Then at 4pm I meet with another family for the funeral on Saturday. Then from 6-9pm I have marriage prep with a couple.

Yes, it is a busy day-a little busier than most others. But I am so thankful to be a priest and live in the name of Jesus. To live in the love and power and goodness and beauty of Jesus. First class. Heaven all the way to heaven. Goodness, all the way to goodness. Forgiveness, all the way to the land of the forgiven. Jesus.

JOY - Jesus Over You

"The Son of Man did not come to be served but to serve and give his life as a ransom for the many." Matthew 20:28

There is a story about a person who was given an opportunity to see both heaven and hell. She chose to see hell first. In hell all the people were gathered around the dinner table to eat. Each person had 4 foot long utensils and they were trying to feed themselves. They were getting very mad and angry. Because they could not feed their own faces, there was swearing and fighting. It was an ugly and hate-filled scene. Next it was time to go to heaven. In heaven were the same dinner table, food, and utensils. But it was a whole different scene. Everyone was using their utensil to feed the person across the table from themselves. There was great joy and laughter in heaven.

One of the surest signs of a Christian is **JOY**. **JOY** can stand for Jesus Others You or Jesus Over You. If our whole paradigm is to put Jesus first and others second and ourselves third- that is the recipe for **JOY**. That doesn't mean that we don't love or take care of ourselves but that we seek to have the spirit of Christ who came not to be served but to serve and give his life as a ransom for the many. There is no way to spell **JOY** or to have true and lasting **JOY** unless we live in the spirit of Christ. If we truly allow Jesus Over You, then we will imitate our master in serving all and living a life of **JOY**. And the **JOY** God gives lasts forever! No one can take it from you!

Polycarp, a bishop who was martyred for our faith in 155 ad, said, "If we love one another and praise the Trinity, we will be faithful to the deepest vocation of the Church." Yes if we love and serve one another and fully give ourselves in worship and praise to the total self-giving of The Father and The Son and The Holy Spirit in the Trinity, we will be true to our deepest vocation in the Church. And there will be **JOY** because when we are in union with God it is impossible not to have **JOY! Everlasting JOY!**

I wonder how much of our depression and sadness in our country is due to the image of hell where everyone was trying to feed their own face with the long utensils. In a culture of "me, myself and I", we are bound to get depressed. Because when we focus on "me, myself and I" that is all we get! That is my definition of hell: only having me, myself and I! Not promising at all. But when we focus on Jesus first and what he asks of us, we will know the joy of living as he gives. We are created to give and it is in giving that we find our joy.

There is a good chance that the answer to our sadness, anger and depression is to serve. Put Jesus over you by serving others first and fin **JOY**. So, serve, serve, serve. And let there be **JOY!**

Remember, there is only one way to spell and have joy—Jesus must be first!

Blessed

One day while walking through my favorite store, the dollar store (the dollar store is my favorite store because you can get everything for $1), I said, "Hi", to a man and he greeted me back. Then, his next response literally stopped me in my tracks. I asked him how he was doing and he replied, "Blessed." I thought, "What an awesome, true and invigorating answer." We are so blessed. I asked the man if he had a copyright on that answer and if I could use it. He just chuckled and told me to use it.

So, I have been teaching that when someone asks us how we are doing we can say, "Blessed." Yes, we are so blessed! Just count your blessings. You have eyes, eyesight, and you are reading this now. You just took another breath. This day alone you will have at least 100,000 reasons to say you are blessed because that is how many times your heart will beat. We were created by God who loves us with an everlasting love! We know that God is good- all the time! We are forgiven and beautiful in his sight. Jesus died for us so that we could go to heaven. God invites us to live with him forever. Yes, we are so blessed! Count and count and count your blessings.

Many of you have shared with me how you have stopped other people in their tracks when they have asked you, "How are you doing?" You have told them, "Blessed." Why does saying we are blessed stop people in their tracks? Because that response causes all of us to go to the heart of our lives. When we tell others we are blessed, we are pointing our lives to the source of all blessing--God. Yes, we are blessed because we are beautiful, loved, forgiven, and invited to live with God forever. Could we possibly be more blessed than that? No! Please continue to let others know how blessed we **ALL** are.

My dad has Alzheimer's disease. He is losing his ability to remember things. He is a bright man and has always been a creative thinker. As you can imagine, it can be frustrating to lose your mind when you have used it so well and creatively. He shared the following touching story with me. Going to sleep at night is difficult for him because his thoughts were so jumbled and confusing. It was frustrating for this to happen so my dad decided to pray the rosary for peace. But dad said to me, "I tried to pray the rosary, John, but I cannot remember all of the words of the Hail Mary. So now I just keep repeating, 'Thank you, Jesus' until I fall asleep. It works."

The words that dad wants on his tombstone are, "Thank you, Jesus." My dad is a blessed man.

How are you doing?

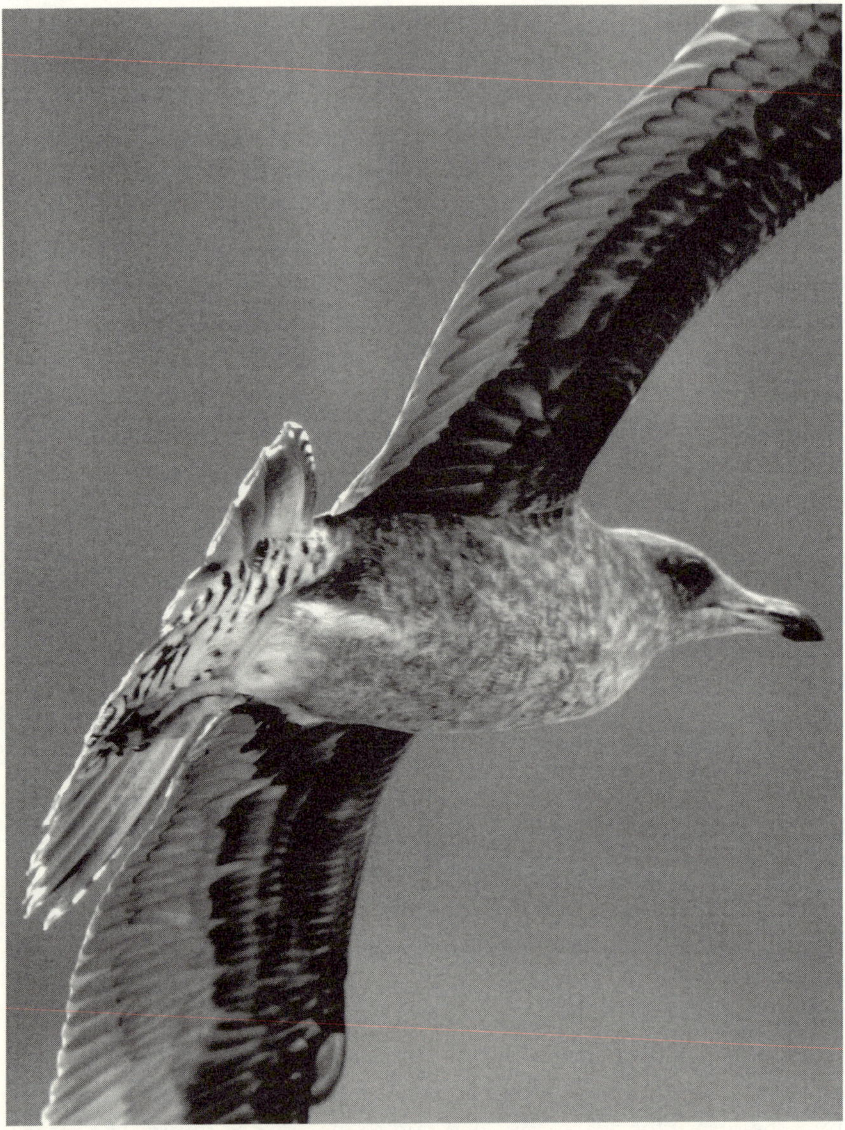

Reaching Out

"The Lord is enthroned over all the flood." Psalm 29:10

This is a true story of a little girl who survived a devastating hurricane. On the top apartment balcony, the raging flood was rising and the whole complex would be consumed within minutes. She had no place else to go and the mean waters would soon devour her tiny body. As she looked for help, a helicopter came and hovered over her. On the brink of being gobbled up by the storm, her rescuers had arrived.

When asked about the whole experience, the little girl shared how scared she was of drowning. But, hope came on the scene and she was rescued. About the rescue, she said it was easy, "All I had to do was reach out and they pulled me up."

Imagine the little girl reaching out and being saved from the devouring flood. This can be an image for our lives. In the devouring flood of broken families and broken promises and suffering and death, we have someone to reach out to. It is someone who will save us from death. But not only will he save us from death, he will give us eternal life. It is our Rescuer. His name is Jesus.

Jesus, our Rescuer, wants us to know that he is bigger than all the flood. He reigns over the devouring waters. I hope that our lives are all about reaching out to Jesus for rescue. May we be given the wisdom to know that there is only one who can save us from the devouring flood. And as we reach out to our Rescuer, may we know the indescribable JOY of living with him this day and forever. One main wish I have for this book is that it would inspire us to always reach out for Jesus who is "enthroned over all the flood."

Let us pray, " Jesus, thank you for coming to rescue me from the devouring flood. Like the little girl reaching out for rescue in the midst of the raging flood, may I reach out to you with all that I am. May I reach out to you all the time. May I reach out to you knowing that my very life depends on you rescuing me. And, in the reaching out, may I find you pulling me into heaven. May I see the angels and saints and community of believers praying for me and loving me as you pull me to you. And in finding you, may I know the rescue, JOY and eternal life you came to bring. Amen. "

YOU ARE LOVED
YOU ARE LOVED
YOU ARE LOVED
YOU ARE LOVED
YOU ARE LOVED
YOU ARE LOVED
YOU ARE LOVED
YOU ARE LOVED
YOU ARE LOVED
YOU ARE LOVED
YOU ARE LOVED

You are Loved!

One time I took a group of kids to a youth conference. On Saturday night a girl shared with me that her mom and dad were getting a divorce. Pain filled her eyes and words. I did not know this girl very well at all. After we were done talking and praying I was curious why she had shared with me. She said, "Because you told me I was loved and I haven't heard that." The crushing blow of those words shot my heart like a burning arrow and the tears came. I hurt so badly for this girl who did not hear that she was loved in her home. **FROM THEN ON I VOWED THAT I WOULD TELL AS MANY PEOPLE AS I COULD THAT THEY WERE LOVED.**

You are loved! Your mom and dad are loved. Your brothers and sisters, sons and daughters, your family and friends are loved. Your enemies are loved. All people are loved, all the time. God loves you with a love that is bottomless and never-ending. Overflowing love being poured out to you all the day long. Filling, washing, healing, forgiving. Uncontained, unrestrained. Looking for an opening to fill your heart.

Who are you? You are loved! We are defined by love. The deepest meaning in our lives is that we are sons and daughters of our God who loves us very much. We live from that truth. And all we think, say and do is with the purpose to utterly convince every person we meet that they are loved.

So, how do we teach others who they are? How do we share with others the core meaning of our lives? What can we do to let everyone in our path know that they are loved without end? We need to tell them! Just like I told that girl at the youth conference that she was loved. And I have come up with a way to do that. Here it is… When someone asks you what time it is you say, "It is_____ (the time) and you are loved!" For example, if someone did not know what time it was and asked me for the time I would say, "It is 9:15 and you are loved!" Do you know how common the question is, "Do you know what time it is?" Very! And so we have tons of chances in life to employ, "It is_____ (the time) and you are loved!" So, just start doing this and watch the miracles happen.

People, all people, need to know they are loved. And they need to be reminded and reminded and reminded. You can be creative beyond using it with the time, too. Like, "The final score was 21-7 and you are loved." Or, "I will see you tomorrow night at 5pm and you will be loved." How about this one I use in church sometimes when people come late, "For all who came late today- you were late and you were loved!" Maybe say, "It is your birthday and you are loved." Or, "It is Monday, and you are loved." Be creative about how you tell others that they are loved.

The three words, "You are loved", have saved lives. I have had kids tell me that those three words have stopped them from taking their own lives in quiet desperation. Please vow with me to tell others, at every chance, that that are deeply loved by God forever. You know, many inspiring homilies, talks, books and songs do not issue forth a concrete challenge. But here is my challenge for you: Let people know they are loved. OK?

YOU ARE LOVED!

You Are the Pearl of Great Price

"The Kingdom of heaven is like a merchant searching for fine pearls. When he finds a pearl of great price, he goes and sells all that he has and he buys it. Mt. 13: 45--46

A man was surfing when a shark attached him. About one month earlier his wife gave birth to their treasured son. The miracle of their first born son filled this young couple with joy. As the shark clamped down on the father's lets, all he could think about was his son. He did not want his son to grow up without a father. He was going to do whatever it took to defeat the shark so he could live for his son. Miraculously, he was eventually able to break free from the shark by beating its head with his fists. Even though this young father lost his leg, he was alive for his son. His son meant everything to him.

You mean everything to Jesus. In Matthew 13: 45--46, we read about the man who sells all he has in order to buy a field that has the Pearl of Great Price. This parable is usually interpreted that Jesus is the Pearl of Great Price and we are the ones who give all we have to gain Jesus. But, let us look at it this way. You are the Pearl of Great Price and Jesus gives all that he has on the cross for you! He doesn't want you as a son or daughter, to grow up without a father – i.e. God our Father. He gives his life away so you can know the Father and his love. You are the Pearl of Great Price!

Say "No" to Wrath

One thing that I tell every couple that I prepare for marriage is St. Paul's words "Do not let the sun set on your wrath." Yes, deal with conflicts in a timely fashion and do not let the hurt/resentment fester and grow. Mountains are made out of molehills because we do not talk with each other and work out our relationships. Taken to the extreme, we can see the greatest mountains of war and terrorism.

It is a given that there will be conflict in our relationships with each other. What is not a given is how we will respond to it. We can either draw apart from each other or draw together to each other when hurtful words or actions have occurred. Guess what God wants for us?

When things bother us we should, in humility, peace and gentleness, seek to reconnect with that person in the mercy of God. If we choose not to deal with that person, then we need to let it go. It is not fair to bring past stuff that we chose not to deal with into the present conflict. If we do not deal with stuff, but choose to hold onto the hurt, our resentments may become mountainous and can emerge as a bomb in the present conflict. Thus, God urges us to deal with conflict or to let it go.

When we do not deal with conflict in God's mercy, divorces of all kinds happen-- and I am not just talking about husband and wife. Who have you divorced yourself from? Don't let the sun set on your wrath. Either let it go or seek the forgiveness you are looking for to bring it all under God's mercy. I know I have got lots of work to do in this area.

Let us pray, "Lord Jesus, fill me with the endless font of mercy flowing from your cross. Help me either to let go of past hurts or seek out those people who I have divorced myself from and ask for your mercy to bind us together in peace. May the sun not set on my wrath. Thank you, Jesus, Font of Infinite Mercy." Amen.

Surrender

"All things have been handed over to me by my Father." Luke 10:22.

Non--stop and without end, Jesus is coming to us and offering us non--stop life that is without end. Amen?! He is planted right smack dab in the middle of humanity so that all humanity can hear and know his invitation, "Come, go with me to that Land."

Divesting himself of heaven so that he could totally invest himself in us so that we would become fully vested with Eternal Life.

What a deal! Jesus is coming to bring us the Kingdom of God. Infinite joy! Uncontainable love and life that will never end. God the Father has handed over all good things to Jesus and Jesus wants to hand over to us that which the Father has handed over to him-- all good things.

This wonderful handing over of all that is good sounds so enticing until we see what Jesus went through. Yes, God the Father did hand everything over to Jesus but it is probably not in the way that most of us would have designed. However, we see Jesus as surrendered to the Father. He is going to receive and hand over the Kingdom in the way that the Father wants.

Each of us wants to get to God. We want the Kingdom. We want infinite goodness now and we want to fully experience it forever. But how do we get to God? Maybe some of us try to get to God without God. With honorable intentions we pray, go to church and try to live a holy life in order to "get" to Jesus. The whole process can become ego--centric and we leave Jesus in the dust while we are trying to "get" to him. We do not allow Jesus to hand over the Kingdom to us in his perfect wisdom. We are not totally surrendered to the fact that we must receive the Kingdom according to his leading.

So, I think a big thing is instead of trying to "get" to Jesus, we should focus on letting Jesus "get" to us and take us by the hand to The Land. Let Jesus hand everything that is good over to you in the way in wants to hand it. Surrender to his way. Receive. That is how we "get" it.

Divesting himself of heaven so that he could totally invest himself in us so that we would become fully vested with Eternal Life.

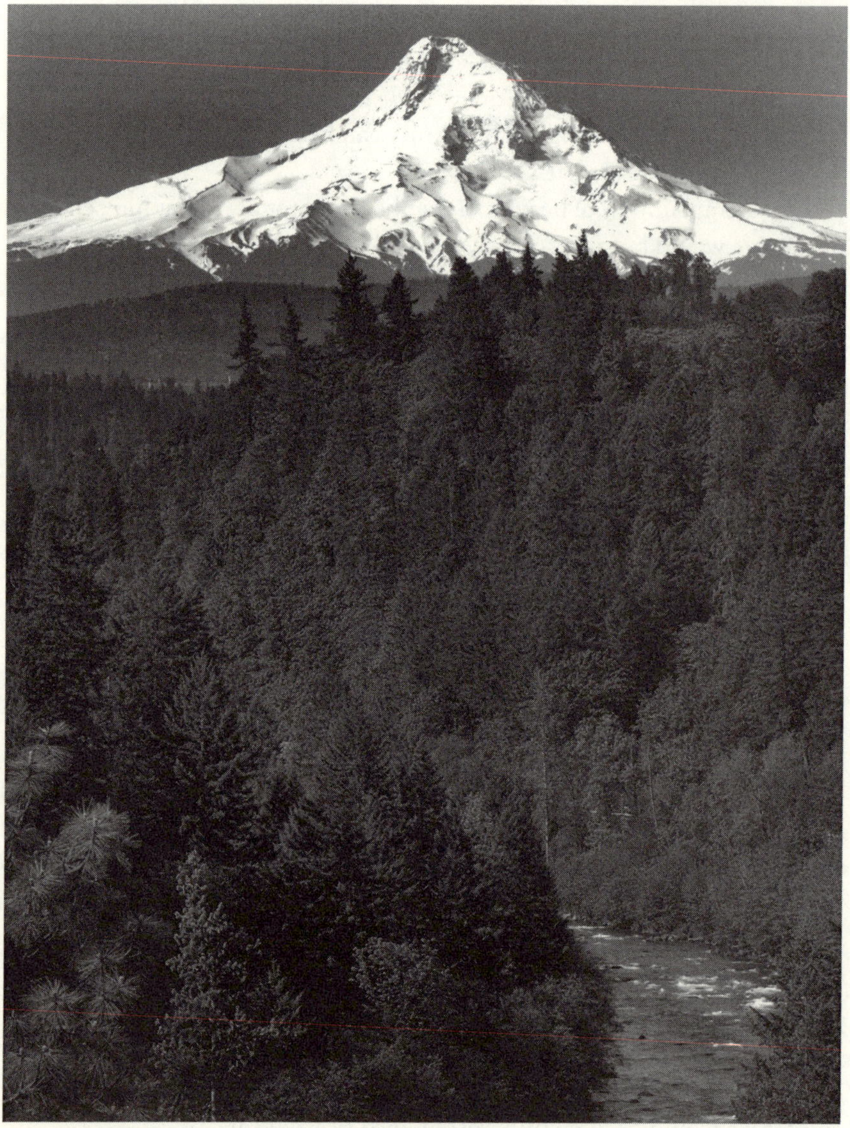

Only God is Good – All the Time

""But not everyone has heeded the good news; for Isaiah says, Lord, who has believed what was heard from us?" Romans 10:16

God is Good all the time and all the time God is Good. God is Love all the time and all the time God is Love. God is Mercy all the time and all the time God is Mercy. God is with us -- all the time. All the time – God is with us. And so on…

Do we get the picture? There is only one that is "Good" and that is God. What does that mean? There is only one who is perfectly good for us and that is God. Only God can deliver endless goodness each and every time. God can never deliver "bad" because his nature cannot change. His only and constant preoccupation is to pour out all goodness into our hearts.

Now, we human beings and all of creation share in the goodness of God but we must remember we are not "The Good". As part of beautiful and broken creation, we do not deliver goodness all the time. In the world we live in, hurricanes can devastate, the dog can bite, and friends can turn away in bitterness. So, it is important to remember that we can cause each other pain or experience it in creation but God will never cause us pain. God will always be good to us regardless of the sufferings and circumstances we face in this broken world.

Only God is good – all the time.

Let us pray: Loving God, I want to be filled with goodness but there are many times I look for that in something besides you. Help me to be wise and know that only you are good – all the time. May I always live by this truth. Amen.

Money, Sports and Peace

"A nation of firm purpose you keep in peace; in peace, for its trust in you." Isaiah 26:3

A little six year old girl takes measures in her power regarding her future financial security. Call her very prudent or highly neurotic, she puts pretty much every penny she makes in the bank so that when she grows up she will have the means to take care of money matters. She is bound and determined to take care of any future financial needs with the money she has amassed.

The coaches have always seen the young boy as an exceptional athlete. He seems to especially excel at baseball. He loves playing sports and his parents might even love his playing sports more. It is time to start thinking about high school and a college scholarship and then who knows? How will we get him to perform at the highest level? How much time each day will he need to devout to baseball? What camps and coaches will we seek out? How much money will we spend in specialized coaching and training?

Now, it is truly important to be prudent financially at the same time remembering that money is not the cause of peace in our hearts. Have you ever seen a u--haul following a Hertz limousine to the grave? Peace comes from knowing, loving and serving the One who will raise us from the grave.

We have bowed down to the God of sports in this country. It is not wrong to want to do well in sports but how much is too much? Most athletes who do well in high school will not play in college. So, what are all the hours and days and $1,000's for? What does it all have to do with God's peace?

What if our firm purpose was to have God and his peace? In the big picture, our money, games, physical bodies are here today and gone tomorrow. Money and sports can provide a temporary security but not eternal blessed assurance. Eternal blessed assurance is the peace of putting our whole lives in the hands whom will make all things well today, tomorrow and forever.

What do you invest in that is lasting? Make it your firm purpose to invest in Jesus and know everlasting peace and blessed assurance.

If we have the peace of Jesus in our lives, we have everything. If we do not have the peace of Jesus, we have nothing.

Who Are Your John the Baptist's?

"A voice cries out: In the desert prepare the way of the Lord!" Isaiah 40:3

I like to be right. I joke with my friends that no one is going to tell me what to do. I have got it figured out and I know what to do. I do not like to admit it but I do have this attitude-- I hope not too much. It is not the ideal disposition for growth.

Today the prophet Isaiah is foretelling of the coming of John the Baptist. He will be the voice crying out in the desert to prepare the way of the Lord. He will tell us all to give up our sin and let Jesus in. He will point out to us the Lamb of God who takes away all the sins of the world and leads us into all life. Sin cuts us off from life but as we get rid of it then we will have more life. Want more life? John the Baptist is pro--life to the core and we are wise to heed his words to do all that we can in our power to get rid of sin in our lives.

But I like to be right and I do not want anyone telling me I am wrong. I can look at anyone who is calling out my sin and easily call out theirs. I can reject or deny the truth of what someone might be saying to me about my own sinfulness and continue on like nothing is wrong-- like I have arrived at a state of perfection and therefore I do not need to change. How absurd is that thought?

How good am I at allowing others to be a John the Baptist in my own life? When someone points out to me my sin am I willing to listen, reflect and be open to any repentance and change God might be calling me through their words? Or do I deny, reject or point out their sins with an unwillingness to really examine my own sin?

We should be thankful for the John the Baptist's in our lives. Sin kills but when we ask Jesus to come and replace the sin with Himself we are filled with life. We should pray for a hatred of sin in our lives so that we can come to the fullness of life.

Let us pray: "Lord Jesus, thank you for all those who have been a John the Baptist to me and pointed out my own sin and how it was taking life. When someone points out my sin to me, help me to be open to listening, repentance and change. Send people into my life to show me my sin so that I can ask for forgiveness and live in the infinite fountain of your life. Amen."

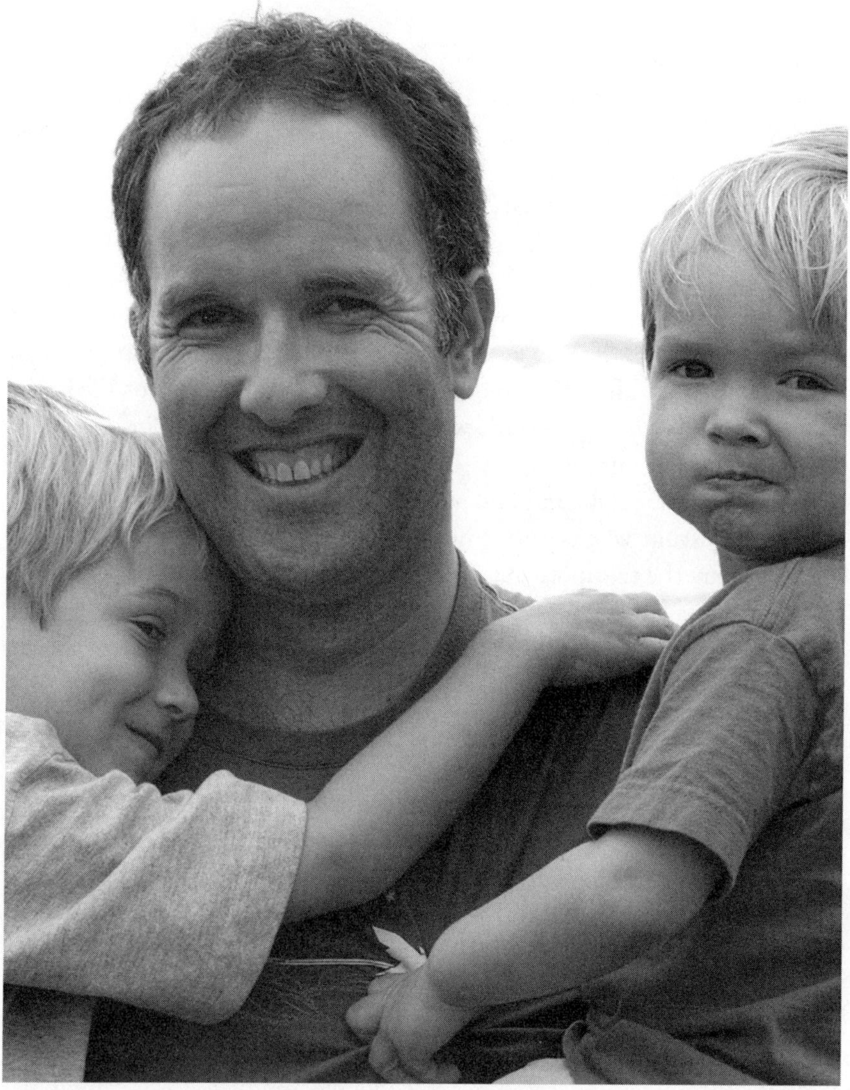

Give Without Counting the Cost

"Without cost you are to give." Matthew 9:6

My thoughts often turn to parents when I think of those who give without counting the cost. I am the youngest of eight boys. I know I was somewhat of a precocious little boy (I do not know how much that has changed!) and it wasn't always a walk in the park for mom and dad to raise me. And I am just one of eight boys.

Dad worked in the challenging profession of children's dentistry for 40 years and mom poured herself as a mother of eight very active and uniquely different boys. Mom was also a nurse but she did not get a chance to practice too many years because she had eight sons to raise. I think if the countless needs to be met. Here is one. The 1,000's of diapers that dad and mom changed. I think of the constant financial pressures. At one point there were five of us in college or post--grad and I think the total number of college and post--grad years all for all of us adds up to 77 years. And this is just the beginning of the list of all the pressures and needs of raising eight sons.

How mom and dad gave without cost points me to the life of Christ. Giving without cost means expecting no return from your giving. You just give and give and give. That is all Jesus ever does. He just pours and pours and pours his life out for us. When we truly give without cost then we have become like Jesus.

The heart of the question in our lives should not be, "What am I going to get out of this?" As a person living in the Spirit of Jesus our refrain should not be, "What am I going to get our of church, God, family, friends, this community, this person, this event, etc?" That is the question our narcissistic culture has trained us to ask. It is a superficial and selfish mode of existence-- one I am too well aware of personally. The question a mature Christian asks is, "What am I going to give to church, God, family, friends, this community, this person, this event, etc?"

Life in Christ is not about what I can "get" but about what I can "give".

All that we will have in heaven is what we have given away on earth.

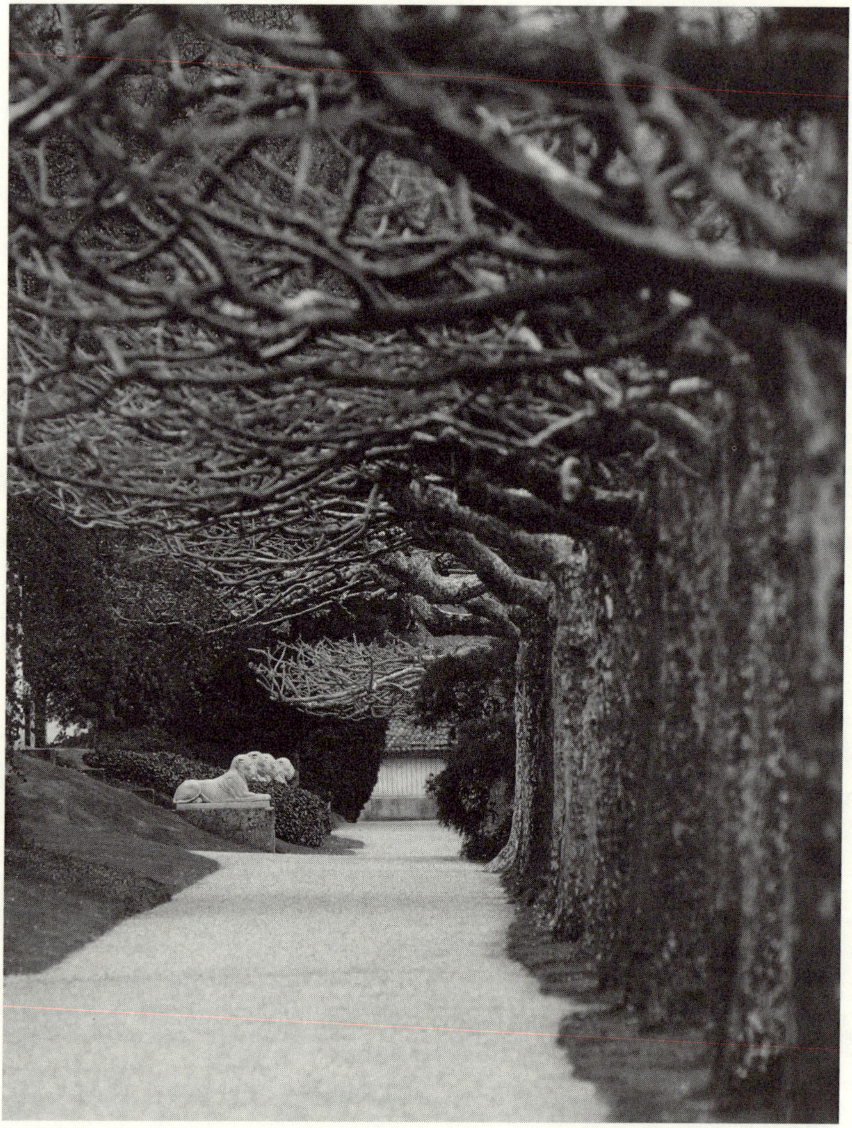

R U on the Right Road?

"A highway will be there, called the holy way; No one unclean shall pass over it, nor fools go astray on it." Isaiah 35:8

I was giving a men's retreat in a country setting with lots of roads on a vast expanse of land. One of the men was walking to meet us at the outdoor altar for Mass. The only problem was that he was walking down the wrong road. If one of the other guys had not found him he would have continued down the wrong road. He would have missed out on celebrating with the whole group how Jesus had died for us and given us all the gift of salvation. A provoking question we can garner from this scenario is, "Am I on the right road? Am I on the holy way?"

If you are on the wrong road you cannot get to the right place.

No one who is unclean may pass over the holy way. The holy way purges and purifies us from sin. Jesus forgives us for our sin and the Holy Spirit helps us to become holy. We stay on the holy way by being faithful to God in church and prayer and service and by having a holy family and friends. We choose to surround ourselves with people who will not let us be unclean or go astray. Like the man on the retreat, we will have a whole army of people who will not let us go down the wrong road and miss out on the only true celebration there is in life: Jesus.

Is your life buzzing away like driving down the highway? May it is time to pull off the highway of shallow or no reflection and see if you are on the right road. Where is your road leading to? Slow down! Stop. Think. Reflect. Pray. Ask God, the church, the gospel, holy family and friends to scrutinize the road you are on. Is it the best possible road you can take to heaven? Remember, if you are on the wrong road you cannot get to the right place.

As a Christian song goes, "There's no better place on earth than the road that leads to heaven."

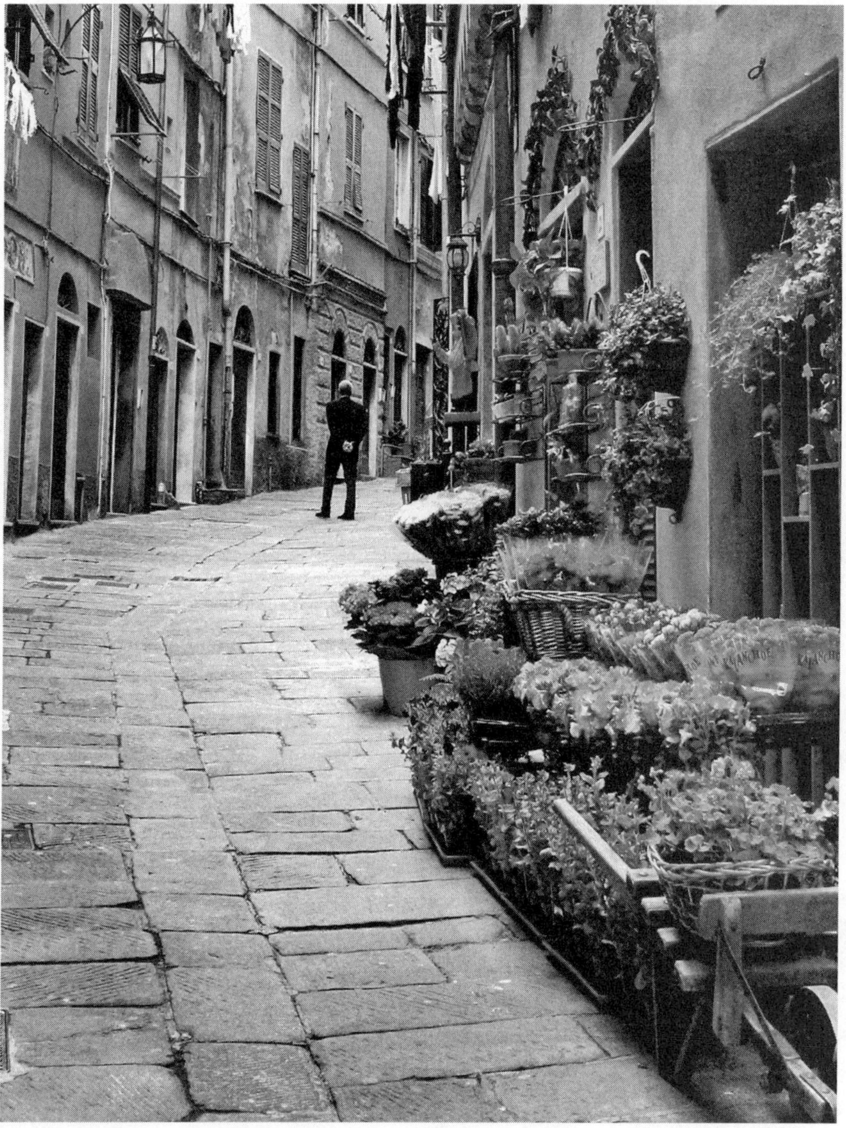

Do Not be Afraid --
Come Out of Hiding

"The Lord God called to Adam and asked him, 'Where are you?' He answered, 'I heard you in the garden; but I was afraid, because I was naked, so I hid myself'". Genesis 3:10

Our verse today speaks of the first sin committed by humans, which is commonly known as Original Sin. God told Adam not to eat of the fruit of the tree in the garden but he did and from this disobedience many things like guilt, shame, fear, sin and death entered into our world. This story of Adam and Eve doesn't necessarily mean there were an Adam and Eve and a garden and tree that God told them not to eat from. It is story construed from pagan mythology in order to teach the truth of creation and fall. Our Loving God created the human race good but we sinned and evil was introduced to the world. The word used for the first man, Adam, is Hebrew for man, human being or humankind.

Once sin entered the world, humankind went into hiding out of fear. In many ways, we have been hiding ever since. We want to hide from God in fear and dread because of what He will do to us if He really found us out. Well, that is kind of a crazy thought. He has got every hair on our head counted (for those who are bald that is an easy job!). Read and spend time praying with Psalm 139 to confirm God's total knowledge of you. "You know me through and through." "You had scrutinized my every action." God knows us better than we know ourselves. He also loves us a whole lot more than we love ourselves. So, that means we would be wise to come out of hiding and move towards God.

God is endless love, mercy, goodness, kindness and embrace-- all the time. So what are we afraid of? We live in fear because we do not know him. We do not know He is endless love, mercy, goodness, kindness and embrace-- all the time. If we truly knew him we would not hide anything from him but we would run to him with everything. Perfect love casts out all fear.

How can we come out of hiding? Two things. First, you can go to Confession. Now, if you are not Catholic you can go to a priest or someone who is and ask them about the reality of God's endless love and mercy he pours out in Confession. It is a graced encounter with the One who loves us so much more than we love ourselves. But, we have to come out of hiding to experience this graced encounter. Second, come out of hiding with others. If you think you have hurt someone, come out from hiding from them and ask them if you have hurt them. Do not live in fear that they are in some way rejecting or condemning you.

From the beginning and throughout his pontificate, Pope John Paul II, proclaimed, "Do not be Afraid". If God is for us, who can be against us? You know what is amazing? Do you know how many times that in some way, some messenger in the Bible says, "Do not be afraid"? 365! "Do not be afraid is spoken to us 365 times in the Bible. That sounds like one "Do not be afraid" for each day of the year! So, every day we must say, "Do not be afraid!"

Do not be afraid. Come out of hiding into the presence of Perfect Love.

So John Gave In

"Thus says the Lord" Isaiah 48:17

Growing up, I had visions of being rich and having a big family full of love. I also had the outlandish dream of playing in the NBA and being famous. As to the more attainable plans of making a lot of money and having a big family full of love, I never really consulted the Lord because I knew what I wanted and how I was going to get there.

When I was a junior in college I started to really open up to the Lord because I wanted to know if he was for real. I saw many people at Franciscan University who had such a deep love, joy and peace and their lives and they all told me is was from Jesus. I wanted what they had. So, how to get there?

I knew I had to seek and seek and seek. Just like any friend I want to grow closer to, it was obvious that I needed to spend time with Jesus in prayer. I also learned that once you get serious with seeking the Lord, he will reveal to you how awesome He is! One night when I was 20 years old I had about eight people pray over me that I would really know the reality of God's love and power. In this defining moment in my life I did not see visions or have any miraculous healings or insights. I just heard God asking me, "Will you pray to me each day?" And I said, "Yes."

Praying each day makes all the difference. A big thing I have learned in prayer is that God really wants to speak to us. And God has the best plan for us. For so many years I was telling God what my plan for love and happiness and it was so far off from what His plan was. I was settling for the scraps when God wanted to serve me the finest and freshest food!

One day while praying I was reading the scripture where Jesus came out at the start of his public ministry and wanted to be baptized by John the Baptist. John said, "No, you should be baptizing me." But Jesus said (loose translation), "No, I need to be baptized by you." As I was reading this scripture the next four words hit me-- big time. It was like they jumped off the page and got five times bigger, "So John gave in." And that is exactly what I needed to do in my life-- give in to God. Give into God the Father who knows best. Give into Jesus who died for my sins. Give into the Holy Spirit who leads us into all Truth. God does not need to give into me. I need to give into God.

I am so thankful I gave into God. He showed me the best definitions for being rich and having a big family full of love. I have the true riches of love, joy and peace. And in light of my desire for a big family, I have an enormous family called the world and communion of saints. I have an eternal joy in my heart and praise on my lips because I know that God is good for us all the time.

Give into the Lord. Stop settling for scraps and let God feed you with the finest and freshest food!

Go With the Flow?

"Woe to the city, to her God she has not drawn near." Zephaniah 3:1--2

Gonna go with the flow and really not know where the flow is gonna go? UT, Oh No!-- That is a line from a song I wrote about how we can throw away our God given ability to choose what we will draw near to in life. It is the Monkey-see, Monkey-do syndrome. Well, I am just going to party because that is what everyone else is doing. Since everyone else in not faithful to their marriage, I do not need to be faithful. I don't see other people in my situation getting up early to pray and draw near to God so why should I?

But where is the flow going? If I choose infidelity in my marriage, look at all the hellish havoc it wreaks. When I choose drink and drug, it most often leads to very bad choices and physical, relational and spiritual headaches. Since I am lazy or have a priority greater than God in my life-- the fool says this in his/her heart-- then I will not get up earlier to pray. So, God who is LIFE is shut out of my life and I die in my heart.

Jesus did not just go with the flow. He went with his Father. He chose the good. We, too, have a choice. If we just go with the flow of the world we will end up in the sewage of sin. Or, we can use our free will to draw near to God and reap infinite good. So, the choice is sewage or infinite good. Are you choosing sewage or infinite good?

Gonna go with the flow and really not know where the flow is gonna go? Oh, Oh No!

What are you doing with your Friday and Saturday nights?

What are you doing with your time?

What are doing with your life?

Are you drowning in the sewage or swimming in the good? Wherever you are, you are there because you have chosen it.

Do you want to change it up? You can. It's up to you. What's it gonna be?

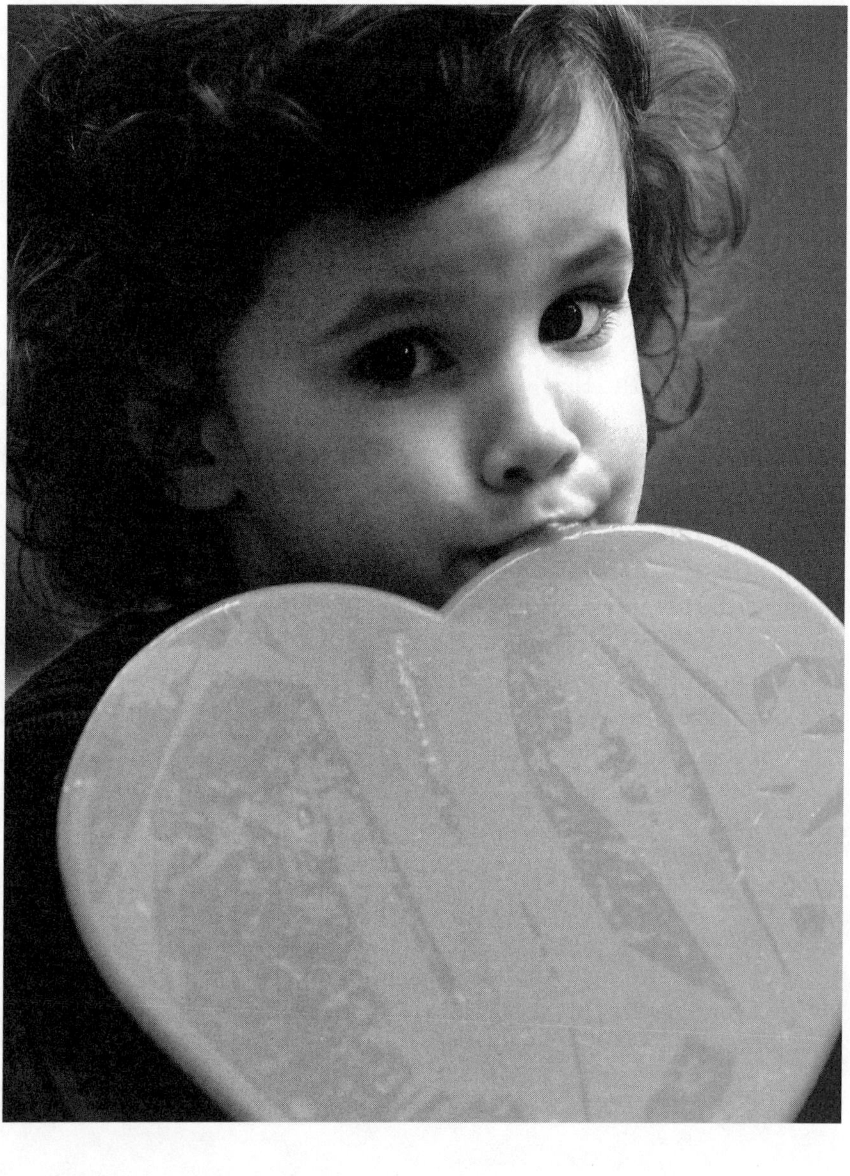

Be A Sacrament

"Rouse your power" Psalm 80:3

In the deepest and most exciting sense of the word, a sacrament is anything that makes the invisible love of God visible. Anything that connects us to the reality of God can be considered a sacrament. So, when you see a parent feeding a small child it can remind us of how God wants to feed his children with the food of his everlasting love. When we see people give each other a hug we can link that to how Christ embraces us in our sin, forgives us and raises us up in new life.

With our most universal understanding of the word "sacrament," we can say that Jesus is the sacrament of God. In the incarnation of the birth of the baby Jesus, God becomes most visible to us. Jesus, par excellence, is going to make God real for us. And oh the power of what Jesus is bringing.

Jesus is descending so we can ascend. Jesus divests himself of heaven so that has can totally invest himself in us so that we would become fully vested with Eternal Life. Talk about a power play of the best kind! The God who created the entire universe lives in power through you and me. We, in turn, make Jesus, visible, real, see--able, touch--able, hear--able, etc. In the deepest and most life--producing sense of the word, we become sacraments for God whenever we connect other people to God.

God shares his unlimited power with us so that we will share it with others. I remember the story of someone who came to a priest with a broken leg. The priest was sick and bed--ridden so all he could muster was a simple prayer that went something like this, "Lord, heal Bill's leg." Guess what? God healed Bill's leg!

Do you believe? God has poured out all of Heaven in the God--man's heart, i.e. Jesus, and the God--man has poured out all of heaven in our hearts.

Be a sacrament! Use the unlimited power that Jesus has poured out in your heart to do good for others. The possibilities are limitless. Let heaven pour through you to touch all. Sling love, joy, goodness, peace and forgiveness out all the time, wherever you are. Believe and live it!

"Lord, rouse your power. Amen"

Our Faith is in the Facts, Not Feelings

"The one who calls you is faithful" 1 Thessalonians 5:24

"Yes, God so loved the world that he gave his only Son, that whoever believes in him may not die but may have eternal life." (John 3:16) In essence, this scripture verse tells us the whole of our faith. Jesus came to die for you and me so that we might have eternal life. While the birth of the baby Jesus for us is a most beautiful and joyful story there is also something else going on that might not seem so wonderful. Looming not too many years after his birth, that baby Jesus will grow into a man to climb upon a cross. There he will be crucified for the entire world to see. In extreme agony, he will give his life for us that we might live forever. This is a fact. Better phrased, this is The Fact of our existence.

Did Jesus have feelings? Yes! He got upset at unrighteousness-- changing the house of prayer/temple into a marketplace. He often was perturbed by Pharisees lack of compassion. Jesus cried for people in his own great compassion. And what about fear, even to the point of agony? He sweat blood the night before he was taken to be put to death knowing what he was facing.

Can you imagine, however, if Jesus let his feelings run his life? Would have ever climbed upon the cross to die an excruciating death for you and me? Thank God, Jesus was not driven by feelings. He was driven by the fact of the Father's love for him and in that love; he trusted that God would work all things for good. Before Jesus lifted a finger to enter his very public ministry at age 30, he went to the Jordon River to be baptized by John. In watching that baptism, we see the fact that Jesus based his existence on. Coming out of the water after being baptized, the sky tore in two and the Father said to his Son (Jesus), "You are my Beloved Son. On you my favor rests." Jesus based his whole life on the fact of his Father's love and favor for him.

Romans 8:28 says that God works all things for good for those who love him. Jesus came to work all things for good for us so that we might have eternal life. Like Jesus' faith in the fact of his Father's love, we have faith in the fact of Jesus love working all for good. And the fact of our faith is the cross. Our whole following of Jesus is based on the fact of the love and forgiveness he gave us on the cross.

We are all going to have feelings in our lives-- anger, fear, sadness, confusion etc. But we do not put our faith in feelings. Can you imagine if our lives were run by feelings? We would probably regret many of our impulsive actions.

Let us imagine our lives in this way. Our life is a train and it is powered by our faith in an engine. Now, this engine can be either feelings or fact. If we have faith in the feelings of our lives, that will make following Christ really confusing. But again, we do not put faith in feelings. We put faith in the fact of our existence-- the cross and all that means. We live according to Jesus mandate of love, forgiveness and service. As we live according to the fact of our existence, that will help sort out all the feelings that come and go.

Offended by Jesus?

"Blessed is the one who takes no offense at me." Luke 7:23

Growing up, I thought my mom and dad were pretty cranked. Let me explain what I mean by "cranked". They loved God. They were excited about God. They wanted to know about this love which was like no other love that they ever experienced. Not only did they go to church a lot (mom went to daily Mass); they went to prayer meetings and talks and conferences. They watched Christian shows, went to Christian Conferences/retreats, read the Bible/Christian books, and listened to Christian tapes etc. in order to go deeper with Christ. When they started to going to prayer meetings, I thought my parents were pretty "cranked." I would say to them, "Are you going to another prayer ball meeting tonight?" Then, I thought they were totally cranked when they started having those darn prayer meetings at our house! I could not get away from my "cranked" parents following of God!

I hate to admit it, but I was offended by my mom and dad's desire for God. And so were other people. I remember one incident with the red Ford Pinto car that I drove to high school. It had a bumper sticker on it that read, "Christians aren't perfect, just forgiven." Now, even though that is not one of my top ten favorite Christian bumper stickers, I have to ask why my classmate made fun of the sticker and Jesus and how my family was "cranked" on Jesus' and why I was offended that I had to have parents love God so much that that sticker would end up on the bumper of the red Ford Pinto that I drove. I remember thinking it was not cool and trying to hide the fact that my mom and dad were so into this person called Jesus.

Why would I be offended by Jesus who loves me like no one will ever love me? Jesus is perfectly good and loving to me at each and every second and I am offended by Him? That just doesn't make sense! Why would I not want the whole world to know about Him? What is there not to be proud about our infinitely good God who wants to bless us with goodness all the way to heaven? John the Baptist is wondering if Jesus is the real deal, i.e. The Messiah, and so he sends his disciples to find out. Jesus sends the reply, "Go and tell John what you have seen and heard: the blind regain their sight, the lame walk, lepers are cleansed, the deaf hear, the dead are raised, the poor have good news proclaimed to them." Luke 7:22

How could life get any better for us than having Jesus?!?

We have been invited to an eternal celebration of perfect love that we can enter into now. Let us get "cranked" and proudly tell the whole world that Jesus has come and He is with us in all power and love!

Dear fellow Christian believer: Go and tell all you meet "what you have seen and heard: the blind regain their sight, the lame walk, lepers are cleansed, the deaf hear, the dead are raised, the poor have good news proclaimed to them." Luke 7:22. Take no offense at Jesus.

The Battle of the Mind

"You did not let my enemies rejoice over me" Psalm 30:4

It is said that we think ten times as fast as we can speak. If we just consider the course of a day that can add up to an awful lot of thoughts. It would be interesting to add up all the thoughts we have about ourselves in one month and determine an average amount of thoughts that we think about ourselves each day. I wonder in how many of those thoughts we would be embracing ourselves with mercy and kindness? And how many of the thoughts would be critical and condemning?

Thoughts can be a mighty powerful enemy that seek to rejoice over us. There is such a battle that goes on in the mind. One moment I can think that I am a loving person and the next I think a cruel thought. It really is a battle of the mind and what spills out in our words and actions comes from how we have decided to think about things. So, if the source of either our love or condemnation comes from the mind, it seems paramount that our minds be transformed by God. We read from Romans 12:2, "Do not conform yourselves to this age but be transformed by the renewal of your mind, so that you may judge what is God's will, what is good, pleasing and perfect." Yes, the potential enemy of our thought life needs to be taken seriously due to the havoc it can wreak.

There is a line to a song directed to God which says, "You tell me who I am". Yes, God tells us who we are. We are often far from his thinking but we come to him so that we might know his thoughts. Our condemning way of thinking is transformed into understanding that God has come to forgive sinners and have us live according to the truth of his love.

Since all we say and do hinges on our thinking, it is essential to think like God thinks!

I want to close with some words to meditate on from Psalm 73:23--26

I am continually with You;
You hold me by my right hand.
You will guide me with Your counsel,
And afterward receive me to glory.

Whom have I in heaven but You?
And there is none upon earth that I desire besides You.
My flesh and my heart fail;
But God is the strength of my heart and my portion forever.

May God's counsel guide us into everlasting glory. Amen.

Nothing Short of Sainthood

"The book of the genealogy of Jesus Christ, the Son of David, the son of Abraham." Matthew 1:1

God's plan for us is to be saints. He wants us with him forever in heaven. But, you say, I am a sinner. Absolutely! You think, " How could I ever be forgiven for all I have done or how will I ever be able to stop committing the same sins over and over again?" And, Jesus says, "The power of the cross is the power to make you a saint." I will make you a saint if you surrender totally to my work in you.

Think about this one, "Every saint ahs a past and every sinner has a future." Every saint was just like you and me in being a sinner but, as fellow sinners, our hope is to join the fullness of life with all the saints (who were former sinners) in the future.

In Matthew 1:1--17 we read about the genealogy of Jesus Christ, the Savior of the World. Yes, Jesus is a family member of the human race who has come to offer every sinner sainthood. And our family of the human race has had quite a beautiful, sad, wonderful and colorful history. Jesus, the one who is like us in all things but sin, comes to the human race to save us from all the skeletons of our sin. Reflect on some of the sinners in the Bible who became major players for God and his Kingdom. Some of the most beautiful writing we have about God comes from a king who was an adulterer and murderer-- just pray the psalms. Think about the first leader of our church-- St. Peter. When push came to shove, he flat out denied that he knew the one who would eventually ask him to lead the church on earth. So, we must take hope that if King David and St. Peter could move from their sins into the future of God's eternal glory, so can we.

Every saint has a past and every sinner has a future.

Be Stirred 24 -- 7

"The spirit of the Lord stirred him." Judges 13:25

One time I was watching the post--game TV interviews of the high school team who had just won the state championship in football. One senior said something like, "We have focused on being a team. We are all brothers and brothers die for each other." That statement and emotion stirred me to think about what a great love you must have to die for someone else. The Holy Spirit stirred me the whole time by showing me that Jesus died for those who loved him and those who hated him. The Holy Spirit moved deep within me reminding me that Jesus died for his crucifiers.

They interviewed another senior whose mom had been just diagnosed with cancer the week before the championship game. I was stirred by his statement. "I did this for you mom! It is the best thing I could do for you." Then, with the Holy Spirit stirring I was brought back to the best thing anyone of us could have done for us. Enjoying a state championship in football is nice but enjoying victory forever in heaven is incomparable. Thank you for your victory, Jesus! The Holy Spirit always is stirring us to focus on the victory, joy and goodness that will last for ever.

The Holy Spirit is open and ready for business 24-7 like 7-11 convenience stores. Twenty--four hours a day, seven days a week, the Holy Spirit is seeking to inspire us to know and live the truth of God's love. Are we open to the Holy Spirit's business 24-7 like 7-11? Or maybe we are just a 9--5'er. Or maybe we look for stirrings just when we are in trouble and crying for some healing, truth and peace. Maybe we are not really open at all because we never set aside time daily to pray and run with the Holy Spirit stirring.

Let us be servants of the Holy Spirit. Always coming to us, let us be open to live, speak and breathe the Holy Spirit's stirrings. Let others know the incredible love of Jesus and how He will lead us to the never ending victory of LIFE.

Let us pray: "Holy Spirit, stir me to love like Jesus loves. Inspire all my thoughts and words that others may choose your holiness. May I be open to your leading twenty--four hours a day. In my heart, stir into flame the God of the universe that my life may be on fire with your love. Amen."

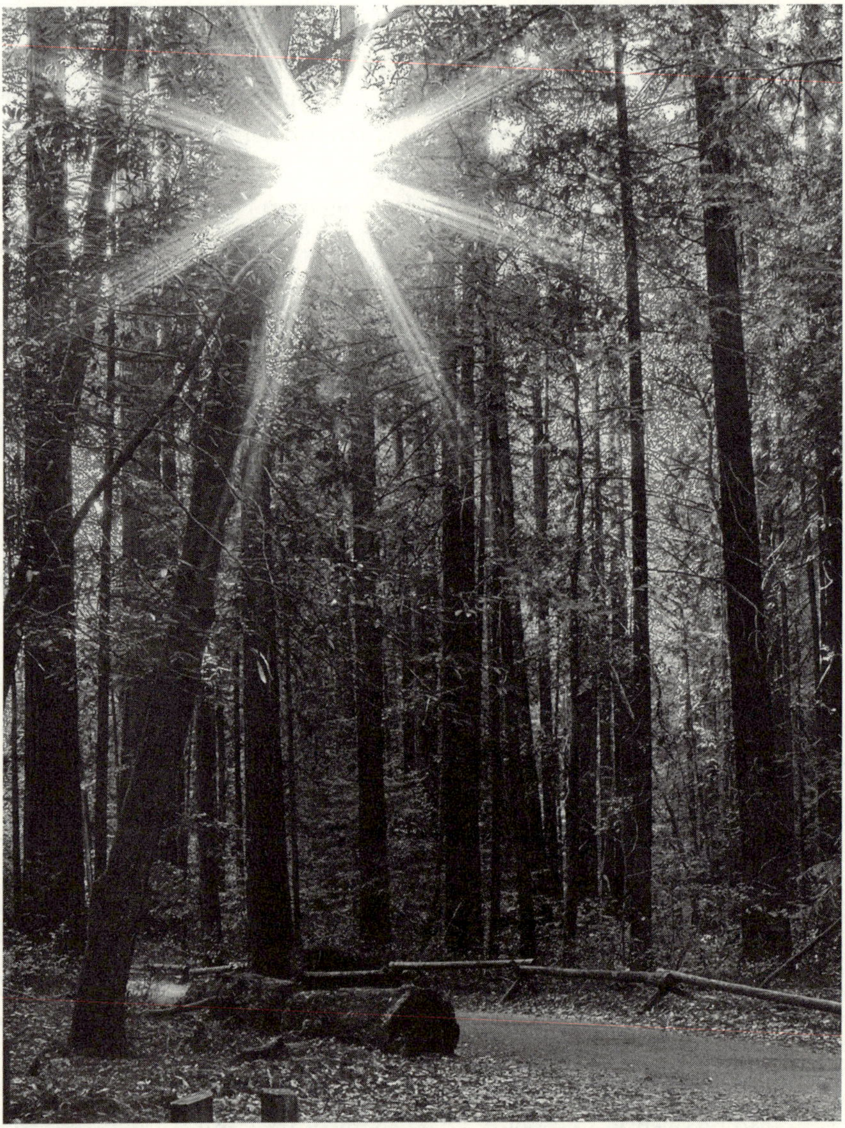

Light

"The light shines in the darkness and the darkness has not overcome it." John 1: 5

In the Gospel of John we read about how the light has come into the darkness and that the darkness will not overcome it. We need to cling to this truth and let the light come into our darkness. It doesn't say that you or I have come into this world to be The Light and not be overcome by darkness. Jesus is the one and only light that overcomes our darkness. We want his light as we confront confusion, suffering and sin.

Jesus comes to us in the darkness of our confusion. He is the Light that lights the way. Imagine this. You are invited to this incredible party that is going to consist of nothing but love and celebration. But if you are not given the "light" of directions on how to get to the party how will you ever get there? God wants to clear up any confusion as to why we are here on earth and the feast of love we are created for. He sends Jesus, the Light of the World, to give directions and light the path home to heaven for us.

Jesus comes into the darkness of our sin. I was praying about St. Paul's verse how God wants us to be holy and full of love. That is exciting. It is God's intention for us to be holy and full of love. But not is it only God's intention, he is also the provision. Jesus will conquer sin and we can share in the victory! Now, it might be well and good that you and I want each other to be holy and full of love but ultimately we do not have the power to make that happen. In the end, only Jesus can make us holy and full of love. Thank God for the Light of the World who intends holiness and love for us and can make it happen!

Jesus comes into the darkness of our suffering. Can you imagine the suffering Jesus went through for us? He takes all of the suffering for all of time onto his body on the cross. Imagine the weight. He takes your suffering to God the Father and asks him to bless, heal and raise you up forever. Jesus lifts you out of darkness into God's own wonderful light. Let HIM!

Spend some time with the following prayerful exercise:

Imagine yourself as a young child. You are suffering. Jesus lifts you up and embraces you. Then he hands you over to God the Father to be embraced. What are you thinking and feeling? What does God say to you?

Get Your Laws on my Body

"To the only wise God, through Jesus Christ be glory forever and ever. Amen." Romans 16:27

I saw what struck me as an angry bumper sticker, "Get your laws off my body." The problem with that statement is we do not have a free license to do what we want, when we want, with who we want, with our bodies. Our bodies are not our own; they are the Lord's. Our lives should be about how we use our bodies and all that proceeds from them to glorify God.

Once I was giving a retreat to a group of high school kids. A mother of one of the kids was helping on the retreat and she told me that she adopted her daughter and I needed to ask her daughter about the story of her adoption. I was able to ask the daughter and she told me that when her birth mother was 17 years old she went in for an abortion. Thankfully, they would not do the abortion because they did not do late term abortions. All I could think of was that this girl has the chance of a life filled with love, good deeds and dreams fulfilled because she was adopted and not aborted.

At the end of the retreat I had the kids share one thing they learned or one thing they were going to change to follow God more closely or one way they experienced the Lord's love and power on the retreat. Purposely, I had the girl tell the story of her adoption. She shared how thankful she was alive and on the retreat. She told us that her life in her mother's womb did not belong to her mother but that it belonged to God. And God wanted her to live.

Right here I want to speak to all men and woman who have been involved in an abortion and are suffering:

Jesus loves you. He wants you to come back to Him. He offers you healing and forgiveness. Do not live in your own condemnation. Jesus is mercy, within mercy, within mercy and He wants you to know that. Jesus does not condemn you but embraces you with mercy and forgiveness. God wants to offer you healing through a priest in the sacrament of reconciliation. He wants to offer you love and hope as you speak to someone who can help you and pray with you. He wants to offer you a ministry called Project Rachel. Project Rachel is a national organization that reaches out in unconditional compassion and forgiveness to anyone who has had an abortion. The whole purpose of this incredibly powerful ministry is to invite God's everlasting love, forgiveness and healing to fill anyone who is suffering from an abortion. Project Rachel uses a retreat format called Rachel's Vineyard Retreats which provides a spiritual and psychological healing process for receiving hope, healing, and wholeness. For forgiveness, healing and new hope call the national Rachel's Vineyard Retreat number 877--HOPE--4ME (877--467--3463). Website is <u>www.rachelsvineyard.org</u>. The national Project Rachel number is 800--5WE CARE (800--593--2273). Website is <u>www.hopeafterabortion.com</u>.

Our bodies are not our own. We exist to glorify God with our bodies. Every thought, word and action that proceeds from our bodies should be to glorify the only wise God, through Jesus Christ.

The bumper sticker for the Christian should be, "God, get your laws on my body." The whole purpose of our bodies is to glorify God and we do that by following His way. If we are not clear what that means we have the duty, as followers and glorifiers of God, to find out. One place we can start is with Christopher West: http://www.christopherwest.com/

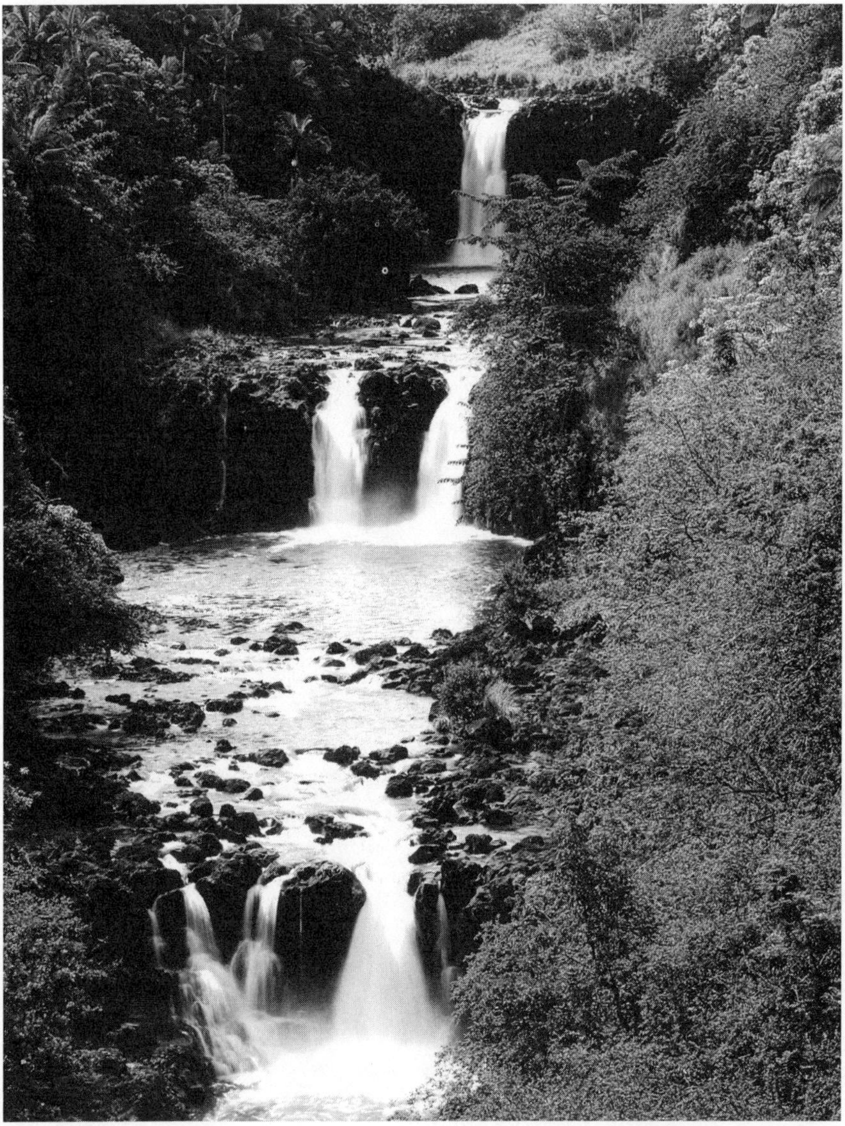

Expect Perfection From God

"The Lord founded the earth and those who dwell on it." Psalm 24:1--2

A couple comes to me and they want to get married. They ask what they must do in order to have a wedding in the church. In the initial meeting for marriage preparation I always ask the man and woman about their relationship with God. If God is not the foundation of their relationship then I do not foresee great results for their married relationship.

The following is not an atypical scenario. A couple desires to get married in the church and one person has faith and practices it regularly. The other person doesn't really know what they think about God and God could or could not become important to them as time rolls along. This is always a red flag for me going into marriage.

We all look for something to be our God for us. If we are not looking to God for that we look to something else. The list can be endless but in a married relationship if we are not looking to God to be God, then we can be looking at the person we are married to and expect them to be God. Obviously, that is not fair. The person you are married to is not God and never will be God. It is not fair to expect perfect love, grace, mercy and kindness from your spouse. Only God can do that.

Ultimately, only God can deliver the kind of love and friendship we want. He delivers it in the gift of Jesus. Only Jesus can bring us saving love and perfect friendship. It is not fair to expect anyone else, including your spouse, to be that for you. But it is absolutely fair to expect saving love and perfect friendship from Jesus Christ.

What do you found your life on? Where does your hope come from? Where have you found perfect love and friendship? Remember, there is only One who is perfect. Go to Him. Expect perfection from God.

Set Out and Bring Jesus

"Mary set out" Luke 1:39

I love the quote, "Many men would become Gods but only one God would become man." In our faith we celebrate the great reality of the Incarnation, i.e. God becoming man. Jesus set out from heaven to earth for us. He left his home to put flesh and bone on the Good News. He not only talked about the Good News but he was the Good News. He set out for us so that we could be with him forever.

Mary set out to visit her cousin Elizabeth when she said "Yes" to giving birth to the savior of the world. She left her home in order to share the Good News of Jesus coming to us. The Hope of our lives would be with us to conquer sin and personally deliver to each of us an invitation to heaven.

Pope John Paul II set out from Rome to the world. He was criticized for not staying in Rome enough and looking after the Administration of the church. But John Paul was compelled to go out. He said, "I must be with my people." And look how he brought Jesus Christ to the world. Do you think all the diplomats, dignitaries, heads of state, etc. and all the world would have come to his funeral if he had not spent his heart, soul, mind and strength on reaching out to all?

I know there are some who complain about me being gone a little much from the office. They think I should be home "running" the church more and around all the time. But I will continue to set out. I will not wait in my office for someone to come shine my shoes. If there is a chance and no one is coming in, I will set out with the Good News of Jesus. I will set out like Jesus, Mary the Mother of God and John Paul II. What would our world look like if we all stayed home and did not share Jesus with others?

When you set out from your home each day, what are you setting out to do? As Christians, whether we are dentists, bus drivers, schoolteachers, religious/priests, etc., the most important thing we should set out to do everyday is to bring Jesus to our families and all we meet. I truly believe that one of our greatest treasures in heaven will be the people we have shared Jesus with on earth.

My good friend did a concert for me recently at my church. One thing I really like about him is that he often says, "You know I was praying about…" This friend, who has written songs for the visits of Mother Theresa and John Paul II to the United States said, "You know this is what I feel God wants for this concert." How cool is that? He shared how he did not just want to show up and sing but he wanted to bring something. That something was someone whose name is Jesus, Yes, my friend set out to do a concert at my church but he also bought something. He brought Jesus.

Pray! Meet Jesus. Set out. Bring Jesus.

The Most High Becomes Most Low

"He has lifted up the lowly." Luke 1:53

Think about the birth of the baby on Christmas morn. There was no room at the Inn so The Holy Family went to the home for the animals. What words can be used to describe his in breaking into our lives as one of us? Rejected from the Inn. Small. Tiny. Insignificant. Dependent. Unnoticed. Lying in a manger in a barn with its dirt, smells and chill in the air. Lowly. Humble. Powerless. Vulnerable. The Most High becomes Most Low.

Though he was in the form of God, Jesus did not deem equality with God something to be grasped at. Rather he became Most Low and took the form of a slave for you and me. With infinite desire and ability, Jesus wants to raise the lowly.

The Most High became the Most Low so that we could live with the Most High.

Jesus traded life in heaven for life on earth so that we would trade life on earth for life in heaven.

So badly, I just want to be filled with mercy and love. I want to love others the same way Jesus has loved me. I think about his love and sometimes feel so far off.

Where can I turn in my desire to love and serve and help and love? I go to the baby Jesus in the manger and see the lowliness of it all. Rejected from the get--go. Tiny. Lowly. Insignificant. Unnoticed. Powerless. Vulnerable. Surrounded by the smell and chills of the barn. Lowly Jesus. I kneel before Lowly Jesus in my own lowliness. And I pray:

Baby Jesus. So many times I feel like you. Rejected. Forgotten. Unnoticed. Vulnerable. Powerless. Not worth much. A failure. I fall down on my knees for you. Help me Jesus. Lift me up. Change me into you. Save me. Raise me. Lift me up into you. May others see you when they see me. To you I give all my condemnations and in return I beg for your mercy. I cry for your mercy, Jesus. Change me into you. I love you, Jesus. Amen

Take heart! The Most High became the Most Low so that we could live with the Most High.

Mercy, Within Mercy, Within Mercy

"Elizabeth's neighbors and relatives had heard that the Lord had shown great mercy towards her, and they rejoiced with her." Luke 1:58

I loosely remember a story about a man living in a marine barracks. He had opened his heart to Jesus and was fired with God's love, joy and passion. He wanted all the other marines to know what he was knowing. Forgiven! Loved! So, he freely shared the Good News. One marine did not want to hear and told him to shut up, but he kept sharing. The marine who did not want to hear, proceeded to beat him up. He hit him time and time again. With a broken nose and blood everywhere, he fell to the floor. He did not retaliate. The aggressor yelled, "Why can't you shut up?" bathed in pain and blood, his response was, "Because Jesus loves you." Long story short, the mercy the beaten man showed led to the other man's conversion. No matter how we try to shut up, beat up or deny God, he will always be mercy. God is mercy, within mercy, within mercy!

Thomas Merton said, "God is mercy, within mercy, within mercy." How wonderful is that? You peel off one layer of God's mercy and you get another layer. You peel off that next layer and you get another layer of mercy. And so on, forever! Great News! Jesus came to show us a God of mercy, within mercy, within mercy.

Change Up Your Diet

"Whoever eats my flesh and drinks my blood has eternal life." John 6:54

What we are hungry for has a lot to do with out diet.

I remember the time of my ordination to the priesthood. Beginning about a week before I was ordained I got cluster migraine headaches. Oh, the pain! One thing the doctors told me to do in order to break the cycle of headaches was to change up my diet. True confession – I wasn't the healthiest eater in the world. I like my pizza, hamburgers and junk food. Well, I started eating a much healthier and balanced diet with the four food groups. As my diet improved I felt my improved health, digestion and overall physical well--being. My body was craving this healthy eating but until I changed up my diet I did not realize this way of eating was what I was truly longing for.

But we are simply not people who have a hunger of the stomach for the body. Our deepest hunger is a hunger of the heart. We hunger for meaningful relationships filled with lasting joy and love. Our greatest desire is to be in relationship with God and others. The most beautiful thing in life is to be in friendship with God and to share that friendship with others. That is the "diet" we all long to be on. Unfortunately and to our own unhappiness, we forget about the hunger of the heart. We miss out on what we long for most in this life – the diet of love.

Once we realize that we are not feeding the hunger of hearts, we can respond to meet the need. Knowing that we want to feed on God's love, there are countless ways to change up our diet. And the more we change up our diet to feed on God, the more we will want to feed on him.

What we are hungry for has a lot to do with our diet.

Some possible diet plans to feed the hunger of the heart: 1) I am preparing a young couple for marriage that has been praying together each night for over 2 years. Right now they live 5 hours away from each other but they pray each night on the phone before they go to bed. Talk about God feeding! 2) A teenager who rides the bus for 1--1/2 hours each way on Sundays to come to Mass. This is a true story of a youth that comes to our church each week! Talk about choosing the best diet possible! 3) And the possibilities are endless to feed on God.

Do you need to change your diet in order to feed the hunger of your heart?

You've Got Mail

The angel said to the shepherds, "For today in the city of David a savior has been born for you who is Christ and Lord." Luke 2:11

"You've got mail." This is the phrase that computer users hear when they open up their email on AOL, "You've got mail." Now some of it can be junk mail, spam, or unwanted forwards but other emails can be great stuff especially if it is personal from a friend or loved one.

Expanding on this notion, we remember that we have mail. God has sent us His Son and tells us in our hearts, "You've got mail." And the mail we have been given is Jesus, who is Christ and Lord. What is different about this mail? It is totally free-- no stamps, electricity costs, monthly server payments. It is instantaneous. Now, we could say email is instantaneous but it is not in the sense that Jesus is. An email takes time to write and then someone on the other end needs to open and read it. Plus there could be a power outage and there would be no way for email to be quick.

Also, have you ever had an email written directly to you from God? There is no doubt that people have sent you scriptures (which, I know, can be argued as God's personal email to us), stories or other words that have touched your soul but has God ever logged on and sent a personal email to you via the internet? Now, we've got personal mail all the time. Each and every second God is saying to us, "You have the mail of my Son who is anointed, appointed and able to save you from your sins. Rejoice, oh highly favored daughters and sons of God, because you always have mail-- Jesus the Lord. He is Emmanuel-- God is with us. All the time. You've got mail."

Any time you hear or think, "You've got mail", I hope you will go right to Jesus knowing that He is the only one anointed, appointed and able to bring us to heaven.

You've got mail – all the time. His name is Jesus.

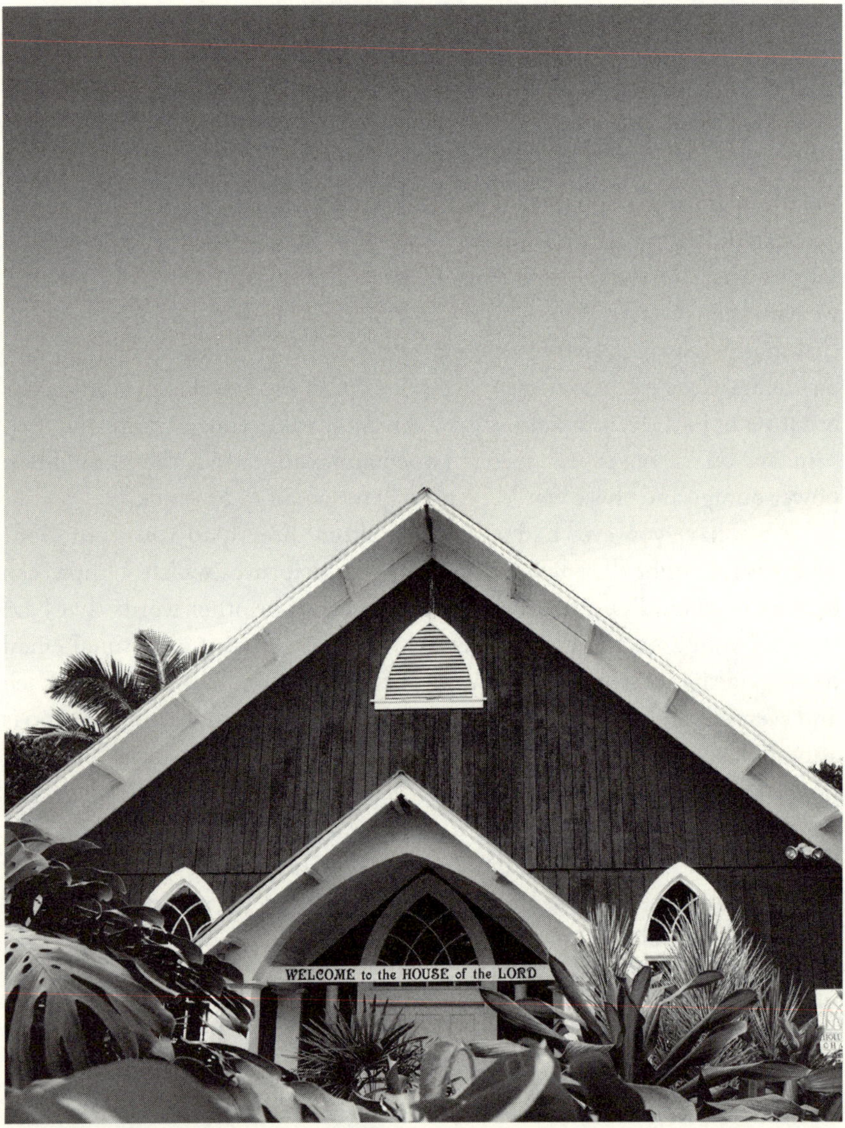
WELCOME to the HOUSE of the LORD

Go First Class!

"Call an assembly." Joel 2:15

The prophet Joel says, "Call an assembly." That is what church is all about. We are all called together to God. The meaning of church is to be "called out from" our busy lives of action, stress, and doing and "called into" the heart, will, and life of God. And because of Jesus, we can go first class in the Church.

It is such an unbelievably awesome wonder to serve as a priest. God is so good---- all the time ---- and ya'll show me that-- all the time. God's people, that is you, just keep blessing and blessing and blessing me! One blessing was a woman who sent me and my friend to Hawaii for 10 days ---- first class. Coming home I was not used to first class treatment. Since I have never flown first class before I kept forgetting that you get special treatment like boarding first, two or three attendants serving you the whole flight, nice food and drinks, cushy and roomy seats. So, I am sitting there in my first class seat watching all the people board the plane and this woman and her husband come on and all she says as she is walking by and looking at me is, "What time is it?" I surmise that she knows me somehow. And that just makes me smile all over! If you do not know, I teach that when some asks you what time it is you are to say the time and then add, "And you are loved!" Yes! The King of kings loves me, loves her and her husband, and loves all people. There is nothing more first class than that!

Life is all about whether we choose to go first class or not. Jesus invites us to a first class way of life. The key is just to be the best friend you can be to him. Living in his love is first class living. Talk about first class treatment – unconditional love, forgiveness of sins, and eternal life! Name something better! And you don't need money to go first class. Just a surrendered heart to his way and love. And guess what – everyone is invited to go first class. Are you in?

The church offers us three disciplines to help us choose a first --class life with Jesus: prayer, fasting and almsgiving. Remember, church means to be "called out from" our busy, hectic lives and "called into" the life of Christ. The whole purpose of prayer is union with God. As we are more and more united with Christ, we are more and more united with perfect love and goodness. Talk about going first class! Fasting reminds us that what we are looking for is Someone. We are hungry and we want to be satisfied and only one can satisfy. The psalmist cries out, "Whom do I have in heaven but you? And there is nothing on earth I desire but you." Talk about a first class feast! In alms giving we care for the poor. We make sure no member in the body of Christ (i.e. all people) is lacking Christ and his care. God wants us to reach out with first class love and service to the poor so that all people will go first class-- all the way to heaven.

When we are united with God and his love and way, we are going first class.

Go first class!

Sentenced to Joy

"Jesus, answered them, 'Can the wedding guests mourn as long as the bridegroom is with them?'" Matthew 9:14

One of the disciplines that can help us draw near to the Lord is fasting from food. Of course, we can extend the meaning of fasting to refraining from gossiping, lusting, judging, swearing, watching TV, unnecessary noise, etc. The context of today's scripture is John's disciples are asking Jesus why his disciples do not fast from food while the Pharisees fast so much. Jesus replies to their question with an analogy of a wedding. Jesus is the groom and there is great joy at the happening of this wedding. It is a time of celebration and not mourning.

Here is an incredibly sweet fact. **It is impossible to be in the presence of Jesus and not have joy!** Looked at another way, we cannot be in Jesus' presence and be sad. Joy happens when we are with Jesus! And this joy will flow from the fact that Jesus has "wedded" himself to us. Jesus, who is perfect in love and goodness, has made a covenant with each one of us in which he says, "I will be true to you, in good times and in bad, in sickness and health, forever and ever." And he has sealed that covenant in his blood. There is no possibility of revocation.

Here is another incredibly sweet fact. The joy of knowing Jesus is greater than any suffering we will ever have to face. As a priest I have had the utter privilege to journey with many people through their suffering and death. Some of these people have been in extreme pain. But it always strengthens me when I see the lived reality of those who know the groom. The joy is always greater than the pain. When you are united with Jesus you have to have joy and the joy is greater than the suffering.

I think we do a lot of fasting in our world today. But it is the wrong kind. We fast from Jesus. We refrain from Jesus. We stay away from Jesus. We get so busy focusing on our jobs, reputations, houses, cars, retirement, sports, grades, or even our family members and yet we forget about Jesus. We fast from the one who will make it all come together in the joy of our salvation.

Fasting is a trumpet sounding to remind us to stop fasting from Jesus. He is our groom forever. You will have joy when you are in the presence of Jesus.. Joy is greater than the suffering.

The Greatest Leaders are the Best Followers

"Jesus saw a tax collector named Levi sitting at the customs post. 'He said to him, Follow me.'" Luke 5:27

The greatest leaders to Christ are the best followers of him.

Think about the people who have been most like Christ to you in your life. What have they done with their lives to become like Christ? How have they spent their time? I bet you they are people who have prayed and reflected a lot. I am sure that they have experienced a lot of healing and forgiveness for their personal sufferings and sins. I imagine their life faithfully reflects the life of Jesus we find in the Gospels. Wisdom, humility, service, and joy are just a few of the many life--giving gifts they bring to all they encounter. And all the good that flows from them is because they are good at following.

From our reflections on who has been most Christ--like to us I would again like to reiterate that the greatest leaders to Christ are the best followers of Christ. We are followers of Jesus and that means he is in front of us leading our path.

I recall one study on silence and church congregations. I do not know the exact statistics but I think the following is fairly accurate. The results showed that a congregation can *cope* (my word for emphasis) with silence for about 14 seconds and then it starts to get restless and people begin to twitch (smiles), cough, and shuffle their bodies or the books in front of them. 14 seconds! If we can't still ourselves and be a follower of Christ, how will we ever be a great leader for him?

I know a priest who was the president of a Catholic University, writing books, speaking internationally and so on, who was also praying two hours a day. As his life became busier, someone asked him about how he had time to pray. He said, "You are right. My life is getting so busy now I need to pray more."

Countless people have been touched by this man's life. The greatest leaders to Christ are the best followers of him.

Turn to Each Other and God

"Repent, and believe in the gospel." Mark 1:15

    I am the youngest of eight boys. Recently one of my brothers called his wife and children together for a family meeting that would turn out to be a great experience of repentance. One definition of repentance could be asked in the form of a question: "Would you kindly turn around from the direction you are going and move towards God and the Gospel way of life?" Saturday was not atypical with soccer games, errands and the stress of trying to get so much done and pack it all in. Nerves, tensions, stress, impatience were definitely on the rise. Waking up on Sunday morning, my brother pulled the family together and had everybody answer questions about the hardest thing and the best thing in their lives. I think the answers they shared with each other are telling. It all had to do with relationships and whether they were working and loving or not. The hardest thing for family members is when they were fighting, being selfish, bickering, being exclusive. The best thing going on was when they were loving, including and sharing with each other. As each person shared what was difficult, it brought the importance of relationships to the fore. Individual members recognized their own sin and they turned toward one another and God in repentance. The whole family meeting ended up in forgiveness, reconciliation, and hugs.

    Fathers, call a family meeting so that you can talk about the "hardest" things in your family and forgive one another. Mothers, do the same. Do it once a month. Children, ask your families to gather together so that instead of turning away from each other you will turn to each other and to God. Let us deal with each other in our lapses of love and turn to God to find Gospel life and forgiveness. Friends, you can do this, too! Repent!

    The Holy Mass contains so many beautiful prayers. I want to close with one from the Eucharistic Prayer of Reconciliation II. Fathers, mothers, sons, daughters and friends---- Perhaps you can use this prayer as you gather to turn to God and one another to experience of fullness of Gospel life and forgiveness as you repent.

God of power and might,
We praise you through you Son, Jesus Christ, who comes in your name.
He is the Word that brings salvation.
He is the Hand that you stretch out to sinners.

He is the way that leads to your peace.

God our Father,
We had wandered far from you,
But through your Son you have brought us back.
You gave him up to death
So that we might turn to again to you
And find our way to one another.

Therefore we celebrate the reconciliation
Christ has gained for us.
AMEN

Daily Bread

"Give us this day our daily bread" Matthew 6:12

My mom relays the following story. After she gave birth to her sixth child, my dad had a reaction you would not necessarily expect with the miracle of a new baby. He cried but it wasn't exactly for joy. Dad was wondering how he was going to raise, feed, clothe, insure, and educate all of his children. It is understandable how that stress, worry, and fear can come into play.

In the Lord's Prayer, Jesus teaches us to pray, "Give us this day our daily bread." He doesn't say pray this way, "God, show me every eventuality and how you will exactly work it out so that I will not have to worry about anything." But he does ask us to trust and depend upon him day by day knowing that he will work all things for good (see Romans 8:28). God does not want us to worry. If we ask him to feed us with his presence daily, we will know His perfect and sure arms holding us in provision.

Just a few days ago I had a dad--like experience, that is, when his child number six was born, of non--trust. I was worshipping with the NET (National Evangelization Teams---- www.netusa.org) and thinking about the four Masses I would be celebrating on Ash Wednesday. I was kind of overcome with fear and wondering how I was going come up with homilies for all those Masses---- two of which were at my church and two more in two of our Catholic high schools in Portland. I was also thinking of many other things like the demands of Lent, being a good pastor, all the needs of my thousand ---- household member parish. How was I going to do it all? Where would I find the words? Where would I get the strength to be there for everyone who comes to me? Would the wisdom of God be made clear to me in the plethora of situations I face daily? And so on... I think you get the point by now! You have your own over whelming schedule. As we were praising God, it was like he took me back through time and showed me how He had always provided the words, strength, and wisdom. He asked, "When have I ever not been faithful to you in your preaching?" And I answered, "Never, Lord. You have always been faithful to me." Next, God gave me the heart of my Ash Wednesday homilies in about 15 seconds---- something only God can do. And then I melted into God's presence. Humbled and quivering in his faithful embrace.

Jesus is faithful and true. He is our provision. He wants us to depend on him second by second. We pray, "Give us this day our daily bread." It is a daily, second by second thing.

Remember, "We do not know what the future holds but we know Who holds the future."

True Mirrors

"Jonah walked through the city announcing, 'Forty days more and Nineveh shall be destroyed,' when the people of Nineveh believed God; they proclaimed a fast and all of them, great and small, put on sackcloth." Jonah 3:3

The people of Nineveh changed at the hearing of the prophet Jonah's word. He called to repent and turn back to the Lord and they did. Do we?

The way the church is set up and the way any family should be set up is that it is a school of love. It is where we should perpetually and deeply learn about the love Christ has shown us the cross. The heart of Christ's love is forgiveness. We are all God's children and we all have sinned but if we believe in Christ and fully accept the gift of His salvation we will live forever in sinless heaven. The way of forgiveness is the way to heaven. The heart of a Christian's life, like the heart of Christ, should be about forgiveness. We should all forgive much and be forgiven much.

Life can be looked at as a retreat in which we focus on strengthening our relationship with God and each other. One way we can do that is to use the analogy of a mirror. It is a time to look in the mirror and reflect on what we see. It is a time to look in the mirror of God and have him reflect back what he sees. It is a time to let other people become mirrors to us and let them reflect back what they see. The true mirror is not the one that hangs in the bathroom or on the wall. That only shows the exterior and we can usually be pretty good about putting on a "happy face." No, the true mirror is the one who is able to reflect back to us what is proceeding from our heart. Our true mirror is our God who knows all about us and forgives us for whatever we have done or failed to do. Our true mirror is our spouse, son, daughter, family member or friend who shows us that we are in need of forgiveness and that forgiveness is absolute in the power of the cross.

How open are you to the true mirrors in your life? Stop. Look. Listen. Be aware of how Christ and the true mirrors are calling you back to the way of forgiveness.

Promises

"For you have made great above all things your name and your promises" Psalm 138:3

Promises. Lent is a time for promises. One Lent I promised to God, my family and friends, my parish that I would not watch TV. That is big because my favorite thing ever to watch on TV is March Madness. I try to do several extra things during Lent and one of those things is to give up something. I had been praying about what to fast from and I felt God very clearly speaking to me as I was praying before Ash Wednesday, "The TV. Give up the TV." Of course I jumped with joy at God's command. OK – I am not being totally honest about that.

God is the Promise--Keeper. Whatever He has promised to us throughout all of history, He has delivered in Christ. My mind turns to the Beatitudes now. It would be good to spend some time in prayer with the Beatitudes-- Matthew 5:3--12. Jesus starts his teaching out by saying "how blest are the poor in spirit; the Kingdom of heaven is theirs." What a promise! Those sinners who cry out to God for salvation and receive his gift will live with God in the glory of heaven for ever. Jesus makes good on the promise of his offering as he seals it with his blood.

I think it is safe to say that we all make promises. Some people might have made the promise not to speed in their cars. (After a couple of infractions/citations in my earlier driving career, I decided I would not speed anymore.) Some people have promised eat right, rest more, study harder, and not to lie, cheat, steal, be lazy. The husband and wife in marriage have promised to be true to each other in good times and bad, in sickness and health, and to love and honor each other all the days of their lives.

Christ has promised us everlasting life. What have you promised Him?

Really think about what promises you have made to Christ. Write down what your present promises are to Christ. He is the first one we should promise our hearts to. Then, pray to Christ and ask him what additional promises you can make to Him to guarantee Christ has primacy of place in our lives.

God's Plan for You

"My soul waits for the Lord more than sentinels wait for dawn." Psalm 130:7

Think about your nearest local sit--down for dinner--type restaurant. How much food goes to waste there each day? I am sure we would be amazed at the amount of food that goes to waste in just one day. Now, think about the fact that an average of 40,000 people starve to death each day in our world. This is a sad reality. Something is wrong. What if each person in the world waited on the Lord and followed his will? I know we would have a very different reality regarding 40,000 people starving to death each day on our planet.

One time I had a senior sitting in my office right before he was going to graduate from high school. He was all set to go to one of the most prestigious academic universities in the USA. I had spent a fair amount of time with this young man and I knew the two areas of study he most deeply loved were history and theology. So, I asked him what he was going to major in at university and he said engineering. I said, "Engineering? If you love history and theology, then why aren't you going after that?" It seemed to me so incongruous that his major did not line up with his deepest passions for learning. I am just speculating here-- maybe just because it has always been a person's dream to go to a big--name university doesn't mean that is God's dream. Above all else, Jesus is the big name school we want to go to!

God has a plan for our lives!!!! We need to wait on Him, pray to Him, and seek His light revealing ourselves to ourselves. Other people can help reveal that plan. And not only does God want to reveal that plan to us, he wants to show us day by day how to more fully live out that plan. We wait on the Lord to see if he wants us to be married, single, a priest/religious/minister and he shows us that major plan. And we believe that He will reveal His plan to us if we seek Him with all that we have. Our lives, then, are not based on shaky speculation but on the true revelation of God personally showing us his plan day by day. God unpacks his plan for us. Just because I am a priest, does not mean that I in any way, shape, or form fully know what it means to be a priest of Jesus Christ. Hence, like a sentinel, I daily pray and ask God what it means to be His priest. I keep growing and learning and growing as I wait on the Lord to more fully reveal what it means to be a priest. By analogy, that is true for all of us---- whether married, single, or consecrated.

A rock star, known to be a Christian and activist, addressed the President of the United States, dignitaries, and all of us at The National Prayer Breakfast. He was talking about doing what God wants us to do in life. I close with his words, "A number of years ago, I met a wise man who changed my life. In countless ways, large and small, I was always seeking the Lord's blessing. I was saying, you know, I have a new song, look after it. I have a family, please look after them. I have this crazy idea..."

And this wise man said: "Stop. Stop asking God to bless what you're doing. Get involved in what God is doing ---- because it's already blessed."

God has a plan for your life and how you live your days. Find it!

You Are Loved - Be That Love

"For your heavenly Father makes his sun rise on the bad and the good, and causes rain to fall on the just and the unjust." Matthew 5:44

I was standing in line ready to board a plane in an East Coast airport. I had just finished speaking at youth conference with 3,000 kids. God, as usual, worked so powerfully, and the grace of the Holy Spirit was pounding in my being. I, like always, just wanted everyone who was in line to board the plane, and everyone who was in that airport, and everyone in that city, and everyone in the world to know God's love. But the way to go about doing that is to share it with the person God has put in front of you. So, I was talking to the person who was right in front of me as we waited to be called aboard our flight. If you do not know, I wear a "You are loved" watch. On the top of the inside of the watch it says, "It is…", and at the bottom of the inside of the watch it says… "and you are loved!" I looked for an opening to share God's love with this senior--to--be in college and it happened. Using my watch, I was able to share with her that God loves each of us---- all the time. God's love for us is unconditional and everlasting. God does not pick and choose who he will love. He pours out his heart for every person---- all the time. As I talked with this collegian, she asked me if I was a Catholic priest (hint: I had my collar on). I replied, "Yes." And she said, "Well, I am a Jew." And I said, "You are a Jew and you are loved!"

Our God causes the sun to rise on the good and the bad, and he makes the rain fall on both the just and unjust. In other words, our Heavenly Father does not discriminate in who He loves. He loves you and me and each human being fully, freely and forever. You are loved! Whether Jew or Greek, slave or free, rich or poor, pagan, atheist, agnostic or saint. You are loved! That is the deepest truth of our existence. In the preface of marriage, the following prayer is found, "Love is our origin. Love is our constant calling. Love is our fulfillment in heaven."

The indiscriminating love that God has poured out into our hearts is the same indiscriminating love we are to share with others. I found myself having an interesting thought some time ago. I was thinking about the four World Youth Days I have gone to in Paris, Rome, Toronto, and Germany. World Youth Day happens every couple of years when Pope invites youth from all over the world to come to a big gathering and enter more fully into the life and celebration of the faith. Over the years, these gatherings have ranged from 1 million to 8 million people. It is amazing what people will do to even just see the Pope. If he is coming down the street in a car, people will be jammed for miles and miles waiting hours in anticipation for his passing by (kind of sounds like what happened for Jesus). Some will climb trees and buildings just to get a glimpse of him (kind of sounds like Zacchaeus who climbed the tree in order to see Jesus---- see Luke 19:1--10). The reverence, love, affection, honoring, and seeking of the Pope is truly beautiful. Now, here is the thought I had. What if we treated everyone the way we were reaching out to the Pope? What if we lined the streets for hours and climbed buildings and trees in order to even just catch a glimpse of each other? How beautiful would that be? That is the stuff of Jesus' love. That is the enormous and indiscriminating love we are to have for all people. Wow! I do not know about you but I have a long way to go to get there.

Let us pray: "Heavenly Father, you do not pick and choose which of your children you will love and which ones you will not love. You never withhold love from any child of yours. You love us all, all the time. Just as the sun rises on all and the rain falls on all, so too does your love come to each of us at every moment. Help us to open our hearts wide, Father, to your ever present love. Help us to love like you, O God. May we love the person in front of us with the same intensity that you love us. May you make our love beautiful and for the glory of your name. Amen!"

House of Love or Fear?

"Brothers and sisters: If God is for us, who can be against us?" Roman 8:31

At the core of who we are there are two primary emotions: love and fear. And when I refer to fear I am not talking about that mechanism that warns us that real danger is possible like walking down a dark alley in a dangerous neighborhood by yourself late at night. That is a healthy kind of fear and we should pay attention and act accordingly. Rather, I am thinking about things like fear of failing, social situations, looking stupid or ugly, unworthiness, not belonging, public speaking, people with HIV/AIDS, and ultimately, death. Sadly, I think many of us live our lives out of fear.

An acronym for FEAR can be-- **F**alse **E**vidence **A**ppearing **R**eal. It is illusory and stifles love, flourishing, and fulfillment. For example, a child grows up in an abusive household. He learns that he is going to a new home, which happens to be a great family full of love. But this child moves into the new home full of fear because he knows home as a place where he gets abused. When he moves to his new home, the fear grips him.

That this will be a place where he is abused. But this is illusory in his new situation.

All of us live in one of two houses: love or fear. If you think about it, fear and love cannot coexist. You cannot feel both emotions at exactly the same time. And fear has to do with the past and the future. Fear is based on the past and keeps us from doing, acting, loving, and risking in the future. Love, in contrast, is all about the present. We can only experience love in the now. We can only experience God in the present.

Again, I think many of us live in fear. We are afraid to do, act, love and risk. Our culture sells fear. Why do you think our insurance companies and security alarm companies make billions of dollars each year? I know we have to be prudent, but it does point to all the fear we live in.

What do we do with our fear? We have to move from the house of fear to the house of love. We have got to be present to the present in which Jesus is loving us. That is the only place he is loving us. How will we transcend fear and move into love? We will move into Jesus who is perfect love who casts out all fear. If we have Jesus, we cannot have fear.

Live in the present. Move to love now. Focus on Jesus in the present moment because that is where he is. Now, let his perfect love come in and cast out all fear. Your home is with Jesus, now, forever present in his love.

Brothers and sisters: If God is for us, who can be against us?

Jesus Loves Sinners

"This man (Jesus) welcomes sinners and eats with them." Luke 15:1

In Romans 5:8 we read, "It is precisely in this that God proves his love for us: that while we were still sinners, Christ died for us." Jesus Christ loves sinners! He does not disdain, exclude, or cast out anyone who comes to him with a cry for mercy. Whether the sin is murder, adultery, stealing, abortion, gossip, lying, or watching porn, the mission of Jesus is to love and forgive sinners. From the infinite power flowing from the cross, every sin of every sinner for all of time is forgiven and washed away in the blood of Jesus. Good News!

The following is part of a song I wrote: "From the cross, on the hill, in the midst of agony. Jesus proved he'd love us---- for all eternity. As we laughed at him and beat him, spitting in his face. Jesus just kept loving, unconditional embrace. He cried, Father, forgive them, they know not what they do. Listen to his cry for love---- a cry for me and you. How could he keep on loving us? How could he be for real? Pouring out his blood for us, the cross on a hill."

If God has forgiven you, why can't you forgive yourself?

Jesus welcomes sinners and eats with them. By having a meal with a sinner, Jesus is saying, "I want to enter into an intimate and abiding relationship with you. In this relationship you will come to know the most beautiful, merciful and enduring love that you can ever possibly know. It is a love that bares all, forgives all and gives all." As a friend, Jesus says these are the words to you. And, that is the friend Jesus is to you all the time.

Let us pray. "Jesus, I know you died for my sins. I know you forgive me no matter what I have done. Please forgive me. Help me to believe in your forgiveness. Amen."

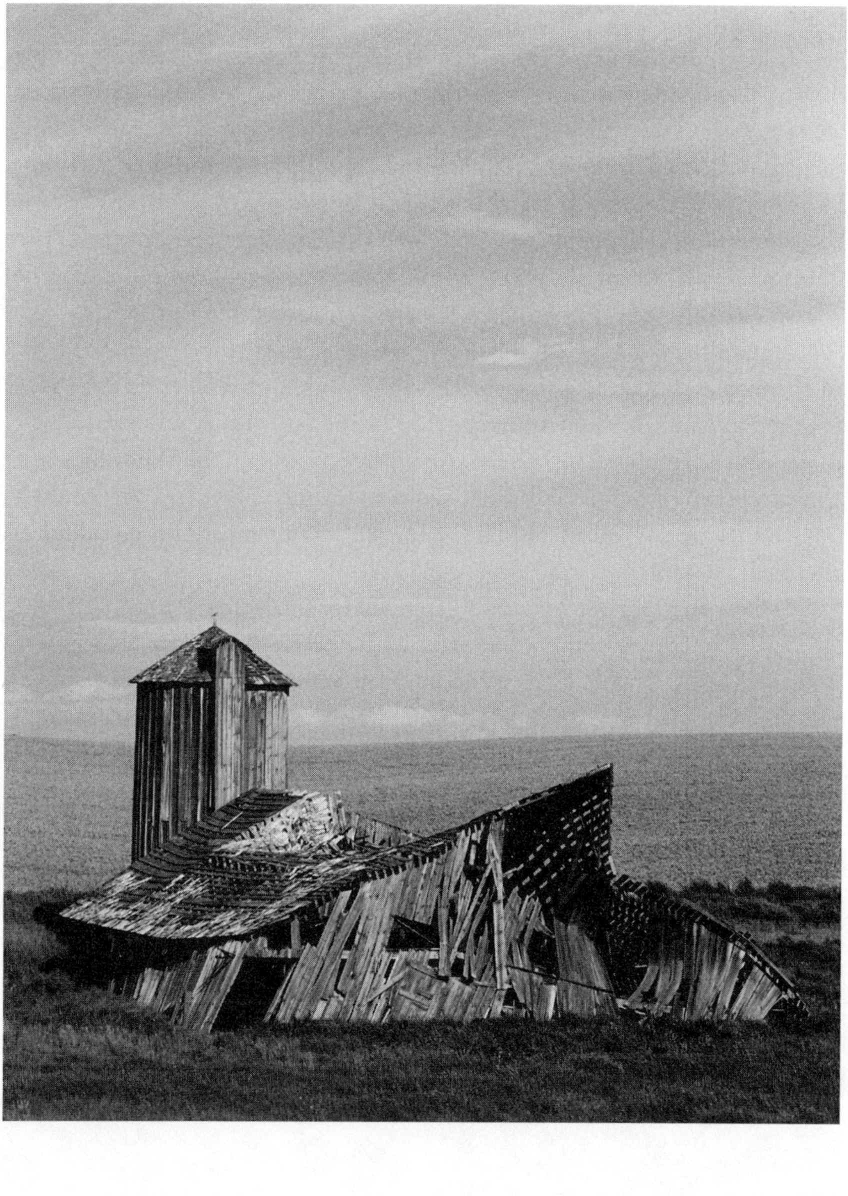

How We Suffer

"Can you drink the chalice that I am going to drink?" Mathew 20:23

Jesus asks James and John if they will be able to drink the chalice that he is going to drink. He is responding to their mother's request that James and John be great in Jesus' kingdom by sitting on his left and right. The chalice is a chalice of suffering. The response Jesus gives about being great in his kingdom is striking and goes against our carnal nature. Jesus asks, "Can you suffer?" Are you willing to enter into your suffering? Our flesh and carnal nature will do anything not to have to suffer. We do not like suffering, we do not invite it in, and we will do what we can to avoid it. But, in this context, Jesus connects his kingdom of greatness to drinking in the suffering that he himself will drink in. The whole reason Jesus came to earth was to suffer and die for us. Our journey is about entering more deeply into the mystery of Jesus' suffering and death for us. Jesus remained loyal to God's call to suffer, and we see the how the fullness of God's kingdom comes as he suffers, dies, and rises for us.

God's kingdom comes to and through us as we loyally follow Jesus and drink in suffering. We taste it, feel it, and know it intimately. It is very much part and parcel of following God in life, and we do not avoid it. We invite Jesus in so that the greatness of God and his kingdom in our suffering will become what is most real for us in our lives. Sadly, I see it so often that people do not invite Jesus into their suffering. They look to other places for relief. Whether it is addiction to drinking, drugs, money, work, gambling, another person, or something else, the answer for help in our suffering will be insufficient.

We do not like suffering. We want to avoid it. It is not fun. But it is also the intersection where we can personally meet Jesus. It is where all the words we have heard about God, especially in the Scriptures, can be crystallized into the word of God: Jesus. It is the place where we experience the fullness of Jesus' power. In the depths of our suffering, Jesus embraces us with his infinite victorious love.

Jesus does ask us to drink in the cup and suffer, but he does not ask us to do that alone. What suffering in your life have you not invited Jesus into?

B Forgiving

"Forgive and you will be forgiven." Luke 6:37

One definition of forgiveness is: Giving up all hope for a better past. Sometimes we are bitter and angry in the present because we feel we have been hurt in the past. The past hurt is poisoning our present experience of life. Unfortunately, many of us are stuck in this bad past. Being bitter and angry in the present over something in the past is not going to change what happened in the past. It is only going to physically and spiritually poison us and all those around us with bitterness and anger. The move the Christian needs to make is to Christ in the now. We need to ask Christ, who forgives every sin for all of time, to help us do the same. We want to move from living stuck in the past with bitterness and ask Christ in the present to give us the grace to fully forgive-- just as he has done. Our goal is to always live in Jesus' present forgiveness and not in some past hurt.

How do we forgive, especially when it is difficult? I want to share a few thoughts. First, look at our command to forgive as a great opportunity to rely on Christ. When we need to forgive someone, we are going to need Jesus to do that. So, our need for Jesus impels us to seek greater union with him, and who could we share a better union with than Jesus?

Many times, when it comes to our need to forgive, we do not invite Jesus into the equation. Big mistake! He is the one we need! Only Jesus can bring the forgiveness that lets the past hurts go and makes the present full of forgiveness. We should always pray for a forgiving heart. Better yet, on the top of your prayer list each day, pray for the person who hurt you. Keep praying for that person every time you of think of him or her. Pray that God will fill that person with the fullness of his love and Kingdom. Do this faithfully over a long period of time and watch what happens. Remember, prayer doesn't change what happened in the past; it changes you now.

Another way to forgive is to do something good for that person. St. Paul says it is like putting burning coals on someone if we repay evil with good. Hopefully, they will take notice and choose to live in the same goodness we are trying to live in. Whether or not the one who has hurt us chooses God, we want to give this person the best witness so he or she will be more likely to choose the goodness of forgiveness.

We all have our own stories of past hurts. When our past hurts are not brought into the present healing of God, they tend to perpetuate and extend out to negatively affect more and more people. It is easier to forgive someone when we realize that person is acting out of his or her story of pain without the benefit of God's forgiveness and healing. Maybe God is calling you to be the one to help a person move from living in the past with his hurts into the present of Jesus' forgiveness. Gently invite him to tell you their story, listen well, and wait for the opportunity to bring him the good news that Jesus is the Lamb of God who takes away all the sins of the world.

Forgive and you will be forgiven.

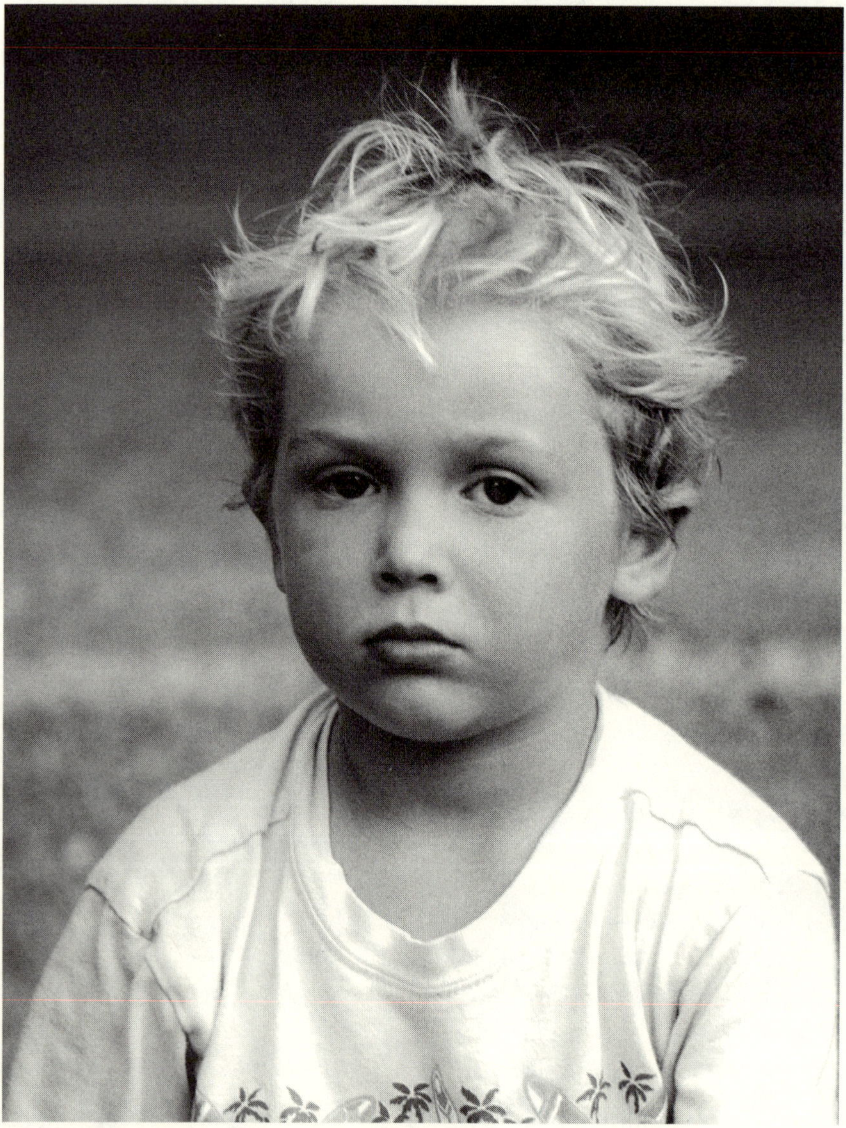

No Orphans

"Hear the orphan's plea." Isaiah 1:16

Imagine what it would be like to be an orphan without any family. The world is big and complicated and it takes so much to maneuver through life to be successful. And the way we do that is by having parents and a family that teaches us "in the way to go." Unfortunately, so many of our families are torn to pieces. Making sense of life is difficult for so many children who, whether they are actually orphans or not, are living an orphan--like existence. There is such a tremendous need for so many to have a stable family system. So many who are living an orphan--like existence, and that includes people of all ages need a consistent diet of meaning and love.

How will the church, that is, you and me, respond to all the orphans in our society? We must always remember that, while we all come from natural families that may range from excellent to fundamentally nonexistent, God has a spiritual family that can make up for what is lacking in the natural family. We, as a church, must reach out to all orphans in our midst and invite them into the family where they will be able to continually grow in love and meaning. God is the Father, Mary is the Mother, Jesus is our brother and the Holy Spirit makes us all come together in the unity of God's family. There are no orphans in God's family. To be a part of God's family is to be part of the biggest, most loving, most beautiful family that will be a family forever.

God has no grandchildren. What does that statement mean? It means God has only children. Every child that is born is a child of God. We are all sons and daughters of the Father who cannot abandon us and will never reject us. As Christian people who know that God wants to gather us as His sons and daughters into one family, we must always reach out, in word and deed, to invite any orphan into the knowledge that he or she is a son or daughter of God. I am the youngest of eight boys. The greatest thing my parents ever taught me is that I am a loved son of God the Father. My mother and father could not be there, front and center, for me much of the time because they were so busy raising eight boys. But they did teach me about the one who was there for me front and center--- all the time. They gave me God and God's family. As a son of the Father, I knew God was always with me, drawing me and all his other daughters and sons into the unity of the biggest, most beautiful, and loving family that would last forever.

Brothers and sisters, the greatest thing we can teach an orphan is that he or she is a loved son or daughter of God and that we all belong to God's family today and forever.

Make sure there are no orphans in your midst.

Who Will Save the Day?

"Cursed is the man who trusts in human beings." Jeremiah 17:6

We all look for someone to "save the day." Who will "save our day?" We do not want life and love and relationships to end with death. On our own power, however, we know that death would surely be the end. Hence, we know we are going to have to trust something outside of ourselves to "save the day" when we die.

The whole of scriptures teach that there is only one who can save the day and that one is not another sinful human being. To our own detriment, we often look to another person to save us. We treat him or her like she or he is God and we trust that person to save the day. We act as if he or she will give us the answers to all of life mysteries including death. To trust another person to save the day is foolish and unfair. It is impossible for another human being to do so.

Obviously, we are all looking for a savior. And if the Lord is not the savior, we will put our trust in something or someone else to save us. I have seen many relationships in which one or both people do not know the Lord. What happens, knowing that they themselves cannot save the day, is that one person looks to the other to save the day. It is as if the person who does not know the Lord as savior puts pressure on the other person to offer unconditional love and eternal life. Regardless of how much pressure is put on, it will never happen. Only a fool would continue in this way of life once he or she realizes that another human being cannot save the day. Sadly, I see many people throughout their lives seeking another human being to save their day.

I think graveyards can be great classrooms to teach us about death and dying. For example, say someone does not believe in the Lord as savior. Go to the graveyard and spend some time looking at the tombstones. Read the about the names, dates, and lives of the people buried there. Perhaps it is your family members. Think about your own mortality. Our physical bodies will all be planted there in less than 120 years. Who will raise those bodies up? Grandparent, Mom, Dad, spouse, best friend? No!

When really uncovered, the most pressing need we have in life is for someone to "save the day" for us. Only the Savior can raise us from the dead. Would not getting to the Savior be the greatest priority for any of us mortal human beings? The graveyard can be a very beneficial place of learning to that end.

Why Reject Abundant Life?

"Jesus said to the chief priests and the elders of the people: Hear another parable." Matthew 21:33--46

Jesus used stories or parables to each his hearers about the meaning of life. I often find myself telling stories in my preaching and teaching in order to bring home certain points. I will share one of many examples that come to mind. I had a wonderful experience in college. Particularly, my experience of God and community life was off the charts. It was a place I did not want to leave when I graduated because I was flourishing. I had this incredible experience of two years as a gift from the Lord and I did not want it to end. As I was thinking about all of this a scripture came to mind. A person who had been healed by Jesus just wanted to physically stay with Jesus after he was healed but Jesus told him to go back to his town. The man had been given a gift that he was supposed to go back and share in his community. For me, by analogy, I knew that I had been given a vision and experience of a community in God that I was to share with the world. Obviously, God has given me a great avenue to give my life in service for community by calling me to serve as His priest.

In Matthew 21: 33--46, Jesus tells a parable about the landowner and tenants. The landowner (God) plants a vineyard (his Kingdom) and leases it out to tenants (here Jesus is addressing the chief priests and elders of the people). When time for harvest comes, the landowner sends his servants (the prophets) to obtain produce. The tenants react by killing many servants until the landowner finally decides to send his own son, thinking they will respect him. But the tenants do not respect the landowner's own son and they kill him. This parable refers to how God has sent many prophets throughout Israel's history to bring the people back to God and how they were killed because of the word they spoke. Of course, when the landowner sends his own son at vintage time, Jesus is referring to himself and that he will be put to death as well.

How can we, like the tenants of the vineyard (Kingdom of God) reject the abundant life and fruit of the Kingdom of God? As disciples of Jesus, let us gaze deeply into the life he is calling us to live. As we prayerfully gaze into the life of Jesus, we see that it is not comfortable, convenient, and easy. But I like my comfort, convenience, and ease. Isn't that what fast food, instant messaging, and cell phones are all about? I would choose comfort, convenience, and ease any day and any time of the day. The only problem is that is not what Jesus has chosen. And, as disciples of Jesus, we choose what He has chosen. He chose things like suffering and sacrifice to forget about his own agenda and live for God, to love his enemies, to get up early and pray, and to forgive his executioners in the midst of utter pain, rejection and humiliation. Yes, Jesus' life was anything but comfort, convenience, and ease.

How have you rejected the abundant life of the Kingdom by choosing comfort, convenience, and ease over the way of Jesus?

Zealously Knocking on Your Door

His disciples recalled the words of Scriptures; Zeal for your house will consume me." John 2:17

Jesus, upset, comes into the temple area and in no uncertain terms tells those who were buying and selling to get lost. In his zeal, Jesus says to stop making his Father's house of prayer a marketplace.

Think about zeal and what it means to be zealous. What comes to my mind are words like excitement, fervor, fire and boldness. Maybe zeal can be defined as the inability for a person to contain what is inside because it has become so important. It is when something has touched a person so much it cannot be held down.

Now, think about the zeal Jesus has for you. Reflect on all the goodness and love you see in just one day from your encounters with other people. See the beauty in the sunrise, the flowers, and all you see in creation. Realize all of the love that comes to you through people in just one day. Now, all of that is just a miniscule fraction of the infinite goodness, love, and beauty of Jesus. His zeal is for you to experience all of this---- forever.

Jesus' passion is you! His constant preoccupation is to fill you with infinite goodness, love and beauty. In his perfect and unbroken zeal for you, he stands before the temple of your heart. But Jesus cannot walk into the temple of your heart just like he walked into the temple to drive out those who were doing business. It doesn't work that way. He will not force his will upon us. We have to give him permission to enter.

Revelation 3:20 says, "Here I stand, knocking at the door." Yes, Jesus stands at the door of your heart and requests permission to enter. From the time you were born until the time you will leave this earth, Jesus in his zeal for you is knocking on the door of your heart. An interesting fact, however, about the door of your heart is that there is a doorknob on only one side of the door. And whose side might that be? Yours. Only you can open the door to Christ. You can keep it shut, open it an inch, or swing it wide open.

How open is your door to Jesus? Would not it be wise to swing wide open the door of our hearts and constantly say, "Come in! Come in, Jesus! Bring it..." Talk about going first class and having heaven all the way to heaven.

Let us pray: "Dear Lord Jesus, I know that I am your desire. All you ever want to do is fill me with boundless goodness, love and beauty. I know you stand at the door of my heart and knock. I open wide the door to you. Please come in now, today, and always. Come in, Lord Jesus. I need your company. And just as I am your desire---- you are my desire. May I be zealous for you in the same way as you are zealous for me. Come, Lord Jesus. Amen."

Gossip

"Whoever does not gather with me scatters." Luke 11:23

A man was feeling bad about all the gossiping he had been doing and so he went to confession. For his penance, the priest suggested for the man to cut open a big feather pillow on the windiest day from the top of a tall building. Then he was supposed to gather every last feather and bring it back to the priest to complete his penance. The man going to confession argued, "I will never be able to gather every last feather and bring it back to you, Father." "Exactly," replied the priest, "and that is how it is with the gossip you spread. It just keeps going and going without ever being able to be retracted. The damage multiplies."

An original understanding of gossip comes from gospa or gospel. The Gospel, of course, means Good News. As it all started out, gossip was all about spreading the good news and things that were happening in the community. It was up building, unifying and life producing. People were using the power of words to fulfill the intention Jesus has for us-- to be united as one family in love.

We either gather or scatter with our words. I think it would be a great idea to put all the words we use in one day under a powerful microscope. What would be revealed? Are you a gossip? Gossips work in conjunction with evil to divide people and destroy relationships. They work in opposition to Christ and his plans. I do not think we can begin to calculate the amount of relational destruction that goes on in our world due to gossiping. Like the feathers flying freely through the air on a windy day, gossip multiplies the evil of being separated from God and each other.

What will each thing I say about another person bring about? Will it cause the hearer of my words to be more united to that person or further divided? Am I a gatherer or scatterer with my words? No one was created by God to be a scatterer.

May we all return to the original understanding of gossip-- spreading the Good News about people and our lives together. As the old adage goes, "If you do not have anything good to say about another person then it is probably best to say nothing at all." How about this for a Gospel challenge? Try saying only good things when you speak about other people. I know I have a ways to go but I will do my best to do the same. Let us stop picking on each other.

Be Quiet

"Be still and know that I am God." Psalm 46:1

Blaise Paschal said, "Our unhappiness is the result of not knowing how to remain quietly in a room." So much truth here!

Here is a scenario that is too common. You are in your home or car and it is quiet. You are uneasy with the quiet and so you turn on the TV, music or somehow else try to drown out the quiet. Why do you do this? Is it perhaps because you do not like spending time with someone you do not love? Is Paschal right when he says that the cause of our unhappiness is that we cannot remain with ourselves?

If you cannot take the quiet, you have a conversion to undergo. The goal is to let God fully embrace all the good, bad and ugly we are with his love. In that embrace, we will find the happiness God created us for. In order for that embrace to happen, we need to be quiet.

Be quiet. Be still and know that God is God. Stop doing all the talking in prayer. Listen! St. Peter said to Jesus, "To whom should we go, you have the words of eternal life?" John 6:68. You do not have the words of eternal life. You do not have the power for eternal life. You do not provide the love or happiness you are looking for. Listen. Be quiet.

Interrogate the scriptures to find out the truth of God's love and happiness for you. In Jer. 1:31 we read how God loves us with an everlasting love. We know that God works all things for good for those who love him (Romans 8:28). God has a plan for each of us with a future full of hope and finding him (Jer. 29:11-14). In Psalm 37:4 we know that if we take delight in the Lord he will grant us the desires of our hearts. And on and on and on…

Be still. Be quiet. Listen. Be embraced.

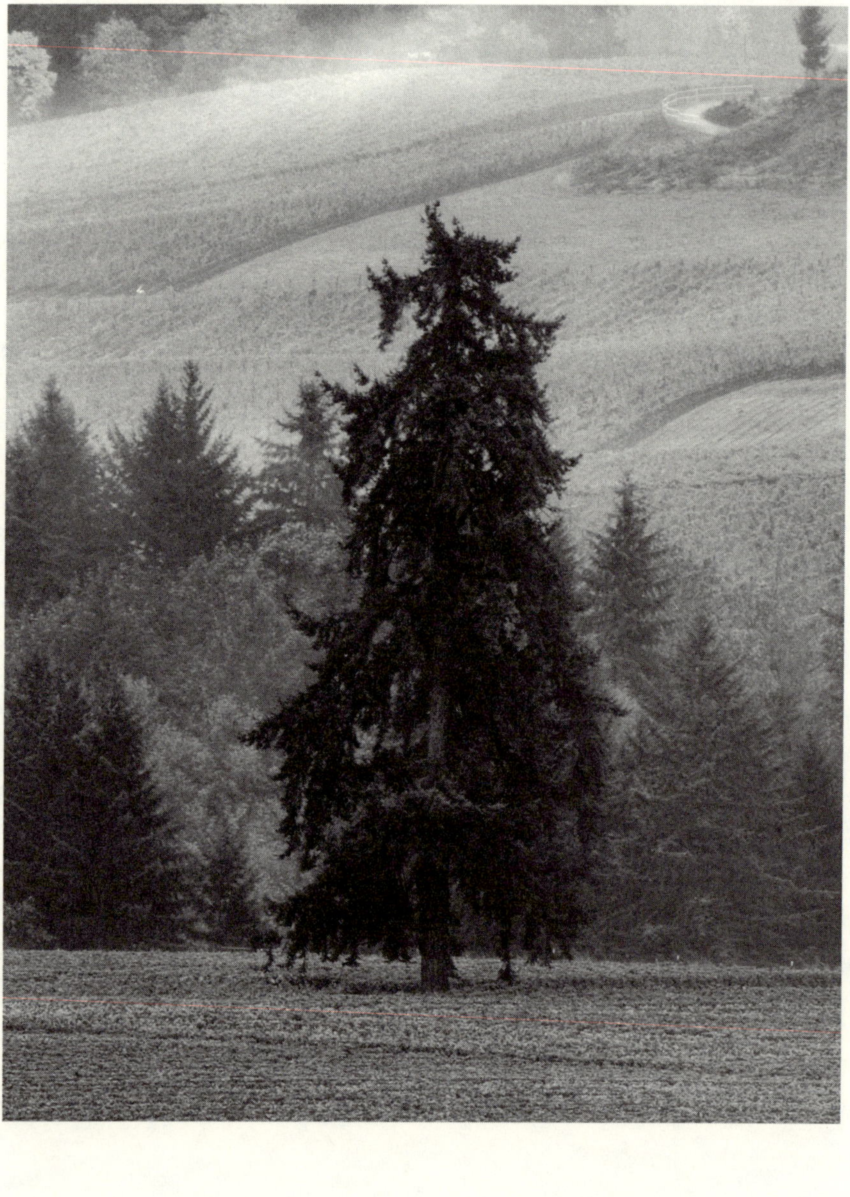

Humility is the Truth of Who We Are in God

"But with contrite heart and humble spirit let us be received." Daniel 3:39

How should we understand humility? Maybe you have heard stories of some of the saints describing themselves as wretches, maggots and worms. Their point might have been to show how small and insignificant they are in relationship to God but that is not how God sees us. God calls us his daughters and sons and he has willed, if you will, all that he has to us. Think of that inheritance! God has handed over everything to Christ who, in turn, hands it over to us. So, in humility, should we describe ourselves as wretches, maggots and worms or as daughter and sons of God who offers us an infinite inheritance?

Humility is about fully receiving and living the truth of who we are in God.

It is interesting to note that humility comes from the word *humus* which means earth. Each Liturgical season of Lent we remember that our bodies are going to be part of the earth someday. On Ash Wednesday, we are marked with ashes as a sign of our own mortality. Think about your body right now. One hundred or so years from now it will be dust. We are headed back to the earth as dust. Doesn't sound too hopeful, does it? Our bodies are breaking down. We are on a collision course with death and decay. It is going to happen. Many people deny this truth but in humility we embrace the fact of our own mortality. But death, decay and ashes are, in no way, the full truth of who we are in God. They are just a minor inconvenience that Jesus totally takes care of.

In humility, we receive Jesus Christ who has died for our sins. The sinless one took on all sin that we might become the very holiness of God. Jesus came from heaven to earth to bring all people on earth to heaven. On the cross he absorbed every sin for all of time into His body so that you and I might come into the infinite inheritance of God. When will you and I act like we are forgiven? When will we rejoice always in the infinite inheritance that Jesus wants us to share in now? At what point will we believe that we are praying for heaven to happen right now when we pray, "Thy Kingdom come, thy will be done, on earth as it is in heaven?" Why don't we believe and know and live and breathe that heaven is with us all the way to heaven? Why do we call ourselves maggots when we are fully forgiven sons and daughters of God with a full heavenly inheritance?

Cast you cares upon God because he cares for you. Cast your sins upon Jesus because he is the Lamb of God who takes away the sins of the world. Jesus loves sinners and that means you! Jesus forgives sinners and that means you! Humble thyself in the sight of the Lord and he will lift you up.

If God gave me the power to make everyone on the face of the earth have a specific experience, a top pick would be to have everyone experience the infinite mercy of Christ in the sacrament of confession. Why? My answer comes in the following story, which I have heard countless times in many ways, shapes, and forms as a priest who hears confessions. A few years ago I heard a confession of a high--school kid. It was her first confession ever. At the end of the confession she cried a few tears as she received Jesus' forgiveness. Right after she left the chapel, her campus minister asked her how confession was. She said, "That was the most loving experience in my life."

Our lives should be the most loving experience-- all the time. In humility, let us let Jesus make it so.

You Can't Earn or Lose God's Love and Acceptance

"Jesus said to his disciples: Do not think I have come to abolish the law and the prophets. I have not come to abolish but to fulfill." Matthew 5:17

How many of us spend so much of our time and energy trying to somehow win the love and acceptance of important people in our lives? We think if we can just prove that we are good enough for our mom and dad or whoever, then we will gain their affection. It is as if we feel we have to earn love through lots of good works. We live with the mindset that we are rewarded with love and acceptance when we are good but, when we are bad, that love and acceptance are taken away.

This whole way of thinking that life is about earning love and acceptance because of all our good works can be transferred to our relationship with God. We think, "If I just do what God wants me to. If I follow his law and do not somehow majorly disappoint him, then I can secure his love and acceptance for me." Now, that might be the way it works in our human relationships that are filled with conditional love. But, that is never the way it works with God! With God, his love and acceptance of us is a preexisting condition. What does that mean? The totality of his love and acceptance is what brought us into existence, and is ours before we "do" anything.

God's love cannot be earned or lost. It is a free gift for the asking. Stop trying to earn it or fearing that you have lost it because it is impossible for that to happen. To help us understand that God's love cannot be earned or lost by the good we do or the sins we commit, let us ponder the following two statements. 1) There is no greater thing you can do in the future to cause God to love you more than he loves you right now. 2) There is no bad thing you can do in the future to cause God to love you less than he loves you right now.

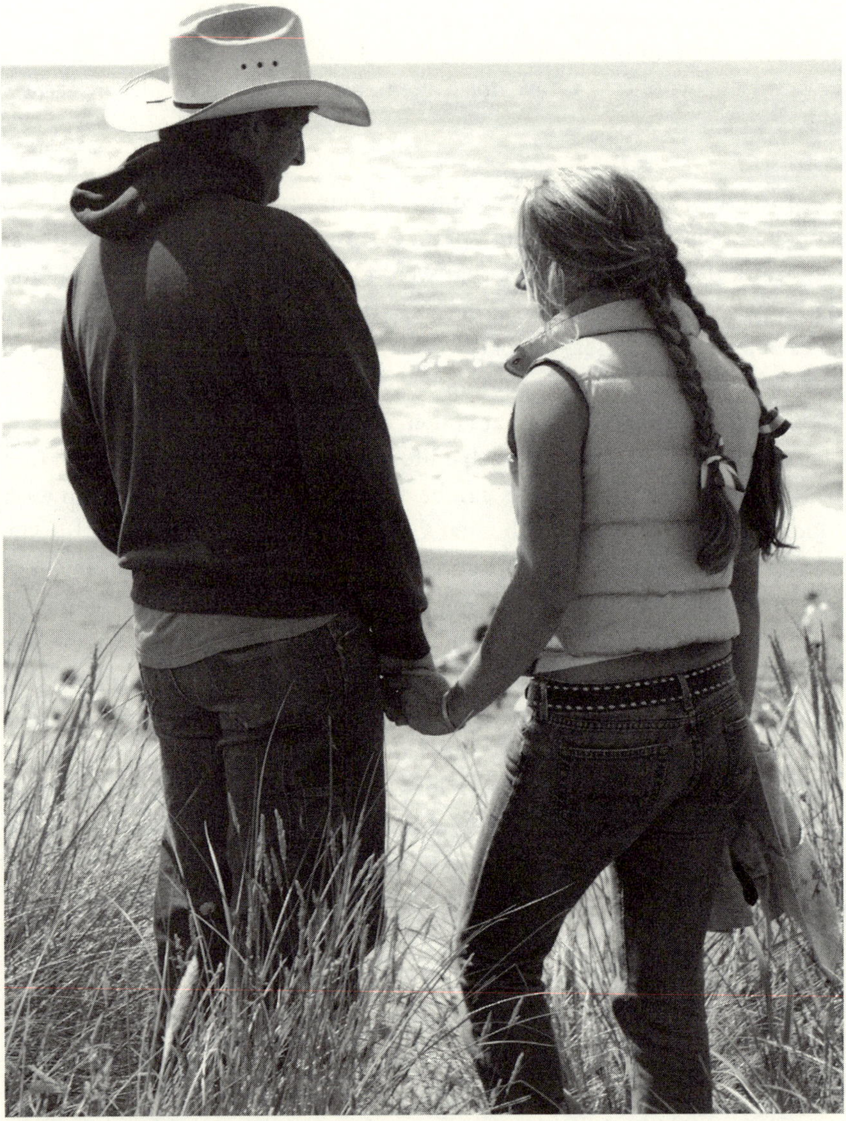

U Love U?

"You shall love your neighbor as yourself." Mark 12:31

We cannot give what we do not have. As I prepare couple for marriage I teach them that the heart of their vocation is to do the best that they can to get each other and, eventually their children, to heaven. But if they do not take time out to receive tastes of heaven then how will be able to give it? The same is true for me as a priest or for anyone else for that matter. How do I share God and love if I do not have God and love alive in my heart?

When Jesus commands us to love our neighbor as ourselves He seems to be teaching that how we love our neighbor hinges on how we love ourselves. The best way we can love ourselves and then, in turn, love our neighbors, is to let the grace of God fill and transform us. For example, if we are using alcohol to soothe suffering then we will most likely bring destruction to all people involved. But if we are seeking God's healing and peace as we love ourselves in our pain then we will bring that to our families and friends.

Sometimes we may think of Jesus as someone who just loved and gave and served and totally forgot about himself in the whole process. It is like He did not have needs, take care of himself or have self--love because He was to busy laying down His life as Savior of the world. But this conception of Jesus is not true. He did have needs and He did love and care for Himself. He went to weddings to celebrate life. He had close friends like Mary Magdalene and Lazarus. He formed a small community of men that was tightly knit with love. He went away from all the crowds to receive the grace and life of God that He would end up sharing perfectly with the whole world for all time from the cross. Jesus let John and his mom and dad and others embrace him. No, Jesus loved himself by receiving heaven and when consummated, became the way to heaven for you and me.

If loving our neighbor hinges on how we love ourselves and we want to do the best we can at loving our neighbor then we have to love ourselves well! Physically, we should exercise regularly so our bodies can be healthy to be messengers of God's word. Intellectually, we should keep growing so that we can plum the depths of God and share that expanding knowledge with others. Spiritually, we should pray, pray and pray knowing that the life and grace of God must be poured out in our own hearts before it we can pour it out to others. The sacraments flood us with grace. Emotionally, we should try to figure out what our unresolved pain is and ask for God to bless and heal us so that we can offer that blessing to others.

    I want to offer a short story to close with. Every 5 years a Catholic Bishop goes to Rome for a short visit with the Pope. One day a number of bishops were gathered, each to have a short meeting with the Pope John Paul II followed by a closing group lunch together. The bishops went in, one by one, to have their meeting with John Paul. But in late morning the Pope stopped meeting with the bishops and they were just hanging out and kind of befuddled as to what was going on. Then, one of the bishops asked the Pope's aides why the Pope had stopped meeting with individual bishops who had not yet met with him. The aide said, "Oh no, the Pope swims from 11am – noon." Now, Pope John Paul II was the leader of the church on earth and arguably one of the busiest people on the planet. There is no doubt he laid down his life for us all. But, he also loved himself and would take time out for a swim.

Miracles

"The Lord spoke to Ahaz, saying: Ask for a sign from the Lord you God; let it be as deep as the nether world, or high as the sky!" Isaiah 7:10

One day after Mass a woman came up to me and said, "Father John, I have got to tell you something. I replied, "Yes." She continued, "I have seen two miracles in my life. (At this point I became mildly irritated) The first one is that my leg was healed." Then I became more upset-- as a matter of fact I did not hear any more words she was saying because I was bothered by her statement that she had only seen two miracles in her life. I am thinking how is it that you have only witnessed two miracles in your life?

I know there are different ways of defining miracles but let us agree generally by saying that a miracle as anything that is made possible by the power of God. And that would be about everything that glorifies Him, huh? I am sure this lady was meaning a miracle to be a physical healing of some sort but I was fuming at such a limited view of the miraculous, everyday power of God that is revealed in our midst. Think about this-- you just exhaled. What a miracle! You are reading this right now and this information is transferred instantaneously through millions of neurons to bring about a coherent meaning for you. An incredible miracle that could only be manufactured by God! You heart is beating and has beat millions of times and you have had nothing to do with making that happen. Who alone but God could make this happen? Miracle after miracle after miracle are being revealed to us each and every second and we fail to praise God for it all!

Sometimes I am asked the question where all the miracles are today? If Jesus is walking with us in the same power as He walked with the people 2000 years ago, then why don't we see all those great miracles that He performed back in those days? He does do those same things today and we must always be open to praying for and receiving such. But sometimes I think we are always looking for the fireworks when we should really seek His boundless power breaking through in the ordinary.

Miracles do not bring about long term change and transformation. Jesus does. Miracles can be the start but they should in no way be our focus. Jesus and having a having an ever--present relationship with Him should be our focus. It is Jesus who will transform us into the holy and full of love saints we are called to be. We have to pray! We must pray that we can see and receive the saving power of Jesus flowing through all that is.

Let us pray: "Jesus, I am yours. Let me see you in all I see. Let me know you in all I know. And in the seeing and the knowing, change me into you. In your mercy, make me a saint. Amen."

Pursue Like the Hound of Heaven

"For God so loved the world that he gave his only son" John 3:16

Imagine a hound dog in full stride using all its strength in restless pursuit to find what it is looking for. Until is finds what it is looking for, it will be relentless in its search. The dog uses all the resources and energy it has to find its object and it will not waver, back down to anything or stop in its mission. By analogy, God has been called the Hound of Heaven. In His great love for us, God has sent His Son to relentlessly pursue us. Jesus' mission is to get us to heaven and He uses all power and every resource of God to do so. He will not waver, back down or stop His mission until it is accomplished. What a God of faithfulness we have!

We all have a deep need to know that we are pursued. The following true story shows how deep down inside, we want to know someone is pursuing us in love. Two eighth graders got into some trouble. One of the boys came from a family where the parents were really involved in their children's lives. There was lots of love, communication, and clear boundaries and expectations for good behaviors. The other boy, in contrast, did not have much of a home life. Basically lacking any parental involvement in a single parent home, he was free to go about and do as he pleased 24 hours a day. Well, when their teacher heard their conversation in the back of her car as she drove them home after they had gotten in trouble, she gained some insight about the importance of being pursued. The one boy from the strong home life was complaining that he had been grounded for one month for getting in trouble. The other boy, who was just basically running the streets looked at him and said, "You are so lucky." Think about this boy's need for a mom and dad to pursue him in love and care about his days, life, and how he is spending his time. This boy with no home life wanted a home life.

How many people in this world do not feel like they are pursued? Here in America we often pursue things over people. Houses can get bigger while families get smaller. What about all the people who are sitting abandoned in nursing homes? I think about all the latch--key kids who so badly want their mom or dad to be home when they walk through the door to their home after school. Think about the homeless, poor, immigrants and those who have no home lives. If we think about the opportunities to pursue and care about another the opportunities are limitless. The next person you talk to is the next opportunity to pursue with God's love, care and involvement.

Families--: Turn off the noise, TV, computers and spend time finding out about each other-- what you are learning, what you like, questions you have, what is good and what is hard, how your relationships might need to come back together in forgiveness and reconciliation. Meet regularly and pursue each other with God's love, care and involvement. Make certain that every member in the family knows they are pursued by the Hound of Heaven. And then, people who have been trained in this school of pursuit in their own families can go out to pursue the entire world with the Hound of Heaven.

Why Just for Lent?

"But you do not want to come to me to have life." John 5:40

One time I was brainstorming with a group of people on the meaning of the word trust. Trust involves relying or depending on someone or something. It involves risk. When you trust someone or something we believe it will do good by you.

Do you fully depend on the fact that what Jesus says and what he does for us is the same thing? What if you were to risk your whole life on Jesus and live like his word is true, "I have come that you may have life and have it to the overflowing?" John 10:10.

A question I ask myself as we give up things or do extra things during Lent is, "Why don't I do this all year long?" If giving up the TV for me has led me to an overall better quality of life because I have read, grown and related with my family/others much more in its place, then why don't I give up the TV for good(which I am seriously praying about)? Think about it, if I spent as much time getting to know my family as I did vegging in front the TV, how much stronger would the family unit be? If I could go to church every day during the year and not just during the season of Lent and have the peace knowing that God has the whole world in his hands, then why don't I do that? If I know that I meet Jesus when I serve the poor and lonely, then why can't I make that part of my life at least every month?

Who said that, "I have come that you may have life and have it to the overflowing?" Was it the TV which is on from about 6--8 hours a day in our homes? No. Was it our work or employer? No. Was it that person-- whether it is your mom, dad, brother, sister, other family member or friend-- who you feel loves you the most? No. It was Jesus who said that in John 10:10. He has come that you may have life and have it to the overflowing, and only he can deliver on his words. But Jesus also says in John 5:40, "But you do not want to come to me to have life."

If what we do for Lent brings us more life, than why not keep doing it all year long? Why just for Lent?

Reverence

"Jesus himself testified that a prophet has no honor in his native place." John 4:43

One time in the seminary we gathered as a whole community in our chapel where we celebrated Mass each day of the week. For about 15--20 minutes we talked about how we should be reverencing Jesus as we entered the chapel and spent time there. Should we bow before the altar or genuflect before the tabernacle as we entered the sacred space? Are we having enough silence or is it getting to noisy? As we were having an important discussion on how to reverence Jesus, I both smiled and was disheartened when imagined Jesus saying to himself, "If only they would learn to treat each other this way."

Jesus' own seemed to shoo him away and Jesus said as much by saying that a prophet has no honor in his native place. Jesus came to reverence them with the gift of salvation but they took him lightly. They said he was just a boy, the son of Joseph the carpenter and Mary. Since they had grown up with Jesus, they thought they knew him but they did not. Even though he was rejected, Jesus would keep reverencing each one of them with the gift of salvation-- all the way to his death on the cross. Likewise, Jesus wants us to reverence each other with the same intensity and faithfulness.

One of the greatest things I have learned in life with Christ is that we are to reverence the human person as Christ reverences the human person. What do you think of when you hear the word reverence? I think of things like holding something in highest esteem, honor and love. Jesus holds you in highest esteem, honor and love. He has gone to the greatest length to show his utter reverence for you. He gave his body and soul for you so that you might live in his reverent presence forever. Imagine that! Jesus reverences sinners. Unthinkable. This reality is astounding and seemingly unbelievable but totally true in the revelation of Jesus Christ.

In our relationships with others, especially with family and close friends, we come to find out how human and fractured our love is. Dishonor and disrespect for the people we know well can creep in because we see their sins and faults up close and personal. The old saying goes, "Familiarity breeds contempt." But we cannot go there. We must reverence each other with the gift of salvation like Christ reverences us. Yes, Christ knows all our sin but he continually holds us in highest esteem, honor and love as He offers us unconditional forgiveness. I would like to offer a different saying based on "Familiarity breeds contempt." In terms of how we treat each other as persons, I say, "Familiarity with Jesus Christ breeds a deep reverence for the human person." I think you can tell how well a person knows Jesus by how much they reverence all other people, especially those whom they live with.

A light bulb went on for a man who was in a faith sharing group that was reading a book on the centrality of Jesus Christ. After pondering the person and message of Jesus, in utter sincerity he said, "Now I get it and it is frightening. The standard of everything I think, say and do is Jesus Christ. I must be like Jesus Christ."

The standard of our lives is Jesus Christ. Reverence others as loved by Christ. Pray for a deep reverence for every person you meet. Never stop reverencing. It is the way of Jesus.

Do You Want to be Well?

"When Jesus saw the man(who had been ill 38 years) lying there and knew that he had been ill for a long time, he said to him, 'Do you want to be well?'" John 5:6

Imagine if there was only one person who could heal us and this person lived across the world. This person is the only source for any physical, emotional, spiritual, relational or any other type of healing that we all need. In our desire for healing, what lengths would we go to find this person and ask for help?

Well, this person is Jesus. He has all the healing power in the universe. We do not have to travel all the way around the world to find him. He is Emmanuel, i.e. God with us, through our baptism. And he walks into our lives and says, "Do you want to be well?"

Picture a beautiful car that is just shining in the sunlight. It is waxed and sleek. What color is it and what does it look like? You have the money to buy it and you are getting excited about the prospect until... you open the hood to look at the engine and there is no engine. Up to this point it all looked good until you found out there was nothing on the inside of this car that looked so good on the outside. This car can represent our lives. We might look all good, beautiful and polished on the outside but have nothing on the inside. We smile and say there is nothing wrong and life is good when we know that we are lying. Jesus wants to change that up for us-- from the inside--out. He walks into our lives and says, "Do you want to be well?"

The 12 steps of Alcoholics Anonymous has so much wisdom for us in the church. The first step of the 12 in recovery for those struggling with an addiction to alcohol is to admit you are powerless and that your life has become unmanageable. Until there is the acceptance that one is powerless in the face of alcohol there is no hope of recovery or wellness. And the truth that there is no hope of recovery and wellness until we admit and accept our powerlessness is true for any suffering or addiction we have. We cannot heal ourselves and so we are in a big bind. We look to other people and things to heal us but they cannot do that and so we are still in a big bind.

What will we do with the big bind we find ourselves in? We can turn to the truth of the scripture 2 Corinthians 12:9 in which we learn that Jesus' power reaches perfection in our weakness.

So, when are we going to be weak before Jesus so that the perfection of His power can make us well? Admit that there is nothing on the inside and let Jesus make you well.

Jesus walks into our live right now and says, "Do you want to be well?"

Do you?

Your Mother and God

"Can a mother forget her infant, be without tenderness for the child of her womb? Even should she forget, I will never forget you."

I want to share with you something I composed about our own mother's and God. It is meant to be a prayerful reflection so I ask that you would do that. Spend some time in prayer with this, either by yourself or you might want to use it in a group. Make sure you are in a quiet place where there will be no distractions or interruptions. Prepare your heart and ask the Holy Spirit to speak. Enjoy the love of God.

The Gaze of Your Mother and God

Imagine yourself asleep as a baby. Go to the room and place where you would sleep at night as an infant. It is late evening and your mother is in the room with you. She looks at you with all the affection that love can hold. You are more precious to her than the entire world. She has a smile on her face and her heart races as she watches you in your gentle sleep. She is in awe because it is you. You are her wonder of wonders and miracle of miracles.

As your mother stares at you, lost and overpowered by the love she feels for you, she thinks about who you will grow up to be. She wants nothing but love, joy and peace for you. She wants you to have the greatest life and she vows in her heart that she will even die for you if she needs to. For a few moments, fear pierces her heart because she knows that some people may reject and hurt you. She just wants to protect and nurture you in any way she can.

Your mother soars again with compassion as she continues to be lost in her gaze on you. She sees you as weak and vulnerable. Without her love, warmth, touch and food, you will die. You totally depend on her to live. She knows of your total dependence and she is going to make sure you are fed with abundant love and warmth. She will not forget about you, lose you or ever stop loving you. She will make sure you live.

Think about God loving you as a mother loves her sleeping baby. Think about the overpowering love a mother feels for her precious, little one and how that is only a dim reflection of the total affection God has for you. Imagine how God looks at you. Get lost in God's gaze for you. Always seek God's gaze for God is with you always.

God is lost and overpowered in love for you. God sees you like a mother sees her child and like he saw Mary, the mother of Jesus. God sees you as vulnerable, weak, dependent and lowly. In light of your lowliness, his heart races and soars even more in his love for you. He fears people might really hurt you but he is going to make sure you live in love and warmth. God will not forget about you, lose you or ever stop loving you.

Taken, Blessed, Broken and Given

"The Lord is close to the brokenhearted" Psalm 34:19

At every Mass the bread is taken, blessed, broken and given. These actions can be an analogy for our lives. We are the bread that is taken, blessed, broken and given by God. As Jesus, the Bread of Life, takes us and blesses us in our brokenness, we become bread that is given for others.

The first thing that happens is the bread is taken. We are taken or chosen by God. The reason you are reading this right now is because you were chosen by God to be alive and live forever. He created you out of love to live in the fullness of his love forever. In no way, shape or form are you and accident or mistake. He personally chose you to be his son or daughter. He picked you to be on His team. You belong to God and His family that will never end.

Next, the bread is blessed. We have all been blessed by the power of the cross. It is the power that has victory over suffering, sin and death and it opens wide the gates of heaven for us. In the power of the Holy Spirit, forgiveness and salvation is offered to all. The blessing of God rests upon us, looking for welcome.

After the bread is blessed, it is broken. We experience much brokenness or suffering in our lives. Illness, death, war, betrayal, rejection, abuse, loneliness, pain from broken families and relationships, etc. are just some of the ways we experience brokenness and suffering. To be alive is to be broken and suffer. If anyone says otherwise, they are lying.

As a priest who deals with a lot of people's brokenness, it seems to me that the whole key of how a person's life will be is determined by how they deal with their brokenness. It is a given that God has chosen and blessed us. What is not a given is what we will do with our brokenness. We might try to drink it away or work it away or laugh it away but as long as we are not asking for God to bless it then it will not be going away. Day after day I see so many sad, lifeless, and hopeless people who have not invited the blessing of God into their brokenness. The key is to invite the blessing of God into the brokenness-- to invite Jesus in and let him transform our unhappy lives into lives full of hope and joy.

It is a given that Jesus is close to the brokenhearted, i.e. you and me. What is not a given is whether or not the brokenhearted are close to Jesus. Are you? Jesus wants to flood you with joy, life and salvation. Open wide your arms and heart to him. And as he gives the fullness of himself to you, then you can give him to the whole world.

Let us pray, "Jesus, I haven't always chosen to run to you in my brokenness. I have sought your blessing in places that could not give it. I come before you now and offer you my broken heart. Be with me. Embrace me, Dear Lord. I am in need of your love and help and wisdom. May your mercy and healing wash over me. Bless me and raise me up in your heart. As you fill me with your giving, may I give others you. Thank you Lord Jesus. Thank you for being close to the brokenhearted. I love you. Amen"

Finite or Infinite Eyes?

"O Lord, my God, in you I take refuge." Psalm 7:2

As we are assailed with all of life's storms, where do we turn for help and refuge? Think about it, we have countless choices in just one hour as to where we will move in our thoughts. Our brains can think ten times as fast as we can speak. The ability to think about so much so quickly gives us an incredible opportunity to turn to Christ in even just one hour. In a few short seconds I can turn to Jesus as my refuge and help and say in my mind, "You are my hiding place, O Lord. In you I take refuge. You are my Portion and Cup, My Deliverer. You are my Safety and Comfort-- my Hope and Salvation. It is you who I claim for my Prize."

There is not doubt that life on planet earth will have its storms and some will be pretty severe. Either the storms can take us down or we can become better or stronger people from them. I think it is important to reflect on what kind of eyes we are looking at the storms with. Are we looking at all that assails us with finite eyes or infinite eyes? Finite eyes come from fearful people because they have placed their trust in something that is smaller from the storm. They know the storm will take them down. Infinite eyes, in contrast, are in the person who is staring down the storm and are saying, "There is no way you are taking me down. All the power of hell cannot hurt me. I have taken refuge in the Lord, I know his love, it is bigger than the air we breathe, and nothing will ever separate me from the love of God in Jesus Christ." Infinite eyes see bigger, way bigger, than any storm.

Take refuge in the Lord constantly. Keep repeating in your thoughts, "You are my hiding place, O Lord. In you I take refuge. You are my Portion and Cup, My Deliverer. You are my Safety and Comfort-- my Hope and Salvation. It is you who I claim for my Prize."

In the reality of the barrage of storms that hit us in life, I love the following quote, "It is time to stop telling God how big our problems are and start telling our problems how big our God is."

See with infinite eyes!

Two Beams and Keeping the Sabbath Holy

"Keep holy the Sabbath." Exodus 20:8

The third commandment is, "Keep holy the Sabbath." Sabbath means "cease." With the Sabbath, God commands us to cease our busy lives for awhile, slow down and come back to him. In the act of creation, God built in a time for resting and being able to be renewed in his covenantal love. Keeping holy the Sabbath is a commandment to rest, relax and be filled with God's presence and plan for our lives. Do you, your family and friends keep the Sabbath holy? Is the Lord, who gives us our every breath, worth 1/7 of our time on earth?

I want to offer a little meditation on the cross. The cross is made up of two beams-- the vertical beam and the horizontal beam. Imagine the vertical beam pointing to the fact that Jesus came from heaven to earth to die for us. Jesus divested Himself of heaven so he could invest heaven in you and me. In his utter humility Jesus comes to earth to give us eternity. Now, we can see Jesus hanging on the cross as he is dying. His arms are stretched out wide on the horizontal beam to the entire world. The Lamb of God hangs on the cross with arms wide open, embracing and forgiving every sinner and every sin for all of time.

Now, let us consider our lives in imitation of Christ. The foundation of our lives, everything we do, must be based on the vertical relationship we have. What does that mean? We can look to the vertical beam of the cross for our answer. It all about receiving the plan of life and salvation that Jesus brings to us from heaven to earth. As we grow in the fullness of his gift, our arms, like Jesus' arms on the horizontal beam of the cross, stretch out wide to embrace all as Jesus embraced all. But if we do not get the vertical relationship right we will never get the horizontal relationships right. However, if we get the vertical relationship with God right, then we will get the horizontal relationships with other right and we will make it most inviting for those others to choose the One who can make all things, all right.

God commands us to give him a day each week so that we will found our lives on Him. As we cease the rat race, slow down and come back to him with our whole hearts, He renews us in his saving love. Renewed, we go out to the entire world with wide open arms and tell all we meet that they are loved, saved and forgiven. That is the plan!

Keep holy the Sabbath but don't just make it one day a week. Make your whole life a Sabbath-- receiving the vertical and sharing the vertical with the horizontal.

Sexuality and Lust

"When the old men saw her enter every day for her walk, they began to lust after her." Daniel 13:8

This story is about Joachim's wife Susanna and two wicked judges. As judges, these two older men were dishonest and evil: passing unjust sentences, condemning the innocent and freeing the guilty (Daniel 13: 53). Joachim, who was very rich and the most respected of all the Jews, had a garden near his house. The judges frequented Joachim's house and would see the beautiful Susanna taking a walk at noon each day in the garden. At his point in the story we read, ""When the old men saw her enter every day for her walk, they began to lust after her. They suppressed their consciences; they would not look to heaven, and did not keep in mind just judgments." (Vv. 8--9) The story goes on with how they tried to have their way with Susanna sexually.

The major reason I chose to highlight this story is to underscore the incredible power of our sexuality and the importance to beg the grace of God that we might reverence others with our bodies. Our greatest desire is to live in loving union with each other because we are made in the image of God who is the perfect loving union of Father, Son and Holy Spirit. Obviously, that union is not essentially about a physical/sexual union because that type of union is reserved for only one person and that one person would be the one you are married to for life(if God calls you to that).

So, what do we do with this, it seems, sometimes almost overwhelmingly powerful and relentless desire to be in full, loving union with everybody? If our sexual drives are left unchecked and are not ordered by God's grace and purpose, the big red flags must go up. We see what happened with the two wicked judges. They saw beautiful Susanna and they let their lusts control their behavior and not God. They suppressed their consciences and would not look to God for his ways and help. They moved to a place where they were going to violate her and be violent to her. Lust that is fed leads to violence in thought and then actions. We must not suppress the destructive role of lust for the sake of all humanity.

At least one--third of the billions of hits on the Internet each day, are for porn sites. Each day! Think about the images that are being imprinted on the hearts, minds and souls of all who are feeding their lust just through the Internet in just one day. As theses images are burned into the conscience and sub--conscience of the viewers (which, by the way, takes years and years to ever go away), a catastrophic damage is happening. What people see in their computer screen is transferred to real life and they will do what it takes to make that happen. Why do you think there is such a thing as a date--rape drug in which one person is sedated such that another person can take advantage of them sexually? Why is there so much abuse and violent sexual crimes? Lust becomes a wild fire that cannot be contained and it is destroying everything in its path. The damage, havoc and broken hearts and lives that unbridled lust has caused are untold. It is time to stop suppressing our consciences about this and look to heaven for healing and a whole re--ordering of our sexuality.

The two wicked judges were tempted and chose lust over love in the garden. Adam and Eve chose disobedience over God in the garden. Jesus, sweating blood in agony in the garden, chose God over the incredible temptation of running from what he had to face.

We need to choose God over lust and feeding that lust. Will we choose to be regularly accountable to other people for any lust and all actions that proceed from it? Maybe choose a person you would report into each week or set it up with another such that you would call and ask permission before you would enter the lustful activity you are tempted to. Will we master our lust in the grace of God's life? Or will lust be our master and wreak all its violence and destruction? Would we be willing to even sweat blood in order to choose God over our temptation?

There is so much we can to extinguish the wildfire of lust and its damage. Ask your loved ones exactly where they are browsing on a computer. If your computer is going to be your downfall, throw it out. What are you reading and watching on TV? We have a lot of choice in terms of what we see with our eyes. Be accountable to God in confession and to others in the faith.

Satan seeks to isolate, conquer and destroy you in this area of lust. If you are trying to win the fight against lust on your own I predict failure. Move out of isolation into a loving relationship with God and others to deal with this temptation with the very power of heaven. God can heal and re--order any pain that choosing lust over love has caused us because nothing is impossible with him. Take heart and choose the love and healing of God's ways.

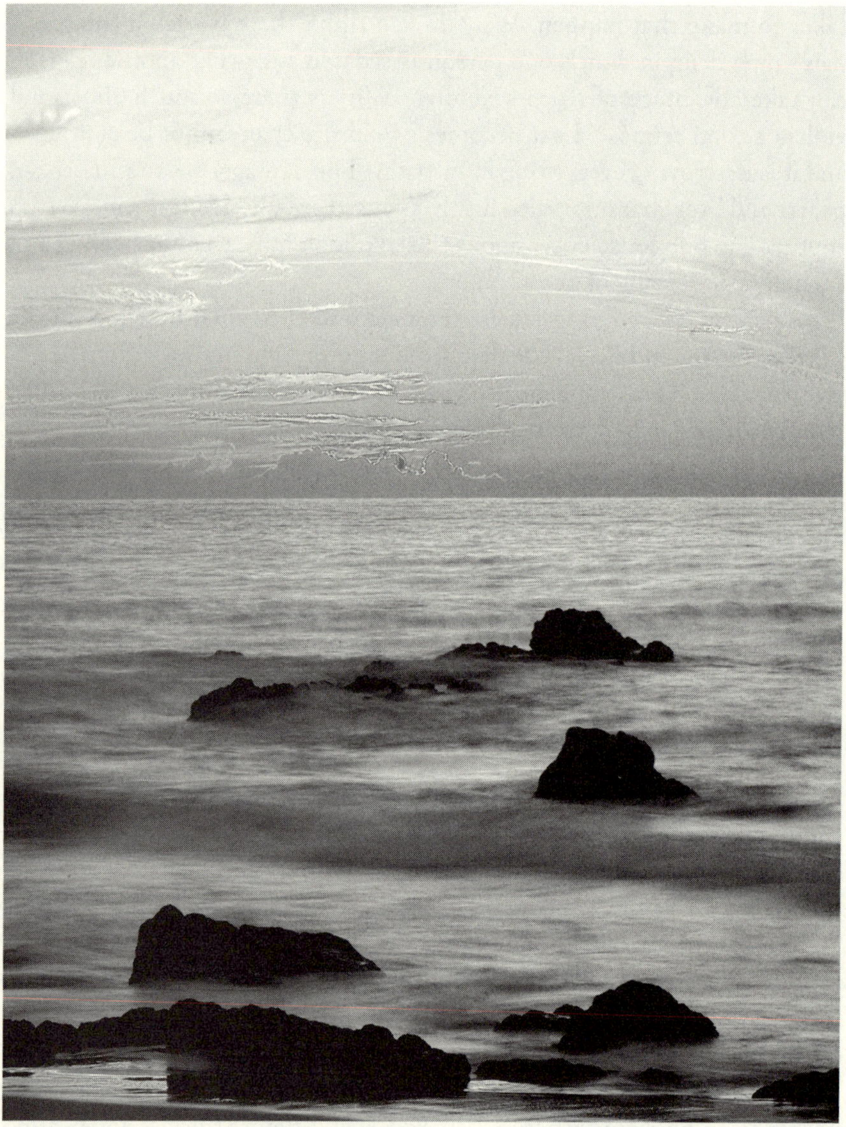

GAP - God Answers Prayer

'O Lord, hear my prayer." Psalm 102:2

We can apply God and Christ and goodness to everything we see. In the Old Testament, the authors would sometimes use pagan myths that the people were familiar with as a foundation for telling a story to teach biblical truths. Thus, God was applied to these stories that were well known to the people. In the New Testament, Jesus would use things his followers were familiar with in order to teach them about the Gospel. Jesus commonly used things like farming and fishing to instruct. As a priest I am constantly thinking how I can apply God, Christ and goodness to our everyday lives such that we are remembering and growing in the knowledge of Our Lord.

One way I like to teach the faithful is through the use of acronyms. Even though it originally probably does not mean this, I teach that **GAP= God Answers Prayer.** If you are really on the look out, I am sure you can see some piece of clothing at least once a day that has the **GAP** logo. When you see it, smile, rejoice and praise God that **GAP= God Answers Prayer.**

Now, some of us may feel that God does not even listen to our prayers; let alone answer them. Well, the truth is that God listens to every one of our prayers. As a matter of fact, He knows every one of our prayers even before we have prayed them. So, we can never say that God does not listen to our prayers because that is a lie. Secondly, we might say that God is not answering our prayers. Well, he does answer every prayer but many times that answer is "No," or ""In my way," or "In my time." God ways and plans are so high above our ways and plans. He will always give us the best as we seek him in prayer – himself. For many years of my life I was telling God what my life was all about and how I was going to get married, have a big family and have big money. I then I learned God's way is the best way and he wanted me to be a priest. And look at me now-- living large in his love sharing that all over the world! I can't imagine having a bigger family then being a priest. I've got the whole world! And I am wealthy beyond compare. I've got everlasting love, joy, and peace. You see, GAP gives me the best – which is HIS way. I can't imagine being happier. **GAP!**

Our greatest happiness in life is the same thing as doing God's will. Jesus says that whatever we ask God for in his name that God will give to us.

To ask for something in Jesus' name means to ask it according to God's will- - not yours or mine! Yes, God will answer our prayers for the of meaning, happiness, and love we want the more fully we follow his will. Remember in the Our Father we pray, "Thy will be done", not "my will be done." If we pray according to God's will for us, then our prayers will be answered and we will live the best life possible.

GAP!

Small Stuff, Big Deal

"Jesus said, 'If I perform my Father's works, even if you do not believe me, believe in the works, so that you may realize that the Father is in me and I am in the Father.'" John 10:38

There is the saying, "Your life might be the only Gospel that somebody else ever reads." St. Francis said, "Preach the Gospel at all times and use words when necessary." Another quote is, "Your life is speaking so loud I can hardly hear any words you are saying." All of these quotes point to the fact that how we live our lives is extremely important.

There is a story of a new pastor who came to town. On one of his first days after arriving, he was getting off the bus and the bus driver gave him 25 cents too much in change. About twenty minutes after this happened; the pastor realized the mistake of the bus driver. So, he had a small dilemma. He thought, "Should I return the quarter? It is only a quarter. That is no big deal at all. There are big things like war, starvation, and AIDS to worry about. Lots of people lose change all the time. It is not big deal and it is not going to make or break the bus company. Besides, it would take a lot of time and effort to track down the bus driver and return to her the quarter." Then the pastor thought about honesty, doing the right thing, living for God-- even in the smallest things. He decided to do what God was telling him to do and he returned the quarter.

It took the pastor over an hour to track down the bus driver. He gave the 25 cents back telling her she had given him too much change. The bus driver looked at the pastor and said, "Aren't you the new pastor in town?" He replied, "Yes." She said, "Great! I purposely gave you a quarter too much in change and wanted to see what you would do. I am looking for a church to join."

There are so many people looking for a church to join (especially here in Oregon and Washington-- the two most un--churched states in the union). All people are in a desperate search for God. St. Augustine said, "My heart is restless and it will not rest until it rests in you, O Lord." With so many people on your right and left looking for belief, what are you offering them? How believable are you? When people see you do they want to join your church and get to know your God? It is the "work" of your love, life, goodness, purpose, selflessness, mercy, service etc. that can draw people into eternity. Is the irresistibility of God flowing from your being?

How fully will we live for Christ? Will we try to please him in everything we think, say or do? Think about the pastor returning the quarter to the bus driver. Small potatoes-- no big deal, right? But it was a big deal. The bus driver was looking for a church to go to and a God to know. That is the stuff of eternity. What if you and I loved God even in the small things like returning 25 cents? By living out even the smallest things for God, how many more people would come to church and know God and eternal life?

Extravagant Love

"Mary took a liter of costly performed oil made from genuine aromatic nard and anointed the feet of Jesus and dried them with her hair." John 12:3

We all know people who love extravagantly. I did the funeral for one such person. This man would reach out to people constantly as he journeyed through his days here on earth. Out for dinner, he would see an elderly couple who he figured was probably living on social security and a tight budget. Assuming they did not have much money, he would secretly buy their dinner. Upon visiting a poor country for the first time, his heart was moved to go back again and again to bring the people there housing supplies and whatever else they needed. He was always helping people in need or distress, whether they were one of his employees, neighbors or someone on the side of the road who looked like they needed care. Droves of people would continually be coming over to his house because he and his wife were so welcoming.

Here is another example of extravagant love. This woman was known for her incredible outreach in care and encouragement. She was writing notes and baking cookies for people non--stop. When I asked the over 1,000 people at her funeral if they had ever received a note or cookies from her, I think almost every person in that church raised their hands. Wow! Just think of how extravagant we can be in our love.

It cost a year's wages for the liter of perfumed oil that Mary anointed Jesus' feet with. It was a foolish, illogical and impractical act. What a waste, huh? How would this affect her financial situation and retirement? But all we see here is someone risking extravagant love. What if the whole world was filled with Mary's? What if it started with you and me?

There is only one thing that Jesus wants from us: everything. Talk about extravagant love! Let us love Jesus and each other with all our heart, soul, mind and strength today because tomorrow might be too late. Risk! Be a fool! Be impractical! Be illogical! And when people ask you why all this extravagant love is coming from you say, "Jesus."

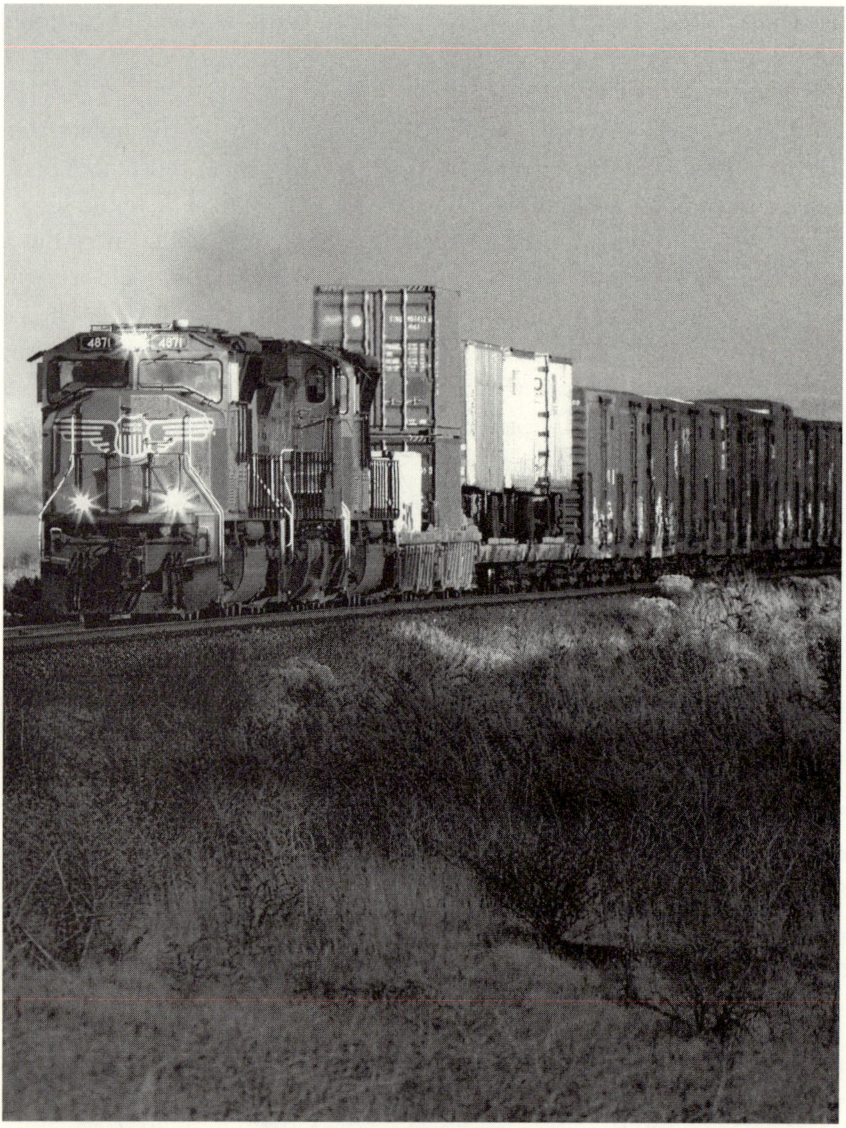
4871
4871

The Longest Distance

"Many of the Jews who had come to Mary and seen what Jesus had done began to believe in him." John 11:45

The longest distance any one of has to travel is from our head to our heart.

There was a great orator who would travel the land and perform for big crowds. One night during the middle of his show a smelly and unkempt man with ripped and shabby clothes walked in and took the only available seat which was right in the front row. This out-of-place, unclean and under-dressed man proceeded to sit down and fall asleep until the end of the show. The great orator decided to close the night with Psalm 23. When the people clapped at the end, it woke up the sleeping man and he went on stage and asked the great orator if he could share something with the crowd. With sarcasm, the great orator said, "Sure," thinking of what a fool this man was going to make of himself. Not knowing that the great orator has finished with Psalm 23, the out-of-place man opened his old and worn Bible and began to read, "The Lord is my Shepherd, there is nothing I shall want..." As he prayed through the Psalm, the crowd quieted and the people's hearts were touched. Tears flowed and many people were weeping with the last words of the Psalm. The crowd stood up and gave this smelly and unkempt man a standing ovation. As this man slowly and humbly walked off the stage, the now indignant great orator, approached him and said, "What is going on here? I am a great orator full of eloquence for all my audiences. Speaking is my life. I gave a masterful presentation tonight, but, stumbling through the same Psalm 23 that I just presented, you moved the people to tears and a standing ovation. I did not get 1/10 of your response." "With all due respect, Sir," the man replied, "you may know the words to the Psalm but I know the Shepherd and that makes all the difference in the world."

Yes, there is a whole world of difference between knowing facts about the Shepherd and personally knowing the Shepherd. The out-of-place, unkept and smelly man knew the Shepherd personally and that is what so moved others. Is that my life? Or do I just know facts about the Shepherd in my head but do not know him personally in my heart?

The longest distance any one of has to travel is from our head to our heart.

We read how many of the Jews came to believe in Jesus. How do we come to believe in Jesus? How do words in our heads about his awesome love become real in our hearts? How do we get Jesus from our head down into our heart?

Here is an idea. Invite, invite, invite. Invite Jesus into your suffering knowing that he is with you in comfort and healing. Invite Jesus into your family knowing he wants your household to be a fortress in peace and happiness. Pray grace before every meal believing that Jesus wants you to enjoy the good company and food he has provided. Invite Jesus into your heart each day in extended prayer that you may show forth His Sacred Heart to the world. The more you extend your wounded heart to his, the more He can extend his Sacred Heart to the world through you. Also, do not forget about Jesus when things are going good. Invite Jesus to share with you in every joy-- do not leave him outside in the cold when things are going well and you are experiencing joy.

Invite, invite, and invite him into everything-- all the time. True, the longest distance any one of has to travel is from our head to our heart. But as we invite and invite and invite-- it will happen. We will make the journey and find Jesus in our heart. We can count on it because Jesus said, "Ask, and you shall receive."

Whatever is not Transformed is Transmitted

"I gave my back to those who beat me." Isaiah 50:6

In the first--century St. Ignatius, a Christian of Antioch was arrested for atheism because he denied the Roman Gods. He was taken from Antioch to Rome where he was martyred for his faith. He gave us these words just before his death, "Now I begin to be a disciple… let fire and cross, flocks of beasts, broken bones, dismemberment come upon me, so long as I attain to Jesus Christ." St. Ignatius was a disciple of Jesus and loved Him more then he loved even his own life and breath. A disciple loves his master more than he loves anything else and will follow him regardless of the cost. A prayer the church prays about martyrs is, "Love for life did not deter them from death." The means that a martyr would choose to sacrifice his life over betraying Christ. If being a disciple of Christ means that I will end up life Ignatius did, how much of a disciple am I willing to be?

Now, being a disciple of Christ probably will not mean martyrdom for most of us. But what about all the other types of attack that can occur in our lives? Being made in the image of God, we are built to experience infinite reverence and dignity. In our fractured world of love there can be so many insults, betrayals, rejections etc. that attack our identity of who we are in God. We are all daughters and sons of Our Sovereign, Loving God and when that is belittled, we suffer. So, what will we do in response to the various forms of attack and assaults?

There is a saying that, "Whatever is not transformed is transmitted." As disciples of Christ, we have an incredible choice to make when we are faced with the insults and attacks. We can extend them or end them. We can perpetuate evil and make it grow or put an end to it and replace it by goodness. For example, say that I hear person A has called me a louse behind my back (and I know that is somewhat true because I know I have some lousiness in my repertoire!). Now I can extend, enlarge, illuminate that evil by saying hateful things about person A in retaliation to what he has said about me. Or, I can choose the grace of God and only say good things or nothing at all about person A. If I choose to retaliate with some form of hate, I am choosing not to act according to Christ and apart from his grace. On the other hand, if I choose to act according to Christ and his grace, good can come from an evil attack. Christ can transform something that starts out as bad into good. The war of evil can either end or extend through me. I choose transformation into good or the transmission of evil. What will it be?

Gaze upon Jesus. That is what the life of a disciple should be. As sons and daughters of the Father, we learn how to be good children by gazing upon Jesus and imitating his life to the T. In the Isaiah's prophecy foretelling Jesus we read, "He gave his back to those who beat him." Jesus offered himself to end war. He gave us his body to end all sin, death and suffering and to make us live in the freedom of God's children forever. He chose to be transformed by the goodness of God and not to transmit the evil of mankind. You and I are called to do the same.

As attacks, insults, persecutions etc., whether in words or actions, assail me as I follow Christ unreservedly, what will my response be? Will I end the war or extend the war? Will I transmit the evil or be transformed by the good?

His Heart Beats for You

"One of his disciples, the one whom Jesus loved...He leaned back against Jesus' chest." John 13: 23, 25

Each Saturday in the United States of America about 44,000 weddings happen. So, if a Saturday wedding can be looked at a dime--a--dozen or just another number in thousands, what makes is so special? Translating this thought to a much grander scale, what makes you and me so special if we are just one person in over 6 billion people who are alive this day? Aren't we just another number or a dime--a--dozen in the multitudes?

To find out how special we are we need to be like John the beloved disciple. On the night before Jesus died he was having supper with his disciples. It was there that we see how John leaned into the heart of Jesus. Jesus' heart is a heart that beats for us and not against us. It is a heart that will not crush our broken lives but heal them. It is a heart full of extravagant love that will enter any other heart that says, "Come." Jesus' heart would have come and beat on this earth if you were the only one he needed to come for. His heart beats for you.

His heart beats for you. Overflowing love being poured out over you all the day long. Eternal beating, flowing and filling. Washing and cleaning and healing and forgiving. Eternal, unrestrained. Looking for an opening in your heart.

You are not just another number among the billions.

Get as close to Jesus as possible. Sit right next to him. Listen to his heartbeat. Pay attention and learn why his human heart beat. Lean in on him as St. John did. And then when you are done leaning in on him to hear His heartbeat, lean in on him, again and again.

"Repent and believe in the gospel, Jesus says. Turn around and believe that the good news that we are loved is better than we ever dared hope, and that to believe in that good news, to live out of it and toward it, to be in love with that good news is of all glad things in this world, the gladdest thing of all. Amen, and come, Lord Jesus." Frederick Buechner

His heart beats for you. Overflowing love being poured out over you all the day long. Eternal beating, flowing and filling. Washing and cleaning and healing and forgiving. Eternal, unrestrained. Looking for an opening in your heart.

Pray Together

"I have set my face like flint." Isaiah 50:7

One survey studied marriages. The resulting statistics are telling. About one out of every two marriages ends in divorce. About 1/5 of marriages in which the family goes to church together regularly get divorced. Now, for the astounding statistic-- only one in over 1,000 couples ended up divorcing where the family was going to church together regularly and praying together regularly. Obviously, if we believe the findings of this survey, we see that prayer is the key to making the marriage relationship successful.

Why is prayer so important in the marriage relationship? Because it forces the utmost importance of relationship, remembering the marriage vows and living by the covenantal love of God. If a couple sits down to pray together and they are somehow relationally divided from each other, God will bring that to the fore. The whole purpose of prayer is to bring us into right relationship with God and each other. Anyone who opens their heart to the purpose of prayer can have a better relationship with their spouse (or whoever) if they are willing to be led by God to that place.

Have you ever felt like bailing in a relationship? It gets too hard, too messy, too hurtful? I know I am averse to relational pain. I know human beings can be pretty unpredictable and unreliable in their love. Look what we human beings did to Jesus. He came to enter right relationship with us all and look how we responded. Never having one lapse in perfect love for every person and we attacked, rejected, mocked and crucified him as the scum of the earth. Don't you think that Jesus thought about bailing? And what if he did? Where would that put you and me right now?

Jesus set his face like flint. Nothing was going to turn his face from looking upon the Father and obeying his will to die and rise. All the lashings, spitting, mocking, humiliation, nails driven into his body would not dissuade Jesus from his focus on the Father. Jesus was in prayer with the Father, he was in union with the Father, and he was in right relationship with the Father. He was doing the Father's will to be the Lamb of God who takes away the sins of all the world, of all the unfaithful who stood by and watched him be crucified.

Brothers and sisters, we need to set our face like flint on Jesus. In our marriages and all of our relationships, we need to look to Jesus to be saved.

There will be tough times and times we want to bail, but as we turn together in prayer Jesus will unite us in his love.

Why is it that spouses will do anything in their marriage relationship besides pray together? Why is it that friends will do anything in their relationship except pray together? .

If we do not commit to praying with each other, we will not pray with each other. Our love will run cold and wither or die. Divorce will happen -- whether legal, emotional, physical, spiritual etc. Obviously, that is not God's plan for us.

Set you face like flint and pray together – all the time!

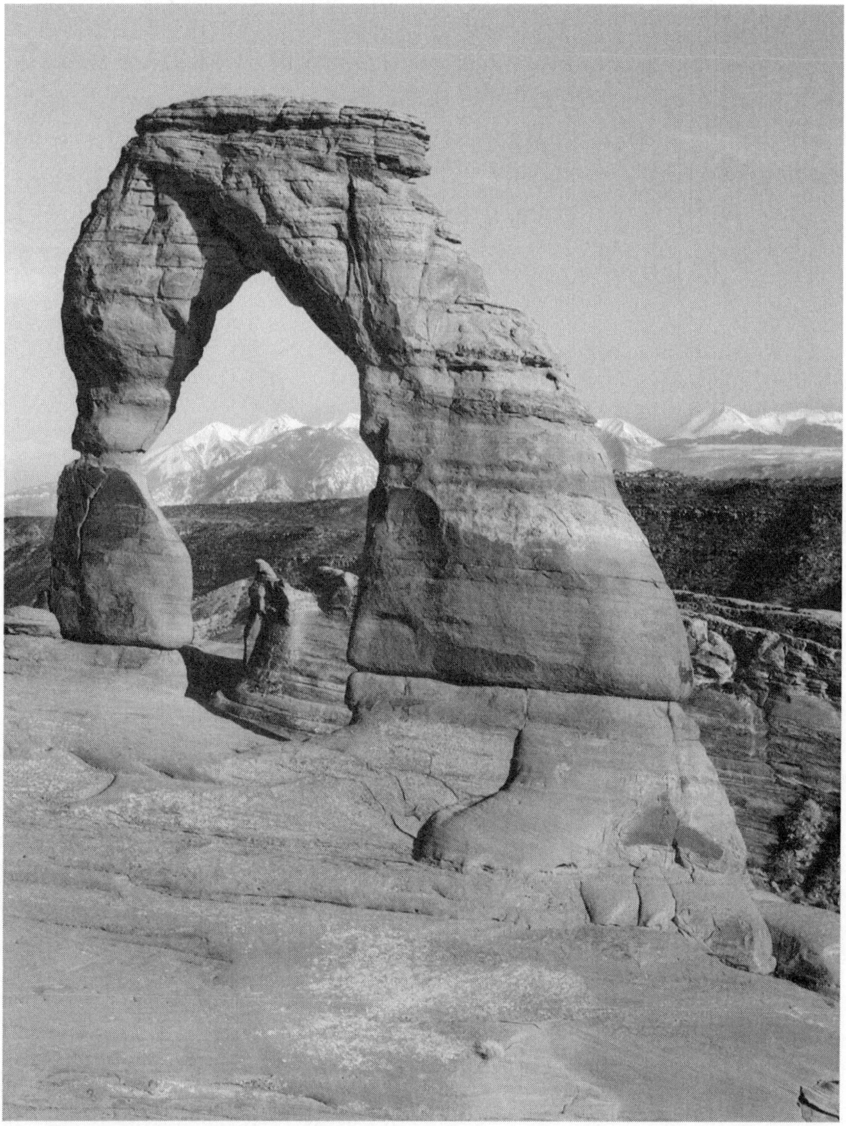

Properly Positioned?

"See, my servant shall prosper, he shall be raised high and greatly exalted." Isaiah 52:13

I have a black T--shirt with a white moon on the front of it. Along with the picture of the moon are the words, "Be the moon." So my T--shirt, which they say will read by an average of 3,000 people in its life span, is telling people to be the moon. What does that mean? Well, on the back of the T--shirt is the cross of Jesus Christ with the words, "Reflect the Son." Our whole being should be about letting Jesus shine through us. While Jesus is the perfect reflection of God the Father we seek to fully surrender to Jesus' perfect reflection in us.

Without the sun, there is no way we can see the moon. It would be just an unknown, pockmarked rock in the middle of darkness. On its own, it generates no light. Properly positioned, however, the moon beams. It is beautiful. The same is true for our lives as Christians. We live in the dark but we were made to shine. But our brightness and beauty is only made possible by the Son who comes to us in the middle of our darkness. The big question is, "Are we properly positioned so that the Son, with his irrepressible light, may shine through us?"

In Hebrews 4:14--16 we proclaim that Jesus is our high priest who has suffered in every way that we have. We celebrate his boundless love coming to us from the cross at Calvary. Hence, we should confidently approach the throne of grace to receive mercy and find grace for help. We read, "Son though he was, he learned obedience from what he suffered; and when he was made perfect, he became the source of eternal salvation for all who obey him."(Heb. 5:9) Jesus is the fullness of salvation for all who properly position themselves by obediently coming to him with their lives. What is your position before the Son?

This world is full of self--help, self improvement, self--will, self--determination, self--enrichment, self--motivation, self--fulfillment, self--service, self--realization, etc. The eternal problem with all this "self" stuff, however, is the self cannot help the self to get the self where the self wants to go. In Isaiah 52:13 we read how Jesus was going to prosper, "See, my servant shall prosper, he shall be raised high and greatly exalted." God the Father was going to prosper Jesus by raising him up to everlasting life through his suffering and death. Jesus was perfectly positioned on the cross to beam

God the Father. He commended his suffering, life and spirit to the Father and it was thus that he was raised high and greatly exalted. And now, all people forever more, gaze upon the cross in praise and sing, "Salvation has come! Behold, the Lamb of God who takes away the sins of the world! Holy, Holy, Holy is the Lord, Our God. Worthy, Worthy, Worthy are you to be worshipped forever."

The proper position for us to take in life is the position of Jesus. From the cross of our own suffering, we commend our sufferings, life and spirit to Jesus. As we throw our lives to the him, he throws his to us and we beam with his life. We beam, and the only reason we beam, is because of what Jesus, and not self, does for us. Jesus raises on high and greatly exalts us, we don't.

Are you properly positioned before Jesus?

What is a Mountain For?

"Go up to a high mountain." Isaiah 40: 9

The whole of scriptures have always talked about the importance of mountains. The people of God have been repeatedly invited and told to go up to the mountain of the Lord. It was on a mountain that Moses received the Ten Commandments which were to guide the Israelite nation recently set free from slavery. Jesus was transfigured before Peter, James, and John on a mountain. The beautiful teaching of the beatitudes was given to us by Jesus with his Sermon on the Mount.

The mountain is a place of teaching, revelation, and divine encounter. The teacher, revealer, and the Divine is the Lord. It is the place where the Lord can "get" to us and reveal the deepest meaning of our lives. It is a meaning that we cannot contrive but that we must receive from the source of any and all meaning in our lives. It is where we come to know and experience the Lord and be transformed into the way of the Lord.

Where is the mountain in our lives? St. John of the Cross urged seekers of the truth to retreat to: "solitary places, which tend to lift up the soul to God, like mountains, which furnish no resources for worldly recreations." Obviously, the mountain doesn't mean a physical mountain only. It means going to a solitary place with no distractions whereby we can totally surrender to the reaching, revelation, and divine encounter of our Lord.

On the mountain we are given infinite vision. We are given the eye of the Lord with which to view the valley of earth below. What we learn above helps us to bless all that is below. What we see on the mountain makes meaning and sense of it all. A poem by Rene Drumal: "You cannot stay on the summit forever, you have to come down. So why bother in the first place? Just this. What is above knows what is below. What is below does not know what is above. One climbs, one sees, one descends. One no longer sees, but one has seen. There is an art to conduction oneself in the lower regions by what one saw higher up. When one can no longer see, one at least can still know."

First Love

"God is love." 1 John 4:16

We are fired into life searching for unconditional love. We crave infinite love that will never wear out, break down or end. There is only one who can provide that for us. As we search and claw and seek and dig to know overflowing love forever, we would be wise to name where we are going to find that love. We name and find our answer in the scripture verse, "God is love." No one else but God is love and so we throw our lives into God's arms to live in the love only he can provide.

It seems logical to state that we should seek first that which we want most in life. And the truth of every human being is that what we want most in life is to share in everlasting love. A way that we can talk about God is that he is our First Love. As our First Love, his love for us is unconditional and perfect. He will never stop loving us because his love is everlasting (Jer. 31:3). He will not break his promises or ever let us down. He always offers forgiveness- no matter how "big" we think the sin. And he wants to pour out that love in our hearts 24-7 like 7-11. Yes, Jesus is always open for business, like the 7-11 convenience stores which are open twenty-four hours a day, seven days a week, three-hundred and sixty-five days a year. Yes, he is always with us to show us that our clawing and digging search ends in him.

Now, second love is the love of our parents, friends, teachers, spouse, co-workers, etc. It is the broken, conditional love that is a part of all human beings who are sinners and have fallen short of the glory of God. We break promises and vows, do not love and forgive as we should, and let others down with what we do or fail to do. This is the reality of second love and we do well to call it like it is and not have unfair expectations as we relate to each other in this life.

We are fired into life desperately craving our First Love. We want God! We want perfect love forever. The great news is that what we want most in life we can have. We can expect our First Love to give us perfect love. We can count on our First Love to provide 24-7, 365(twenty-four hours a day, three-hundred and sixty-five days a year).

But do not be foolish in thinking that a second love can provide what our First Love does. It can't. It will never be able to.

A.S.K.

"So I say to you, 'Ask and you shall receive; seek and you will find; knock and the door will be opened for you.' For whoever asks, receives. Whoever seeks, finds; whoever knocks is admitted." Luke 11:9-10

Are you ready for another acronym as a way of remembering the Good News and sharing that Good News with all we meet? In this case we pull the acronym straight from the Scripture text of Luke 11:9-10. Jesus teaches us to **A.S.K.** **A**- Ask and you shall receive. **S**- Seek and you shall find. **K**- Knock and the door shall be opened for you. How cool is that? Jesus tells us to ask, seek and knock for Him and He will deliver the goods! What kind of goods? How about the land flowing with milk and honey? Forgiveness, freedom and fidelity. A love that only grows brighter and stronger as we **A.S.K.** Life that just keeps spilling out of every pour of our bodies because it is just way too much for us to contain. And that would be happening 4ever!

Jesus says, **A.S.K.** me! And what do we get when we ask the Infinite Good for Infinite Goods? We get Infinite Goods. Let the Infinite Good deliver the Infinite Goods!

Now, in this world of unfairness and suffering, we could say that a lot of times Jesus doesn't give us the Infinite Goods when we **A.S.K.** What about the innocent youth who is shot or the child who dies of cancer? How come God did not answer our prayers to protect and heal them? Well, in the midst of the suffering, unfairness and death that we all face in this life, Jesus is telling us that he will answer the deepest prayer of our hearts that we are asking for. We are built to live in God's love forever and this is what Jesus is asking us to ask for. We do not focus on trying to live forever on earth but we focus on receiving the free gift of eternal life that Jesus offers each of us. So, regardless of the unfairness and suffering of life, we seek the vision to ask for a life that never ends. And Jesus teaches us to ask rightly and delivers the Infinite Goods that we ask for.

How do we know that Jesus will do make good on his promise to deliver the Infinite Goods and give us the best? He has sealed that promise in his Blood. Just **A.S.K.**

Self-Esteem

"You are precious in my eyes." Isaiah 43:4

One definition of self-esteem is sharing God's opinion of us. Can you imagine how radically loving our lives and world would be if we all shared God's opinion of us? Well, brothers and sisters, we want to get there!

Why is there so much loathing and low self-esteem in and around us? It is sad and contradictory for a disciple of Jesus to continually live with low self-esteem. As a matter of fact, it is impossible to have low self-esteem if we are truly living united with Christ. If we truly know Christ's opinion of us, we would know of his infinite esteem for us.

Therein lays the problem of low self-esteem. It is all about whose opinion we let dictate our lives. I can remember two opinions that were shared with me by people within a two week span. One person basically told me I was a horrible pastor and a different person told me I was going to be the Pope. Talk about two different and opposite opinions! Who should I believe? Jesus.

All that really matters is what Jesus thinks about me.

Everybody has their opinion and that is all fine and dandy. But all that really matters is Jesus' opinion of you!

What does Jesus think of you? Base all you are on that answer.

There are billions of opinions out there. There is only one you should base all the other billions on. Maybe you have been off-base in basing your worth on opinions other than Jesus'. Stop doing that! Repent. Turn back to Jesus and let him share his opinion with you. All that really matters is what Jesus thinks of you!

"Repent and believe in the gospel, Jesus says. Turn around and believe that the good news that we are loved is better than we ever dared hope, and that to believe in the good news, to live out of it and toward it, to be in love with the good news is of all glad tidings in this world, the gladdest thing of all. Amen, and come, Lord Jesus." Frederick Buechenr

Practice Choosing Life

"There are set before you fire and water; to whichever you choose, stretch forth your hand. Before man are life and death, whichever he chooses shall be given him." Sirach 15:16-17

If you want some pepperoni pizza do you go to a pine tree and ask it for a slice of pepperoni pizza? No, that would be foolish. You will never be able to get pepperoni pizza from a pine tree. In order to get pepperoni pizza you would go to a pizza place or some store that provides pizza. You would not go to a place that does not provide pizza. That would be a waste of time and you would not find what you are looking for.

By analogy, in our search for life, we can waste our time going to places that do not provide what we are looking for. We want overflowing, infinite life but so many times we turn to finite sources. Well, the finite sources will never be able to provide. It would foolish to ever think a finite source could somehow ever provide the infinite or change into the infinite. There is only one source of infinite life- Jesus. Our source of infinite life says to each of us, "I have come that you may have life to the overflowing." John10:10

If we know where we need to go for the life we seek, then we need to practice going there. Before I baptize a child in the baptismal ceremony, I ask the parents if they are going to bring up their child in the practice of the faith. In other words are they going to teach their child the practice of choosing the life of Christ in prayer, the scriptures, the sacraments, learning more about God and the church, etc?

You can tell that some people are just so filled with life. Life pours out of their eyes, hearts and bodies and they are confident that it is going to be happening forever. When a person knows life like this, do we think they got there by accident? I do not think so. The have been choosing and choosing and choosing life.

Knowing infinite life does not happen by accident. It comes from the practice of trying to continually choose the infinite one. People see the life in me and I tell them it is Jesus. Jesus does not happen by accident in me. I practice choosing life each day by seeking Christ in prayer and the scriptures. I go to confession once a month and obviously I am in church a lot receiving the infinite life of Christ in word and sacrament. I am continually trying to grow in him. Practice, Practice, Practice. As I reflect on the last 22 or so years since I really met the Living Christ and decided to pray daily for an hour us practice choosing his life, all that I can say it that it works.

Know **WHO** life is. Practice choosing life.

FROG

"Blessed are the Poor in Spirit." Matthew 5

FROG = Fully Rely On God.

    Think about how little children run to their parents with arms open wide. This familiar image can speak to how we all utterly rely on our parents or someone else to take care of us when we are babies and little children. We would die if we did not have the care of their food, shelter and nurturing.

    Think about the other end of our earthly life. As we get older we become like little children again. We more and more rely on the care of our children or someone else to provide our needs.

    The reality of how much we rely on others is obvious as little children and when we are old and dying. But if we reflect on how much we rely on others we see that our whole life is filled with relying. We rely on others to keep promises, affirm us, guide us, tell the truth, care for you, etc.

    Ultimately, we rely on someone else for that which we cannot do on our own. And what we want at the heart of all our relying is a life of love that never ends. We want much more than just physical life on earth; we want eternal life. Thank God we can **FROG** it! God provides for that which we cannot do on our own. As we fully rely on God, he gives us eternal life. So, **FROG** it!

    Maybe this metaphor can help us as we commit to **FROG** throughout our lives. A down-syndrome boy was ready for his first day of school. It was a big day and he was excited about taking the bus to school. His mom put him on the bus and told him where and when she would meet him when he came home on the bus after school. Afternoon came and mom was standing on the curbside waiting for her son. Well, he got off the bus a block early but she called out for him. As soon as he heard her voice he began to run to his mother. For a whole block he ran with arms open wide screaming, "Mommy, Mommy, Mommy!" Not caring what anyone else in that neighborhood thought, he just wanted to be with his mom. He ran with his whole life to the only thing he wanted.

    May our lives with God be the same. **FROG**.

NEWS

NEWS is a word that is an acronym for North, East, West and South. When we watch the news on TV we get information on daily events that are occurring all over our city, state, nation and world. Life happenings and stories are covered in the North, East, West and South. The **NEWS**, like FOX or CNN, is constantly available at the click of a remote.

Now, if I were to ask you what the news we see on TV is about, what would you say? Is it good or bad? Does it leave us hopeful or further burdened? Is the focus war, violence, and anger or is it about kindness, reconciliation, respect? Is it about how God is working for good in our world or about highlighting how the family, society and world are falling apart? Growing up as a child, the main thing I remember about the TV news was wars and the threat of nuclear destruction. A lot of good that **NEWS** did for me!

So, let us think about the Good **NEWS**. What if there was primary TV station, say FOX that was completely devoted to presenting all the good things God is doing in our world. Can you imagine the life and hope it would offer a world that is constantly inundated with bad news at the five or six or ten or eleven o'clock or, should I say, around the clock news hour?

The Good **NEWS** is that God is infinitely good to us at all times, in all places, in all circumstances. His power, healing and life are over flowingly available in the North, East, West and South. So, do we believe that? Do we seek His goodness in all the rabble and rockiness of life? Do we know that prayer is the only way that our eyes will be opened to the reality that the goodness of God is flowing over each of us infinitely and eternally in the North, East, West and South?

The Good **NEWS** is that Jesus is good in the **NEWS**! There is no way we can top that Good **NEWS**.

I love the quote, "It is time to stop telling God how big our problems are and start telling our problems how big our God is." Jesus is the Good **NEWS** working all things for our good in His infinite love for us. Whether we are in the north, east, west and south, Jesus' healing and forgiveness are forever greater than the suffering we face or the sin we have committed.

I wish you Good **NEWS** - all the time!

No Fear

"Do not be afraid, Mary" Luke 1:29

When I think of someone who did not live in fear, St. Francis comes to mind. Francis grew up in a wealthy and noted family in Assisi. He was a valiant and successful soldier in war. He enjoyed the social life of friends and was a poet and romantic at heart. But then God spoke to him from the San Damiano cross and began to ask him for changes in his life. God called Francis to live differently than previously and Francis trusted.

Francis basically became a beggar when Christ captured his heart. Think about the fears he might have faced. Would people think of him as an abnormal, crazy lunatic who traded the life of a wealthily nobleman for the despairing life of a beggar? What kind of mocking and ostracization would this lead to? There certainly would be many kinds of physical, emotional, intellectual and spiritual fears going from a valiant and respected soldier in the eyes of the world to a penniless street person. There is the scene in the plaza where Francis takes off his clothes and returns them to his father as the bishop and crowd look on. As he does this, Francis says that he will follow God the Father's plan for his life and he will not follow the plan of his earthly father for Francis to be wealthy and prestigious. Talk about not being afraid to follow God.

Francis truly belonged to God. He was HIS. He was brave. He went against the flow. He was in direct contradiction to much of the accepted flow of his time. He was unafraid and trusted that the word of the Lord would be fulfilled in him. It was! That is why there is a book called, "The PERFECT Joy of St. Francis."

Are we HIS? Are we brave? Go against the flow. We find the message, "Do not be afraid", about 365 times in the Bible. That means that the Lord of all is telling us each day of the year, "Do not be afraid." Be HIS.

The Master's Plan

"Lo, on your fast day you carry out your own pursuits" Isaiah 58:4

I spent two years of my life on a national youth ministry team. Before I began my first year, one of the top leaders of the organization told me that I would lead a team of 12 young adults as we traveled around the USA giving retreats for one year. As it turned out, I was not chosen to be a team leader and I almost quit because I thought they were making a mistake and not using my "great" talents. Lord have mercy - right? I had my plans but God had others. I often look back and chuckle because I was not in a place to be a team leader and God, as always, knew what He was doing.

We all have plans and pursuits. But God has his plans and pursuits for us that will lead to the deepest love, meaning and happiness for us. How many times do I check in with God, the master planner with the master plan? Often in my life I find myself telling God what I am going to do for him without asking him what he wants. That is like giving my friends pizza all the time because I like pizza. Maybe many of my friends don't like pizza!

Each day we make countless decisions about what we will or will not do. In how many of those decisions do we ask Jesus if that is what he wants us to do? A true lover of Jesus is one who will try to please him by asking him first what he wants before making any decision.

Is Jesus the Lord of your life or are you the Lord of your life? Is it about his pursuits or yours? If we do not run things by Jesus before we make decisions then we have to question who is Lord.

May the Master, master your plan!

God Suffers With Us

"When I called, you answered me; you built up strength within me" Psalm 138:2

I remember when my older brother Mike got into a motorcycle accident in our younger days. After the crash, his friends found him on the side of the road. He was unconscious and bleeding from the nose and ears after being tossed 45 feet or more. Mom and dad got to the hospital and found him unconscious with a fractured skull. Dad made the comment, "If there was any way I could, I would take his place right now". Obviously, dad could not take Mike's place but I am sure dad's love was a strength for Mike that built him up as he healed.

The most moving scenes for me in "The Passion of the Christ" were the interactions between Mary and her son, Jesus. As Jesus falls carrying his cross, Mary flashes back to a time when Jesus fell as a boy. She ran after him and said, "Here I am". She could not erase the pain but she could be present to Jesus in love. And as Jesus carried his cross, suffered and died, there was nothing Mary could do to prevent it all from happening. Perhaps the greatest love she could show was to communicate to Jesus that if there was any way she could have taken his place she would have. By knowing that Mary would have taken his place that would have been a great strength to build up Jesus as he cried out in torment.

To be a human being involves suffering. Throughout the scriptures, different men, women and children have called out to God in their suffering and he has answered their prayers. When we call, maybe we don't feel like God answers because the suffering is not relieved or sometimes it gets worse. The fact is that we all have to suffer and our dad, Mary or God cannot prevent us from having to suffer in this life. But God is always with us in our suffering. When we call out with an open heart, the immensity of his love and power will build strength within us. Call out to Jesus and let him embrace you.

For now, we must suffer. But Jesus wants to teach us that the suffering is just for now. When we die and rise in him, he will be able to take our place and there will be no pain or tears or death anymore.

Fasting From God

"Jesus ate nothing during those 40 days (in the desert), and when they were over he was hungry" Luke 4:2

Cell phones ringing, faxes, emails, 16 hour work days. Endless schedules of sports, shopping, buying, and meetings. And we fast from God. We fast from LIFE. And we wonder why there is so much despair and destruction in our own hearts, families and the world. We hunger for peace and happiness and they are so foreign to us. And we fast from God.

We neglect the inner life of the heart. We neglect the life of relationship which is most important and is going to last forever. We don't let God care for our own hearts and so we cannot care well for other people's hearts. In our noisy, busy, endless schedules we fast from God.

Yesterday I heard a song on the radio that brought me back to the TV life story of the singer. I remember him saying that in the height of his career he made $20 million. He looked straight into the camera and he said that even though he made all this money he wasn't happy. Money is tempting but in no way is it the love of God, which we are made for. There is no joy and contentment in fasting from God.

Jesus fasted from food in order to feast on the Father's love. He was going to suffer an excruciating crucifixion and he needed to feast in order to have the power to move through the cross to the resurrection. We all have our crosses. We take them up in a very imperfect world as we journey on this earth toward our home of heaven. There is an infinite difference between fasting from God and fasting for God. When we fast from God there is no feasting and we die. When we fast for God there will be feasting to help us embrace our crosses with joy, peace and hope.

Is your life more about fasting from God or feasting with Him? The barometer that measures your answer is how much joy and peace you possess.

May you choose feasting.

It's an Inside Job

"Thus says the Lord God: But a very little while, and Lebanon shall be changed into an orchard." Isaiah 29:17

It is an inside job. The world tries to tell us that life is all about appearances. The "highlife" of the Hollywood rich, beautiful and famous comes to us every day through the Mass media. A while back I had a wonderful conversation with my niece about appearances. She goes to a university that is inundated with a focus on appearance. As you walk on campus you see the highlife of the rich, beautiful and famous at every corner you turn. But as you investigate some, you realize that the highlife isn't such a great life. The loneliness, tears and lack of true love become apparent. The worldly focus on eternal appearances is in so many ways opposed to God's focus. Jesus taught us that it is an inside job.

Our reading today from the great prophet Isaiah tells of the coming of the Messiah. We hear that when the Messiah comes, Lebanon will be changed into an orchard. Lebanon was a dry, dusty, barren land. But the Messiah will take the dry, barren land and make it a rich and fertile land that will bear much beautiful fruit! When Jesus comes into some place, it becomes beautiful and the fruits of His presence show forth.

When I think where my niece goes go college, I see a dry, dusty and barren land. When I consider my own life, I sometimes feel like Lebanon. What can I, as a measly bag of bones, offer the world? And now, I come across this Scripture verse. I rejoice as the truth sinks into my soul that Jesus can take my dry, barren heart and make it flourish offering beautiful fruit for the entire world. The fruit that he can put in my heart to share with everyone I meet is love, joy, peace, patience, kindness, goodness, faithfulness, gentleness and self-control. And that is just the beginning of the list.

Sometimes we may not feel beautiful or that we have a lot of love, peace or joy to offer. Spending more time at the beauty salon, paying a visit to my brother whom is a plastic surgeon, or a proudly attained weight loss will not alleviate the barrenness in our hearts that longs for beautiful fruit. The barrenness that we need to give full priority to is in our hearts. It is an inside job.

Here is a little story about a boy and his family that I love dearly. Jake and his brother Robert and sister Katie pray with their parents in the car on the way to school each morning. One morning on the drive to school shortly before Jake was going to receive his first communion he prayed, "Lord, just help me to really receive you in my heart at first communion." Yes, Jake, you're prayer is absolutely right! It is all about inviting Jesus into our hearts. When Jesus comes into our heart, we know our beauty and His loving presence shines forth. May you know your beauty- from the inside out!

Faithfulness, Not Success

"Though I thought I toiled in vain" Isaiah 49:3

There are different ways we can question the purpose of our lives works. Many people suffer the fact that their loved ones have left the faith, church, and God. The years of Christian education and example seem to be a big waste. What about when we are really trying to follow God and we lose our job, health, comfort? How about when relationships come crashing down or when bad things happen to innocent people? Life can seem to be lived in vain if we only consider the earthly plain. Without the hope of resurrection, in the final analysis the sum of life is that we are going to toil, suffer and die.

As the author of the book of Hebrews tells us, Jesus is fully able to
relate with our feelings of toiling in vain. Jesus, Our High Priest, was tempted in every way like us but did not sin. As we look at life through his eyes, he must have been tempted many times to question the worth of what he was doing. Many people were rejecting the Good News of forgiveness, healing and salvation. We know that Jesus experiences utter rejection by this world as he is condemned and crucified on the cross. Jesus' life, then, could be viewed as a waste.

Jesus did not put his faith in results, respect, and affirmation from
the people. He put his faith in God. His food was to do what the Father wanted him to do. He sought that out in prayer and lived it out in his life-regardless of the consequences. Any meaning Jesus was going to offer us would come from the author of all meaning. It was through his relationship with the Father that Jesus knew his life would not be lived in vain. In contrast, the meaning that the Father poured out in Jesus' heart led to the most meaningful life Jesus could lead. Likewise, you and I are called to live the most meaningful life we can by opening our heart to the way of God in prayer. We seek to faithfully follow God regardless of results and feelings of vain living.

There will be results if we bring God's meaning to the world. Some will accept and some will decline. When someone accepts, we will see the results. However, whether someone accepts our rejects is not our concern. Our concern is to always bring the meaning and let God worry about the rest. We do what God wants and let him take care of it from there.

One time reporters were asking Mother Theresa why she was so successful, "Mother Theresa, you are known for your incredible work in the hearts and minds of people the world over. What do you attribute your success to?" Her reply, "I have never seen the word success in the bible. I have seen the word faithfulness but not success." That is our call: to be faithful. To be faithful to the unpopular way of Jesus, regardless of results and feelings of vain living.

A plaque on Mother Theresa's desk read, "Faithfulness, not success." Amen.

Make Jesus Big

"Jesus cried out in a loud voice, "Father, into your hands I commend my spirit"; and when he had said this he breathed his last." Luke 23:46

It is time to stop telling God how big our problems are and start telling our problems how big our God is.

Life involves a lot of suffering and it comes to us in many ways. You have just found out that you or a loved one has cancer. The financial pressures are sky high. The family that you have always wanted has fallen apart. Whatever sufferings we might face, they are real and can become overwhelming at times. That is why it is so important to put sufferings in their place.

It is so much about focus. If we fix our gaze on the sufferings that assail us, we can become hopeless or depressed with their weight on our shoulders. It can be a tendency to give our problems all the attention, focus and concern and relegate Jesus, our Savior, to a place where he has no influence on it all. Thus, we go around telling the whole world and God how big our problems are and remain defeated in what we are facing. We do not invite the Savior to come in and save.

Jesus can teach us about focus. Remember what he did? His focus, his food and strength, was his Father. In and through all his suffering he cried out, "Father, into your hands I commend my spirit." Jesus' focus was his Father and he stared down all his sufferings and his crucifixion with the very power of God- and won.

We want to live in imitation of Christ and how he handled suffering. It is about what we focus on. We can focus on the sufferings and they can seemingly become really big and Jesus becomes really small to us. Or, we can focus on Jesus and he can become really big and our sufferings become really small. The bigger we allow Jesus to be in our lives, the smaller sufferings and death will be to us.

Make Jesus big!

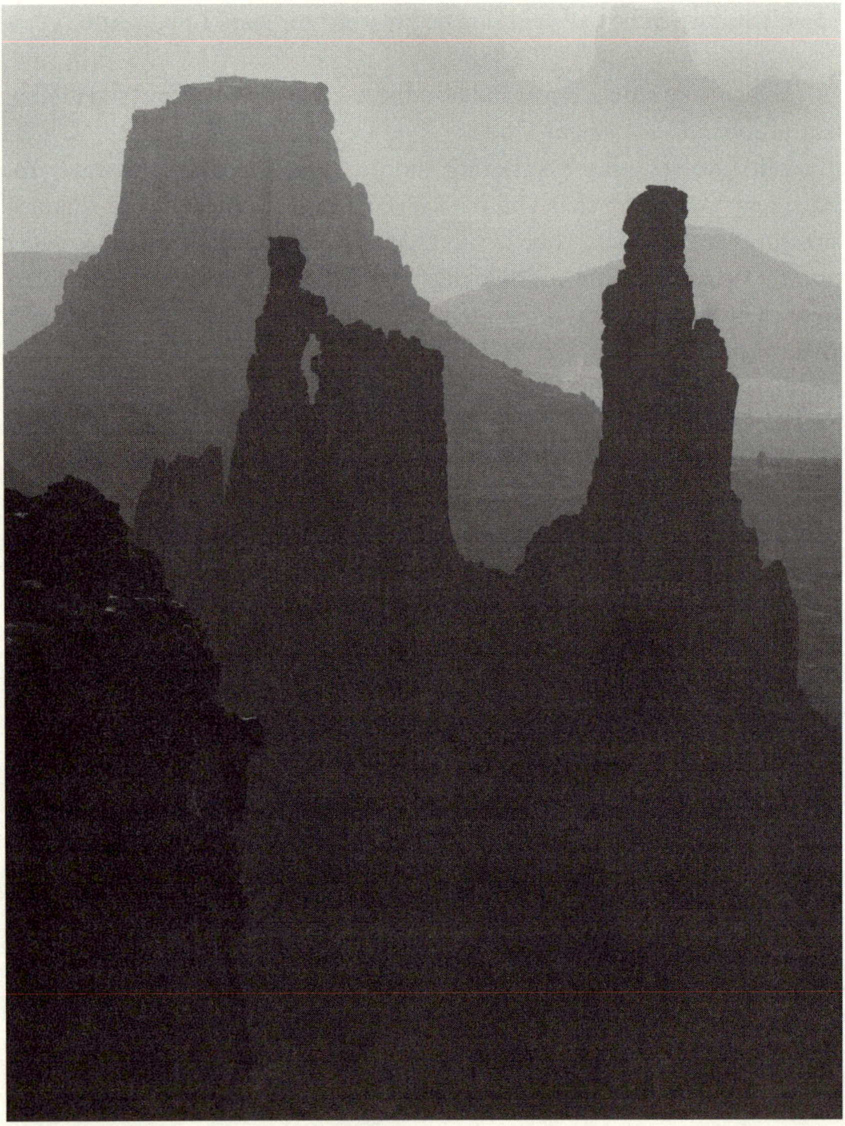

Praise

"Jesus rejoiced in the Holy Spirit and said:" I offer you praise, O Father, Lord of heaven and earth" Luke 10:21

Celebrating the Eucharist on Sundays with the family of God is the heart of my JOY on earth. Sometimes I can tend to get excited with preaching and the Mass may, dare I say, extend beyond an hour! God help us Catholics if we hang out in Church too long! Anyway, one Sunday morning I was in front of Church greeting people after Mass and smiles, hugs and laughter surrounded me. It was 11:20am (and I was loved) when someone complained to me about the length of the Mass. At that point, in some ways the complaint popped my balloon of joy. Sadly, I know that I have many times popped other people's balloons of joy through my own negativity.

We bring others either life or death by our words. The words we say to another person either lead that person closer to or further away from eternal life. There is a reason the tongue is the most coordinated muscle in the body-it has the power to give life or destroy it.

Isn't it amazing how one negative comment can wipe out 100 compliments? Isn't it sad that people will underachieve and sometimes even take their own lives if they have been continually told something like they are stupid or ugly? Isn't it shocking, once we stop and think about it, how much killing of other's spirits we see in our world? Isn't it scary how we can be so negative to others both in front of their faces and behind their backs?

What is the antidote to being negative? Praise. Just before I was ordained a priest I asked a holy woman in her late seventies what advice she had for me as a priest. Basically the advice she gave me was two words; praise God. This advice is some of the best I have ever gotten because the more I praise God; the more I praise and honor everyone around me. And that is cause for JOY.

Jesus' whole life was a song of praise to his Father. Jesus' song was about life and he came that we might have life and have it to overflowing. Thus, every word Jesus spoke, even if it was tough to follow, was intended to build up the life of the hearer.

Let us reflect on our speech. We are called to be a people of praise. In the name of Jesus, negativity be gone!

Let's imagine each other as balloons. Are we filling up each other with the helium of God's love by our words of honor or are we popping each other's balloons by the sharp pins of our negativity?

Perfectly Loved in the Eucharist - Real Communion

"This is my body to be given for you." Luke 22:19

Life is a journey. Between our birth and death we try to figure out what it is all about. As I see it, the issue in life is communion. St Augustine prayed, "My heart is restless until it rests in Thee, O' Lord." We are invited to live in the perfect and loving communion that is the Father, Son and Holy Spirit, i.e. The Trinity. The Trinity has been enjoying perfect and loving unity for all eternity and our hearts will be restless until we are fully united with the Father, Son and Holy Spirit. As we become united with The Trinity, we will learn how to live in communion with each other and all of creation.

If I had a real one-hundred dollar bill in one hand and a counterfeit one-hundred dollar bill in the other hand, which would you choose? Hopefully, you would choose the real one. Well, that is the purpose of following Christ in the Church. The church gives us a great opportunity to choose the "Real One". The "Real One' is Jesus Christ who has come to forgive our sins so that we might enjoy perfect and loving communion with God and each other for all eternity. The "Real One" is the only one that can make perfect and everlasting loving communion possible. As we both know, there are many counterfeits out there offering this perfect and everlasting loving communion that always turns out to be empty promises. We need to counter the fits that the counterfeits bring with the "Real One." The "Real One" always delivers- every time. He is faithful and true. He does what he says and says what he does. He constantly and forever offers us perfect and loving communion. There is no shadow of a lie in him.

For all who are reading this, from people of all faiths or no professed faith at all, I say, "You are perfectly loved by Jesus in the Eucharist." Why? Because it is True! As Catholics we continually celebrate the Eucharist. At The Last Supper on the night before he died, Jesus said he would give us his very body and blood in the bread and wine so that we could have perfect and perpetual communion with God and each other. May we counter the counterfeits and find the "Real One" in the Eucharist offering us loving communion forever.

Speaking Up

"Tell my people of their wickedness, and the house of Jacob of their sins." Isaiah 58:1

God asks Isaiah to tell the Israelites of their wickedness and sins. That is not necessarily a fun task. How many of us like to confront others when we know that we are just as much a sinner as anyone else? Perhaps that is a key understanding to the whole process of calling others out of their sin. We must do it humbly remembering that we can never grandstand in view of our own sin. We do well to resonate with King David, "For I acknowledge my offense, and my sin is before me always" (Psalm 51:5)

What would you do if your child or someone you loved dearly was about ready to walk off a cliff to their death? I hope that you would do everything in your power to prevent them from walking over the cliff. By analogy, we must use everything in our God-given power to make sure that each others souls do not die. Physical death is one thing that we all encounter but the death of the soul is an eternal death that we want no one to encounter. How willing are we to speak up for the sake of someone's eternal soul? Who do you know that is hurting or maiming their soul through sin that you need to speak up to? It may sound strange but some of the times I have felt most loved in life is when someone humbly pointed out how my sin was taking the life out of my soul.

Do not let anyone walk over the cliff to their death. Let us speak up for the sake of each other's souls.

Ask the Inventor

"Jesus said to Levi, 'Follow me'" Luke 5:27

There is only one creator and the rest of us are creatures. The sooner we understand and live by that the better. The creator says to the creature, "Follow me." Jesus looks at Levi in today's verse and say, "Follow me." Our creator says to you and I and every other human being "Follow me." If you will, think about ourselves as inventions. If an invention wants to know how it works, it just needs to ask the inventor. The inventor knows all about how the invention works and its reason for existence. Read Psalm 139 to learn how the creator knows everything about the creature.

Through the mass media and maybe in our own hearts we can get the idea that it is OK to do what we want, when we want, how we want, with whomever we want. But that is not the plan of Jesus who says to each of us, just like he did to Levi some 2,000 years ago, "Follow me." Jesus' love makes big demands. He tells us we must carry our crosses daily. We will suffer and be persecuted as we follow him. Some of the other demands of following him are to forgive our enemies, sacrifice for others, to put others before ourselves.

But let us look at what else is involved in following Jesus. See him forgiving the adulterous woman whom everyone else wanted to kill. Think about how he embraced children or wept at the death of his friend Lazarus. Put yourself in a festive celebration that he was having with friends and sinners alike. Imagine yourself as the blind man crying out for mercy and Jesus answering your plea. Picture his look of love upon you. Yes, he has come to offer you love and love to the overflowing. That is where following him will lead to.

Life is a loving, difficult, adventurous, challenging, grace-filled ride. Jesus is the driver. If you have been doing all the driving- move over. Take the passenger seat and let Jesus do the driving. The creator knows exactly what he is doing.

I Was Hungry

Jesus said, "I was hungry, thirsty, a stranger, naked, ill and in prison, and you did not care for me." Matthew 25:42-43

Jesus is crying out to each of us all the time. He wants our love and affection. He asks if we will clothe and feed him. He is lonely, old, ill and in prison and he longs for a visit from us. Where can we find Jesus? He says he is person who is hungry, thirsty, a stranger, naked, ill and in prison. That is true but even more practically; Jesus is in the next person we see. Think about it- the next person you see is Jesus seeking our love. Maybe that person does not need some sort of material provision but there is no doubt they need more love and affirmation. You cannot love or affirm someone too much.

Jesus says that when we don't care for the person in need, i.e. the next person we see, then we don't care for him. What do I do when someone asks me for help, money or food? What about when I refuse to help? Am I snubbing Jesus? What consequences will I face because I ignore his cry? These are the types of questions we have to grapple with in terms of his command to care for him as a hungry person.

All people are Jesus crying out to you and me for love. We are commanded to answer the cry of Jesus in all people. Wow! That is a tall order that requires divine eyes to see and divine love to carry it out to all we meet. With this injunction, don't let anyone-whether teenagers or whoever-tell you that church and Christianity is boring. We have work to do! Our work is the work of love.

St. Teresa of Avila writes, "Let truth be in your hearts, as it will be if you practice meditation, and you will see clearly what love we are bound to have for our neighbors." Amen!

Our mission in life it to love our neighbors, i.e. everyone. Look at life as a whole bunch of one day missions to love. Pray about this mission each day before you go on your one day mission. Think about the fact that Jesus is in the next person you see and he is crying out for love. Reflect and meditate on your mission. Then, LOVE.

Here is a prayer for the beginning of each day: "Dear Jesus. Let me love, honor and serve you in each person I meet today. May I love you in my brothers and sisters with the same reverence, fidelity and intensity that you love us all. Amen."

Tempted? Be Accountable

"Jesus was led by the Spirit into the desert to be tempted by the devil." Like 4: 1-2

The Devil wants to divide us from God and his life. "Devil" comes from the word Diablo, which means to divide/separate. Any time there are divisions in relationships, the Devil is behind it. He is constantly tempting to divide and separate us from God and each other. And if that is not enough, when I have resisted *Diablo* to the point that he leaves me alone, the bible says that he looks for the next opportune time to come back and wreak havoc. (See Luke 4:13) The assault is constant and *Diablo* is cunning and subtle. He doesn't want us to see that he is coming. He lives in the darkness and he wants us to live there too. He does not want to be exposed for who he is- a sham, the deceiver, The King of Liars. He wants the truth about himself to remain unexposed because he is lying about truth, love, and goodness.

So how do we combat temptation to divide ourselves from God and each other? If we don't have regular accountability to other people in our lives, Satan will have a field day with us. Who in your life right now are you accountable to for your temptation, sins and the evil we are all tempted to choose?

Choose someone to be accountable to. A person trying to make it to heaven on his or her own is set up to fail. Pray about who God wants you to fess up to and ask that person or those people if they would be willing to hold you accountable to resisting evil in your life. Talk with them regularly and give them the permission to ask you any time how you are fighting evil. I know of a bishop who has told his priests that he will show up unannounced at any time to their parish or house and expect to be able to know where they are and what they are doing. How is that for being held accountable?

Also, think about Christianity as much more about doing the good than just avoiding the evil. If you are doing the good all the time, evil won't have a chance. Do the good!

Running Freely in God's Love

The word of the Lord came to Jonah a second time: "Set out for the great city of Nineveh, and announce to it the message I will tell you" Jonah 3:1

An interesting study was done on schoolyard playgrounds across the United States. When a playground had a fence around it the kids would go up to the fence, touch or maybe climb it a little bit but then would leave the fence area to run around freely within the confines of the playground. Playgrounds that did not have a fence, in contrast, told of a whole different story. In places where there were no fences to the playground, the kids tended to not run around freely like the kids in the fenced playground. The kids in fence-less playgrounds were observed huddling in the middle out of seeming fear and timidity. The point is that the kids who had fences had boundaries and they knew where they could and could not go. In the fence-less playgrounds they did not know where they could or could not go which created an undefined, scary and out of control world. What can be derived from this study is we all need boundaries. God has set an order to all creation and we can not, if you will, run freely in love like the children on the fenced playground of life unless we know what we can and can not do.

Jonah is a man sent by God to tell the Ninevites to turn from their evil and turn to God. We are called to be Jonah's for each other. Someone wrote to me the other day and told me we have no right to tell others of their sin because that is being judgmental and self-righteous. But think about what parents do. They are constantly teaching their kids about right and wrong. And if they don't teach them what they can or can not do, the kids may well end up living fearful and crazed lives where nothing seems true all the time. It is the boundaries that allow us to run free in God's love.

Jesus wants us to run freely in his playground of love. But we need to know where we can and can not go so as to remain in the freedom and safety of his love. Thank God we have parents, family, friends and community always calling us to live in the infinite boundaries of his love.

Who have been the Jonah's in your life who have risked their friendship with you so you could run more freely in God's love? Send them a thank-you card or call them on the phone and express your gratitude.

Praise Him

"I will give you thanks to you, O Lord, with all my heart" Psalm 138:1

Wouldn't it be neat to meet the person who wrote this line to the psalm? I wonder what was going in this person's life. Everyone has their own incredible story and I think it would be fascinating to get inside the heart and mind of this person as they experienced life 1,000's of years ago. I would bet that many of the joys and struggles of the psalmist are the same kind that I live presently. And yet, in the midst of it all, this person is giving thanks to the Lord's whole-heartedly.

Someone was talking about how shy we are to say something like, "Praise the Lord." We know how many times God's name is used in vain or cursed but how much is it praised? Think about your day to day conversations and if you are shy or ashamed in some way to give thanks to God before others. You never know but by taking a risk and giving thanks to God before someone you don't necessarily know could lead to big things. It might just open the door of eternal life to them. There are big consequences for sharing and not sharing. We have been given a lot of power to open the door for others to God.

Am I shy, scared or ashamed to share my thanksgiving to God before others? I would honestly have to say that there are times that I use one or all three of these excuses not to thank God. Boy, I am being convicted as I write! God is good all the time and all the time God is good. Jesus loves us perfectly in the Eucharist. He died that we might have eternal life celebrating his love forever. And I am ashamed to share him? Lord have mercy on me.

Let us encourage each other to give thanks to God with all our hearts-everywhere, all the time.

Love All

"For if you love those who love you, what recompense will you have?" Matthew 5:46

There are times when we might want to avoid "certain" people. Maybe they have hurt you or you have nothing in common with them or they just seem to push your buttons. I often wonder what heaven will be like if we forever have to be around people who, for whatever reason, we just find a difficult time loving. I trust that God will work that out to bring us all into the unity of his love.

When I think about the church, my family, social situations etc., I know I can tend to spend time with those who it is easy to love. You know, the kind of people I can trust to honor me and always have my back. But Jesus says even the pagan's love those who love them. If that is all our love is about then we are no different than those who do not have God in their lives. So, the questions begs, "Then what difference is Christ suppose to make in our lives." Christ helps us to love those we do not or can not love on our own power. It is only though the power of Christ that we can love those who have hurt us or do not love us in return or push our buttons, etc. Consider how Jesus loves everyone equally and eternally on the cross.

Who is it in your life right now that you are avoiding? Imagine if you were at a wonderful celebration of friends. Who is the person that you would least like to see at that same party? Reflect on your relationship with this person. Have you acted more like a pagan or a Christian in your relationship to this person? Pray about how you can love this person in some simple way. Maybe it is saying a rosary or prayer for them. Maybe it is a compliment or a kind letter/phone call. It could be offering forgiveness in your heart. Give the Holy Spirit a chance to show you who this person is and how you are to reach out in one, simple act of love. Then, do it in faith. Become more like Christ who loves everyone with the same relentless outreach.

LAW - Love Always Wins

"Blessed is the man who delights in the law of the Lord" Psalm 1:2

A wonderful spiritual principle is that we cannot out give God. No matter what we give to God, he will always give us more. For all eternity, God will not be outdone in generosity. You or I could be the most generous person in world but there is no way we could come close to matching the unlimited generosity of Our Lord. And I am not talking about material goods or even physical health. I am talking about the eternal goods of things like love, beauty, truth, joy and peace. The impossibility of never giving more to God than he gives to us should truly lead us to a life of awe and wonder. Just think about it- we give God our sinful, tattered hearts and in return God offers us eternal life. What an exchange. We trade in our sins for eternal life. In the equation of life, it is blatantly obvious to see that our giving is really pithy compared to the eternal and infinite giving and generosity of our God.

Living the blessed life involves knowing, on the deepest level, the eternal generosity of God. Our psalmist today states that whoever follows the law of the Lord will be blessed. Yes, the one who follows the law of the Lord will know in his or her heart the infinite and eternal life God offers to all people. An acronym that I came up with for the word "Law" is Love Always Wins. If we follow God's law on our earthly journey through this valley of tears (see Psalm 23), he will lead us to victory over sin and death. In unreservedly following God's law, we win as he brings us to eternal life in heaven. It is in seeing with this vision that we can say, "Love Always Wins."

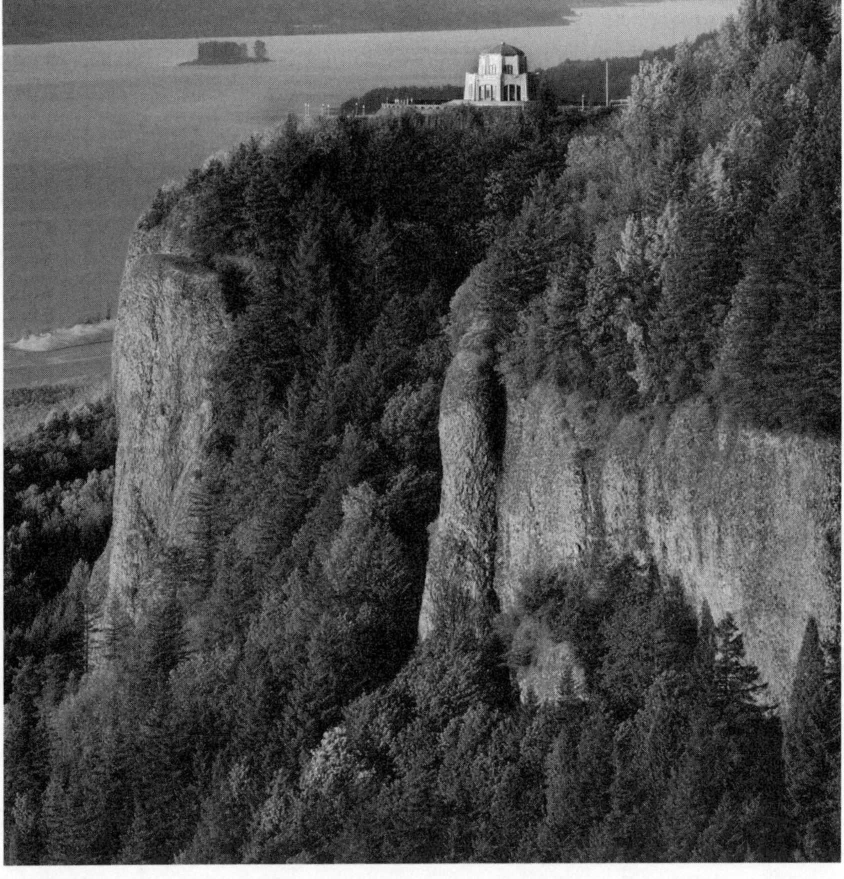

Heaven on Earth

"And Jesus was transfigured before them; his face shone like the sun and his clothes became white as light." Matthew 17:2

Jesus came from heaven to bring heaven to earth and earth to heaven. Day by day and second by second all around the world Jesus is becoming the bread and wine of the Eucharist to feed all people with the taste of heaven. When will we say "Yes" to the reality of Jesus in the Eucharist? When will we say "Yes" to being totally transfigured in his love such that our faces shine like the sun and our clothes become white as light?

In the gospel (Mt. 17:1-9) of the Transfiguration, Jesus takes Peter, James and John up on a mountain and becomes transfigured before their eyes. We read that Jesus' face shines like the sun and his clothes become light. Imagine the brilliance that Peter, James and John saw. Try to imagine shining intensity of only being a few feet from the sun? In this scripture we are once again reminded that Jesus is bringing all his disciples (including you and me) heaven! That is why Jesus came to earth- to bring heaven to earth and earth to heaven.

Where is heaven to be found on earth? Most especially in the Mass! The Constitution on the Sacred Liturgy says, "In the earthly liturgy we share in the foretaste of the heavenly liturgy which is celebrated in the Holy City of Jerusalem which we journey towards as pilgrims" *Sacrosonctum Concilium* 8. The Mass is, "heaven on earth". We have been duped and deceived in so many and various ways that we can find what we are truly looking in so many places outside the Mass. Do not be duped or deceived any longer! You and I must come to terms with the fact that the freedom, healing, forgiveness, love, happiness and salvation for eternal life we agonize for are found in the Mass. Jesus gives us heaven in his body and blood poured out for us in the Eucharist. We must come to terms that the Mass is heaven on earth!

We can always grow in our understanding of the mystery of the Mass.

THE HOLY DIP- Each of us goes for the holy dip upon entering the church. As we re-sign ourselves with the cross using the holy water, we remember our baptism and that we all belong to the Father and the Son and the Holy Spirit. <u>The whole meaning of everyone's life is found in the sign of the cross.</u> **IN THE NAME OF THE FATHER-** You and I were created for total love. God Our Father is love and he desired that we would share in his perfect love. We sinned and became separated from that love. We fell from God's grace and suffering and death entered the world through Adam and Eve's sin. **IN THE NAME OF THE SON-** God Our Father doesn't change his mind or heart. He still wants us to share in his total/perfect love. So, he sends Jesus die for our sins that if we would truly follow and become like him, he would lead us to heaven- the place of the perfect and total love of God. **IN THE NAME OF THE HOLY SPIRIT-** When Jesus rose from the dead the Father sent the Holy Spirit to each one of us that we might follow and become like Jesus- all the way to heaven. The Holy Spirit, if we open up our hearts and allow it, makes us perfect in love. We come unto the very holiness of God though the power of the Holy Spirit.

So, how are the sign of cross and the Mass like each other? In the Mass, we always start out by remembering that God is always with us and God is love. In the Penitential rite we confess we are sinners in need of God's mercy and eternal salvation as we cry out Lord Have Mercy, Christ Have Mercy and Lord Have Mercy. We remember we are forgiven and we give glory to God. Then we are fed by the word of God in both the Scriptures and the Eucharist to become more like Jesus. Just like the bread and wine are transformed into Jesus though the power of the Holy Spirit, so too are we! We pray as Augustine prayed," May we become what we have received." We want to be united with Jesus. This is the story of the Mass, the sign of the cross and of our lives. It is all the same story. God loved us; we separated ourselves from that love but Jesus and the Holy Spirit want to bring us back to the perfect place of love. Jesus came to bring heaven to earth and earth to heaven. It is in the Mass that heaven kisses earth and earth kisses heaven. The Mass is heaven on earth.

Eucharist - Infinite Merciful Covenant

"Lord, great and awesome God, you who keep your merciful covenant toward those who love you and observe your commandments." Daniel 9:4

You are perfectly loved by Jesus in the Eucharist! That is the truth, the whole truth and nothing but the truth. Many people have remarked to me how much they liked that statement. How could life get better than receiving the perfect love of Jesus as he gives us his body and blood in the Eucharist? You think we would want to stay close and hold the Eucharist more precious than anything else. Go to Mass as much as you can. Surrender to Jesus in the Eucharist and you will experience a revolution of peace in your life. You will find Jesus' perfect love in the Eucharist.

If you are reading this and you do not believe that you are perfectly loved by the Real Presence of Jesus in the Eucharist, I pray that you may come to believe and know this in your heart. If you seek with all your heart, soul and mind to find Jesus' Real Presence in the Eucharist, you will! Once I asked a convert why she converted to Catholicism and she answered, "Basically, I became Catholic because of the life of Mother Theresa and her teaching on the Eucharist." Yes, Mother Theresa adored Jesus in the Eucharist in her morning and night prayers and during the day she adored Jesus in all the poor she served. She stayed centered on the perfect love of Jesus in the Eucharist and became that love for the poor. She taught all her sisters to do the same. You and I have the free will to do the same and find the perfect love of Jesus in the Eucharist.

The Eucharist is an irrevocable covenant of God's eternal love to all his people. In the Eucharist, Jesus gives himself fully to us in love, forever! That is where I struggle with today's scripture. We read in Daniel that God keeps his merciful covenant to those who love and obey him. Does that mean that God does not keep his covenant to those who do not love or obey him? Absolutely not! The issue is whether or not we experience the covenant of God in the Eucharist. If we stay close to and love and obey Jesus in the Eucharist, we will know the merciful covenant of God. In the Eucharist, i.e. the new and everlasting covenant of forgiveness of sins through his death and resurrection, Jesus offers every sinner ever born his infinite mercy and love. The Eucharist has been happening for some 2,000 years. It was established by Jesus Christ at the Last Supper on the night before he died. The Eucharist is Jesus' Covenant of perfect love offered to anyone who will choose to believe it. It is all a matter if we will or will not take him up on his offer that he gave us all at the Last Supper.

My brothers and sisters, how will you and I come to know the Real Presence of Jesus in the Eucharist? We will seek, with and open and believing heart, with all our heart, soul, strength and mind the Real Presence of Jesus' perfect love in the Eucharist. Then, the Holy Spirit will show us that the Eucharist is Jesus. The Holy Spirit leads us to all truth. We will learn that for 2,000 years of church history God has kept his covenant in the Eucharist! He has offered every person in every age the perfect love and mercy of Jesus in the Eucharist! And he will do so until the end of time.

What Founds You?

Jesus said, "And so I say to you, you are Peter, and upon this rock I will build my church" Matthew 16:17

"What founds you?" We believe that Jesus founds his church on people- that people are the church. The Vatican II documents call the church the People of God. And in today's verse we believe that Jesus is appointing the first leader of the church, i.e. the Pope, in Peter. But, what is our foundation? What do we build our lives on?

Once I visited a 91 year old, homebound parishioner. I asked her what her greatest memories in life were and she said, "Family, Christmas, Thanksgiving and any times her loved ones were gathered together." It was all about people and not things. As we approach death I think we often more clearly realize that life is about people, love and relationships. That is the way we are hard-wired. We are built for relationship because that is what God is. God wants to be in relationship with us, offer us perfect love and translate that love in all of our relationships. Are you finding yourself "founding yourself" on him? If not, your foundation is shaky at best and it will crumble.

Think about if you founded your life on the stock market. What a bunch of up and downs your life would be. Even if you found your life on the most loving person you know, there will still be ups and downs. But if we truly found our lives on the perfect love of Jesus, he will always be an eternal "up" for all the other up's and down's we face in every other relationship and situation. That is why it is so important to know the Real Presence of Jesus loving us perfectly in the Eucharist.

We are built for relationship and we are to found our lives on Christ. Have we?

Be What You Should Be - Set the World Ablaze

"The stone that the builders rejected has become the cornerstone" Matthew 21:43

I am always sadly bewildered when I think about our rejection of Jesus. Reflect on who he was and why he emptied himself of heaven to come to earth. As we seek greater union with Jesus, we reflect more deeply on the "who" and "why" of Jesus. Jesus was and is perfect love. The reason he came to earth was to die for you and me that we might have forgiveness of sins and eternal life. And how did we respond? We crucified him on a cross. I am utterly stupefied to think that Jesus, being fully God and man, offered us perfect love and we rejected his offer. We said "no" to his love and tried to put an end to it. Who in their right mind would reject the infinite love of God revealed in the life, death and resurrection of Jesus Christ?

All that Jesus ever offered us was unconditional love and we returned the offer by nailing him to a cross. I think of parents who give fully of themselves so that their children can come to know and live in the unconditional love of God forever. Many times, the parents and their offer of God's love are rejected. I know many people who suffer greatly because their loved ones have left Jesus and the church.

Why do people leave Jesus and the church? As a Catholic, I ask myself why so many people have left the church, even after 12-20 years of Catholic education? Why are there so many non-practicing Catholics in the United States? Perhaps the brilliance of Jesus has been buried, hidden, locked-up, denied access...

Everyone wants the perfect love of Jesus. Everyone wants the hope and forgiveness of Jesus. Everyone wants the eternal life that only Jesus can give. So, what is the antidote to all the rejection of Jesus going on in our world? Jesus needs to become so real in you and me. When people see us they should see Jesus. **THE MESSAGE** of the Christian's life is Jesus forgives, loves, heals and saves us unto everlasting life.

We must give Jesus full permission to overflow our lives with his perfect love.

Let us pray, "Lord Jesus, May the message of my life be You. When others see me, may they see you. May your perfect love inebriate all I think, say and do. May you be glorified and made known to the ends of the earth. Amen"

"If you are what you should be you will set the whole world ablaze." St. Catherine of Siena

Shepherds With Staffs

"Shepherd your people with your staff" Micah 7:14

There are special occasions like first communion where I will dress up as a shepherd. One of things that I have to have when I dress up as a shepherd is my shepherd's staff. I use it as a visual aid to teach about what shepherds use their staffs for.

One of the purposes of the staff is to draw the sheep away from danger back into the fold. Whether there was a disconnect from the sheep-fold or imminent danger from steep and rocky terrain, a shepherd would use his staff to bring the sheep back into safety. The staff is also used by shepherds to fight off beasts wanting to kill their prey and thieves wanting to steal their sheep.

Another purpose of the staff is to check for any injuries on the sheep's body. At night the shepherd moves the sheep to an enclosed pasture. He waits at the gate and make the sheep crawl under his staff as a way to carefully check each sheep for blood or injury.

Who are well called to draw back into the fold because they are walking away from God towards the "predators" that are attempting to steal their life in Christ? Also, are we making sure that the sheep in our care are not bleeding or wounded as we carefully observe them each night before they go to bed? Do we pray with our children and each other for peace and healing before falling asleep each night? Are we looking to help heal the bleeding and injuries of all the people who come across our path looking for care?

The Eucharist is Not Fast Food

"A woman from Samaria came to draw water" John (4:5-42)

I invite you to sometime soon read and pray over the story popularly known as, "The Woman at the Well", in John 4:5-42. What is God personally saying to you in this story? It is a story of a dialogue between a Samaritan woman and Jesus at a watering well. It is a story of how Jesus gradually reveals himself as a personal and loving Messiah. Jesus reveals that he knows about her life and that he is the truth she is seeking. This story is kind of like a miniature portrait of our lives. Jesus continues to unfold himself for us. As we open ourselves up to him daily in faith we are transformed by his grace to become more like him. It is a process to come to know the fullness of salvation just like it is a process to become a mature man or woman. Like a good wine, to become a Christian takes time. The same is true for understanding the Eucharist. It takes time to personally know and be transformed by Jesus in the Eucharist. Day by day, we invite the grace of God to act on us and bring us to the fullness of life in the Eucharist. It is a process of allowing God to bring us into perfect communion with his love. The finished product is not NOW. One just doesn't invite Jesus into their heart and become instantaneously a perfectly holy person. There are some theologies that might teach this. Also, our world demands that we have the fullness of everything NOW. We are a fast food and everything society. But that is not the way life works. Growth is a process. The Eucharist is not fast food. We must spend a lot of time bowed down before it in order believe and be transformed by it.

THE EUCHARIST IS **NOT** FAST FOOD

Instantaneous- I hit a button that sends an email to Australia. Do you know how many hours by flight it takes to get to Australia from Oregon going at speeds of 600 mph? The email letter arrived there instantaneously. Living in a credit card, instant messaging, cell phone world gives us things we want "on demand." So many things at our fingertips and so often we want them and we want them **NOW.**

Instant gratification- Anywhere from get-rich-quick schemes to having sex outside of the marriage bond without any serious moral/

relational/spiritual/physical etc. consequences (which is utterly impossible), our society constantly promotes instant gratification. A person doesn't become a doctor overnight. In order to become a good doctor, you have to study, sweat and work a lot and endure a lot of sleepless nights over the course of years and years. It is ridiculous to think that you can instantly become a doctor. All great things take time. But the anthem we hear is get gratification and get it **NOW.**

Fast food- One drive-thru promises food within 45 seconds of ordering. We live in a fast-food world and we want our food **NOW.**

THE EUCHARIST IS <u>NOT</u> FAST FOOD- I want to challenge us all to look at how we look at the Eucharist. Is church just a drive-thru restaurant where we pick up the fast food of Jesus? Is Jesus just a Big Mac to us or is he different? Seriously- what is the Eucharist to you?

<u>Preparation</u>- Being the youngest of 8 boys, I know the hustle and bustle of family life and just trying to make it to church on time. As the car is pulling out from the house, the last kid is jumping in (maybe!)... I am familiar with that routine. The question is, "Can we be better prepared for Mass- so it is not a last second, drive-thru deal? Getting up earlier and going to bed earlier because Mass is #1 priority? Praying together as a family during the week and before we go to Mass? Praying a decade of the Rosary on the way to church? Listening to Christian music before Mass? Reading the Sunday scripture readings before Mass and during the week prior? "

To understand the Eucharist takes time and care. Three things I recommend to grow in understanding the Eucharist: 1) Go to confession and be forgiven for your sin 2) an open and believing heart, and 3) time. Come to Jesus with a clean heart, believing that he will reveal himself to you. Give him time, time, time. **The Eucharist is <u>not</u> fast food!** If given time, he will reveal himself to you and revolutionize your life in the eternal new-ness of his love. Brothers and sisters, do you want to live in a revolution of love? The Eucharist is greatest treasure of our church. To find the Eucharist takes time and your heart. Any great friendship takes a great sharing of time and hearts. Our greatest friendship should involve a lot of time and heart sharing.

What Masters Master You?

"Athirst is my soul for God" Psalm 42:3

"My heart is restless and it will not rest until it rests in Thee, O' Lord" St. Augustine

If you were asked to name the top three things, besides God, that people seek to fill their souls thirst for meaning, love and happiness, what would you name? Three things that came to the forefront of my list are money/material possessions, sex and what I will call self-salvation.

So many people seem like they live to work instead of working to live. Studies show how we are working more and sleeping a lot less. There is the pressure in this country to make more money to keep up with the Joneses and buy more, bigger and better than your neighbors. The "rat race" to accumulate rages on but the only problem with the "rat race" is that even the winner is still a rat! (smiles) The eternal problem with money and things is that they can never grant us peace.

Many look for connection, meaning, love, and belonging in sex without a total commitment to each other in marriage for the whole of life. People then become objects and are used and thrown away like a napkin. Porn is out of control in this country. I believe that over one in three of the billions of hits on the internet each day are for a porn site. Porn has nothing to do with love and the humanity of a person is destroyed when someone chooses to fill their soul with it.

Another way we can try to feed ourselves is through prideful and radical independence. In others words, we live as if we can do it on our own and we don't need a savior. Think about it, how much do our words and feet talk about how badly we need a savior. Do you tell other people how Jesus is saving you- if not, then is he? Let's talk about how our feet tell others that we need a savior. Do they take us to church often and to prayer daily? If someone's feet aren't taking them to daily prayer then I would wonder if that person really believes they need a savior. They must be handling it all on their own if they don't need Jesus. If we don't go to Jesus, then we don't need him, correct?

So, if we serve money/things, sex, ourselves etc. then they become the master. These masters cannot free us from our shame and sin and raise us to life everlasting. They offer no key for the prison of sin we live in. We become slaves to masters who offer no forgiveness and peace.

However, when we become a slave to our master Jesus by surrendering to him, he sets us free in love. In his grace and with his power we can say, "Death, you are a Punk- get lost. Sin, I send you to the foot of the cross where Jesus will deal with you. Satan, in the name of Jesus, be gone." Now, Jesus is the only master worth serving.

Who are the masters you serve? What do they provide you with?

Your words and your feet tell what masters you serve. What do you talk about? Where you walking to? What does that give you?

"My heart is restless and it will not rest until it rests in Thee, O' Lord" St. Augustine

Follow Unreservedly

"So let our sacrifice be in your presence today as we follow you unreservedly" Daniel 3:40

"What's your line? Tell my why you wear your cross of gold. State of mind or does it find a way into your soul?" This refrain from a Christian song has always been a challenge for me. Do I live the creed and prayers I pray at church? Is my life a life of the gospel? Do I carry my cross in imitation of my savior, Jesus? Or is my faith more "in name only" such that my life is not much different then someone who does not believe in God or go to church? The words, prayers and beliefs in church/scriptures must translate into lives of radical love as we follow Jesus unreservedly.

Have you ever been around a professed Christian who seems to have no joy and a lot of judgment going on in their lives? Think about how incongruous it is to be a joyless and judgmental Christian. Jesus did not come to condemn but to save sinners like you and me! He loves us and wants us to live in the unspeakable joy of heaven forever. That should be a great cause for Joy. Jesus' burning desire is to outpour his salvation and everlasting life into our hearts. How can we not have joy when we look at the facts? As a matter of fact, you have to have joy when you have Jesus. It is impossible not to have joy when we give him primacy of place in our hearts and he reveals his overflowing goodness to us. Joy will come as we follow him unreservedly.

But it costs to follow Jesus. If we look at the path of Jesus, we see the hatred toward him being fueled during the last three years of his life until he was made to carry the cross and die the excruciating death of crucifixion. Jesus did come to take away sin but many did not believe him. We would not open their hearts to his work, follow him unreservedly and meet his demands for change. Instead, we put him to death on a tree.

Have you and I done the same? Have we closed our hearts and put Jesus to death because we don't want to hear about the demands and the changes he is calling us to? There is no doubt that Jesus is constantly calling us to change and become holier, better people. Open your heart to his invitation to change as he speaks to you in church, prayer, scripture or where ever. Remember this invitation is an invitation to a life of joy- to live in the overflowing love of God forever with no sting or stain of sin.

I want to leave you with a couple of quotes as we ponder our call to follow Jesus unreservedly. Reflect and pray on these quotes. Go deeper with them and talk about what they mean for you with others.

"Christianity has not been tried and found wanting. It has been found difficult and left untried." GK Chesterton

"God does not desire our comfort but our salvation."

God Sightings

"Take care and be earnestly on your guard not to forget the things which your own eyes have seen" Deuteronomy 4:9

God is good- all the time. And all the time- God is good. God is love- all the time. And all the time- God is love. God is merciful and forgiving- all the time. And all the time- God is merciful and forgiving.

One thing I always want to do is talk about "God-sightings." Where have you seen the Lord acting in your life? Continually, I encourage people to share how they see God working for good in their lives. If we give a majority of our time to the newspaper and TV we can get inundated with bad news. The bad news, then, can dominate our thoughts, words and actions. We don't want that to happen. We want to Good News to win! For the glory of God, we want the Good News to fill all that we think, say or do. Just think about that one- Have you ever met a person who just radiates Good News in that that they think say and do? That, my brothers and sisters, is what a believer should look like.

One name by which God has been named is "The Hound of Heaven." In other words, God is in relentless pursuit of each one of us. He seeks to find you and me and everybody and bring us all home to heaven. If this is true, which it is, then we should see countless signs in our everyday lives that attest to the fact that "The Hound of Heaven" is in relentless pursuit of us. If we really believe that God is perfectly good, loving, merciful and forgiving all the time, then our hearts should be filled with joy because of WHO is pursuing us!

A lot of times we act like the perfectly good, loving, merciful and forgiving "Hound of Heaven" is dead because we never talk about "God-sightings." In light of this not too uncommon phenomena, I want to absolutely urge us to the discipline/practice/grace/gift/joy or whatever you want to call it of sharing "God-sightings" with one another. Families- please do this around your dinner table or when you are having some family times. Take time to share with friends or strangers about the "Hound of Heaven" and his relentless pursuit of us. Talk about how you are seeing God. Talk about the wonder of his goodness. Talk about his infinite upside!

God is good- all the time. And all the time- God is good. God is love- all the time. And all the time- God is love. God is merciful and forgiving-all the time. And all the time- God is merciful and forgiving. Name how God is always good, loving merciful and forgiving in your everyday life. Share "The Hound of Heaven" with the world.

Listen to Each Other

"Thus says the Lord: This is what I commanded my people: Listen to my voice" Jeremiah 7:23

How much time do you spend each day listening to Jesus?

If the Pope or some other imminently holy and wise person were coming over, how would you prepare for their visit? Clearly, you would want to be totally present and affixed to the words and wisdom this person would share. You would not want the kids and pets running all around. No interruptions by the TV, radio or phone would be allowed. Total presence to the words, mind and heart of the person would be called for.

Now, let us put this in perspective. Say your favorite saint was coming to visit you. Can you imagine how incredible your time together would be? Yet, this saint is not your savior. There is only one savior- the Lamb of God who takes away the sins of the world. Only he can rob the grave of its death-hold. So, what will we do in order to get to him? How will we carve out time each day, ridding ourselves of noise and distractions, to hear his voice? I know a woman who, when she had three young children, who used to get up at least ½ hour earlier (i.e. 5am) in order to hear Jesus speak to her in prayer. We should all be challenged by this. She did not neglect her family but she would not neglect Jesus either.

Do you neglect Jesus? How much will you fight, how far will you go, to hear him in prayer each day?

Me-on Trial?

"For I know my offense; my sin is always before me." Psalm 51:5

Are you baptized and do you receive the Eucharist at Mass? If you do- WATCH OUT! Why? Because we are on trial before the King of Kings when we go to Mass. We want to see the Mass and the Eucharist for what it is. We come to Mass to renew the sacrament of our baptism and to receive the sacrament of the Eucharist. We take the holy dip and sign ourselves with holy water upon entering the church as we prepare to receive Jesus in communion. We remember that we are a sacramental people as we renew our baptism and take part in the Eucharist. The word "sacrament" comes from the Latin word for oath, i.e. *sacramentum*. As we remember our baptism, we remember the oath of our baptism. Mass then, in a sense, becomes a court of law. When we make the sign of the cross at the beginning, it is like swearing on the bible in a court of law. We are on trial! We have come to tell the tale of our lives. We have come to tell the whole truth about how well we have lived up to the oath of our baptism. We point the finger at ourselves and say, "I confess to Almighty God, and to you my brothers and sisters, that I have sinned through **my own fault...**" No one in Mass is a spectator- we are all active participants giving witness to our lives.

What is the oath of our baptism that we have professed to live? To love God with all our heart, soul, mind and strength and to love our neighbor as ourselves. Well, it doesn't take long to remember how we have broken that oath. Also, the oath of our baptism is brought out in more detail in the Mass through the prayers, scripture, creed, Eucharist etc, that we assent to through our amen. "Amen" means "Yes! So be it! Truly! I believe!" So, for example, when we say "Amen" to the body and blood of Christ in the Eucharist, we are saying we will live according to the demands of the gospel and the relentlessness of Jesus' love.

Let yourself be tried at each Mass. Confess your sins and call on the grace of salvation.

Whose Telling Who?

"I have come that you may have life and have it to the overflowing." John 10:10

Two of my goals in life were to be rich and have a big family. I thought I would be happy if I reached these goals. When I finally allowed God to come into my heart with a flurry of power, he wrecked me. My goals were shattered and my life was radically changed. God took away my pithy plans and in exchange gave me the most beautiful plan, -- his plan for my life. I thank God that he wrecked me up and changed me up! I found that I was really not interested at all in amassing money. I also learned the family I wanted to have was much bigger than a wife and some children. I knew I wanted all the love and happiness I could have but the trick was finding out how that was going to happen for me. When the Holy Spirit unveiled God's plan for me, I realized I wanted to be a priest. Now I chuckle about how, God, according to his design, has helped me to achieve my two original goals. His way, as always, was just so much better, bigger and brighter than mine. As a priest I have a rich life constantly overflowing with love, peace and joy. I cannot imagine being richer! And, in terms of having a big family I could not have a bigger one- the whole world! Yes, I am infinitely rich and I have a big, big family! Praise God!

A producer of MTV was asked the question, "How do you find out from the viewers what they want to watch on your programs?" The producer responded, "We don't find out from them what they want. We tell them what they want." Whoa- think about that one. MTV is telling us what we want. We are going to let MTV be the master and savior of our lives? We are going to let MTV order us around and believe that it is offering us infinite love and joy?

We know we want infinite joy and love. Let us let Jesus , and not MTV or anything else, be the supreme authority who tells us how to get there.

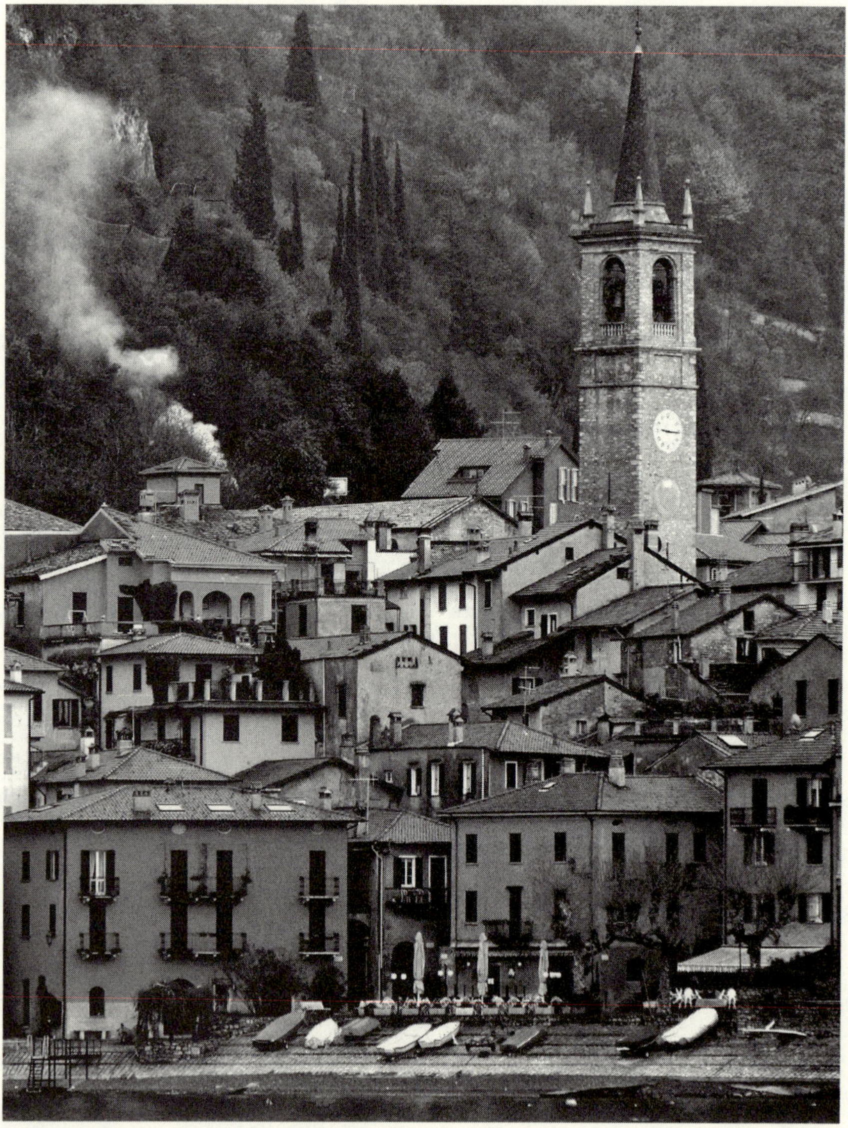

No More Hiding

"As certain as the dawn is coming his judgment shines forth" Hosea 6:3

In Genesis 2:25 we read about the "Original Unity" of man and woman. Adam and Eve lived in perfect unity with one another in nakedness and without shame. They were drawn together without fear of being used, exploited or shamed. Then, the couple chose against God and the "Original Unity" was fractured. With their original sin, the couple became ashamed of their nakedness and they covered up their bodies (Gen. 3:7). From this point forward their lives go into a whole pattern of hiding because of their choice to sin. In their shame, they hide from each other and hide from God.

Like our first parents, we all too easily pick the pattern of hiding from God in our sin and shame. We do not like the sin we carry and we do not want to be found out. We deny, rationalize, drown out in whatever way, and run etc. from the sinful choices we have made. And the sin remains haunting us with its shame.

I constantly preach that there are no end-arounds for the Christian when it comes to facing our sinful choices and their negative consequences. We must confront our sin face to face and let Christ confront the sin in us. We all know that Christ completely takes away sin by the absolute forgiveness he offers us on the cross. Yet, we go into hiding from the one who is the only one that can forgive us our sins. Not very logical thinking, huh?

There is so much wisdom in the sacrament of reconciliation. It is a place where we have the greatest chance to really become honest with our sin and honest with the infinite love that God has for each of us. It is a time where we can truly humble ourselves before the Lord so he can lift us up in his everlasting mercy. It is the experience whereby we can learn in our hearts that God did not send Jesus to condemn us in our sin but to save us. It is the encounter where we are freed from the death of sin and born into the life of the spirit. In my view, I don't really see a better offer in our fallen world.

Someone once asked me if they could go to confession behind the screen instead of face to face. It seems to me that it would be a much wiser practice to go face to face since you will be going face to face with The Judge soon and very soon.

Are you living in hiding? If I could play a video of all your thoughts, words and actions in the past month to your spouse, family, friends, church, pastor etc., what sins would be shown? Confront and confess those sins now and let Jesus heal the pain of their life-taking blows.

Honor

"For Jesus himself testified that a prophet has no honor in his native place" John 4:44

Someone observed a number of practices of one of the best NBA coaches who is really good at getting good at getting his players to play together as a team. On average, this coach was found to give one criticism for every 5 compliments as he led each practice. An NBA coach spends countless hours analyzing his team and undoubtedly could focus on all the faults of the players he knows so well. This coach, in contrast, has chosen the way of honoring those people who are closest to him.

In one book on marriage, the author proposed that he could predict with great accuracy whether a couple would stay married or get divorced. He only needed 20 minutes of observing a couple to access the strength of their relationship. Again, if the positives outweighed the negative 5:1 then that spoke of the staying power of the marriage. As things got less positive in a couple's interaction, the likelihood of divorce increased. When you know someone so well, it is easy to pick on their faults.

There is the old adage, "Familiarity breeds contempt." Maybe this is what Jesus was thinking when he said a prophet has no honor in his native place. There is the scripture where the people will not believe in Jesus as God saying he is just a Nazorean carpenter born to Mary and Joseph. I propose we look at the adage in a different way, "Familiarity breeds deep respect, love and honor." Think about our relationship with the Lord. The more we know him, the more we will respect, honor and serve him in our lives. We should make that same knowing, respect, honor and service our aim in our relationships with others as well.

Think of each person you meet as a flower. Imagine that everything is provided for this flowers growth and health except sunlight. Only you can provide sunlight to this flower. Whether the flower grows and flourishes or dies depends on your sunlight. How intense is the sunlight you bring to all the flowers in God's garden? How good are you at helping others to grow and flourish?

Basketball teams, marriages and people are much more likely to fail when there is little honor going on. May we become familiar with God and the immense love, respect and honor he has for us sinners. May we come to live that honor, especially with those that are closest to us. Bring the Son-light to the flowers planted in your home garden so they will flourish and prosper.

Cell Phones and Calling God

"The Lord is near to all who call him" Psalm 145:18

Where is your cell phone right now? Think about all the advantages they afford. They offer you the convenience of making a call just about anytime you want whether you are walking, biking(be careful), driving(be really careful) etc. When the plane is taxiing on the runway I call and let my ride know when and where to pick me up. As a priest my cell phone is great for emergencies because I can be located pretty much instantaneously and respond. With today's technology, cell phone costs are rather inexpensive.

Now, let us compare and contrast making a call on our cell phone and making a call to God. You don't need a phone to call God but you need your cell to call another person. You have to somehow dial your cell phone, even if it speed dial or voice command etc., but with God no dialing is necessary. While cell phones are so convenient, to make a call to God is the most convenient call you can make. While cell phones are inexpensive, God has given us the free gift of eternal life through his son, Jesus. It is awesome to realize that the "cost" of our call to God is the free gift of eternal life. When making a call on your cell you often get voice mail or no answer at all. When you call God he is always there to answer it. It is just amazing to think that God has the capacity to take over 6 billion calls at once. Sometimes you are in a dead spot with no service for your cell. There are no dead spots when calling out to God. We can call and get through anytime. The batteries on our cell might die rendering it unusable but as long as our heart is beating we can call on God.

St. John Baptist De LaSalle stressed, "Let us always remember, we are in the holy presence of God." Yes, God is with you. You are never alone. It is a fact that God is always with you. He relentlessly waits for your call so he can heal you in the full power of his love.

Isn't it amazing how seldom we choose to make the most convenient call in the world? Isn't it strange that we so often bypass the only call that is absolutely free and offers us eternal life? Isn't it crazy how we look for human beings to sooth and save us before or to the exclusion of our Savior? Isn't it a wonder how we would choose the possibility of dead spots, a dead phone or no answer over trusting the 100% sure connection with Jesus who offers us overflowing, unending life?

Think about all the calls you make each day. How many are to Jesus? The Lord is near to all who call.

Pointing Fingers

"The Lord said to Moses, "Go down at once to your people whom you have brought out of the land of Egypt, for they have become depraved" Exodus 32:7

God is love. The only way he can relate to us is with perfect love. He can never not be perfect love. He is the Eternal Rock of love that knows no change. God is not fickle in love like we are. Sometimes we love and sometimes we don't but God loves us perfectly all the time. Isn't it wonderful to think about the fact that throughout all history, every person with every story could totally count on God to be love? When Moses asked God what God's name was he said tell your people, "I Am." That means that what God was in the past, what he is now and what he will be in the future is all perfectly the same. He cannot be other than perfect love for all people of all times.

Under the leadership of Moses, God frees the Israelites from slavery. But life after slavery in the desert isn't so fun and the freed Israelites turn to a molten calf. They grumble against God because the desert is hot and the food and water do not come so easily. Pointing the finger, they demand to know where God is with goodness and care. They end up turning away from the perfect love of God to a mineralized cow that can offer no love. What a horrible trade off, huh? Forsaking perfect love for a life of depravity.

How can we be like the Israelites? Life gets tough and we point the finger at God and others for our suffering. God did not create the suffering. We chose it by sinning and became depraved of his love. We live in an imperfect, sinful world. The sooner we learn that life is not always "fair", the better. But, when things are tough and are not going our way we can have the tendency to point the finger.

Think about how much we point the finger in our society. Just look up the word "Attorney" in the Yellow Pages. You will find page after page after page of attorney's. We emphasize how others have wronged us and we are going to make them pay. In this context, we become depraved from letting the perfect work of God's love in our hearts and in the world happen.

The world is full of sin, suffering and fickle love. God's love for us in the middle of the wantonness we experience is perfect. Might I suggest a new pointing of the finger? Let us point the finger at God and shout out, "You are perfect love! You have revealed that to me by having your son Jesus die on the cross for me. You did not create suffering and I will not blame you for it." And, let us point the finger at ourselves and say, "Whatever my suffering is, whether self-imposed or done unto me, I have a move to make. Will I move to the Eternal Rock of perfect love or some form of a molten calf that offers nothing in return?"

God is perfect love to us in our struggles and suffering. Point your finger to that reality and ask if you are moving towards that love or turning away to live in depravity.

Close to the Brokenhearted

"The Lord is close to the brokenhearted" Psalm 34:19

At least some of the Pharisees seemingly did not have a lot of tolerance for the unclean, the unlawful, and the sinner. As long as a person was externally following all the prescriptions of the law they were deemed as having a good relationship with God. The love of God, which should impel us to follow God's law, was missing. Their brand of following God was having a relationship with obeying the law rather than the Living God. Jesus, on the other hand, came to bring a love relationship to the unclean, the unlawful, and the sinner. He told the Pharisees that, while they paid him lip service, their hearts were far from living in his love.

Jesus constantly taught how he came for the brokenhearted. He said he did not come for the righteous but sinners. He talked about how healthy people do not need a doctor but the sick do. He would often offer his total friendship to the unclean, the unlawful and the sinner through a sharing in a meal. Never once did Jesus say that he had come for the perfect-hearted. He came for those who suffer from broken hearts.

What is so awesome and paradoxical in living with Jesus is that most broken person in the world can become the most powerful instrument of love. How does that work? In one of my favorite scriptures in 2 Cor. 12:9-10, St. Paul boasts of his weakness because it is in his weakness that Christ's power can reach perfection. When we finally admit that without Jesus we are utterly broken, we are in the privileged and perfect position to come to know the full Jesus. If we cry out to him with a broken heart he will inundate us with the love, forgiveness, meaning and happiness we are searching for.

Unfortunately, I think many of us deny our broken lives. In our plastic, external society we try to act as if nothing is wrong. We project that everything is fine on the façade but it is actually crumbling on the inside. If you have ever gotten the idea that Christianity is only for the perfect-hearted and holy, you have gotten the wrong idea. Christianity is for the unclean, the unlawful, the sinner, and the brokenhearted. It is for you and me! Do not deny this. And give full access to the perfect Christ who came for sinners.

The power of Christ reaches **PERFECTION** in our weakness and brokenness. Let Him!

Sexuality, Marriage, and The Eucharist

SEXUALITY- As Christians, we live in submission to Christ. Submission means to live under the mission of Christ (sub – under; mit – mission). And, whether we know and accept it or not, Christ has a mission for how he wants us to use our bodies as sexual human beings. There is an order to our lives and relationships that God has created. If we follow that order to love and live as God has designed, we will flourish spiritually. In order to live a flourishing life in the area of sexuality, Pope John Paul II and the church have shared with us the theology of the body. As human beings, our deepest longing is for communion with God and each other. Sexuality is about our deepest longing which is for communion. As we seek relationships with each other, our understanding of God's plan for sex must be learned. First of all, God thinks sex is beautiful and sacred. After all, he created it. But God has a purpose for sex. If we don't follow the purpose, we cannot flourish as human beings. So, what is the purpose of sex? Babies and bonding. Each sex act must be open to conception of new life and build up the unity of the couple. The only place where the purposes of sex can be fulfilled, then, is the context of marriage.

MARRIAGE- On their wedding day, the couple makes a covenant with one another. They promise to totally and exclusively give themselves to each other for the whole of life until death do them part. They also say that each time they have sex, it will be open to the transmission of new life. How does sex fit in here? Do you know that a marriage is not considered a sacrament until it has been consummated by having sex on the honeymoon <u>after</u> vows have been exchanged and blessed by God in the wedding liturgy? Why? Because having sex is saying your wedding vows with your body instead of just your words. You are going to live with your body the marriage vows you have made. And having sex is the ultimate expression that what you have committed to in word you will do in deed. Sex says: "I give myself to you entirely. There is nothing more I can give to you. I am entirely yours. Forever." Yes, sex speaks the forever language of marriage such that babies and deep bonding are possible. No wonder we have so much confusion and pain in our society today. So many people have said their marriage vows only by the physical act of having uncommitted sex but are so far away from God's great plan for sex and marriage. Marriage is the mutual, total self-giving to each other for the whole of life with the utter openness to the conception of children.

EUCHARIST- In the Eucharist, Jesus says to each of us, "I give myself to you entirely. There is nothing more I can give to you. I am entirely yours. Forever!"(and that is exactly what sexual intercourse in marriage is saying). What an offer! What a giving!

The Eucharist is a template for marriage (and the Christian life in general). We are made in the image of God and so we are to love as God loves. The Eucharist shows the way and gives us the power to love according to God's ways. Married couples know that their love can be half-baked, weak and selfish, and so they keep going to receive the Eucharist. The Eucharist teaches and empowers the married couple to love as God loves.

What Goes in Your Cup?

"My cup overflows" Psalm 23:4

There is no doubt we have a large quantity of things we do each week. A common refrain from parents is that they feel like taxi drivers who spend most of their time shuttling children to all their games and other commitments. We are a people on the go. Stress is in ample supply. Our lifestyles can become a lot of quantity but where is the quality of it all?

If you would, let us compare our lives to a cup. As the cup, many different things want to fill us up. Work comes knocking and the cell phone makes us reachable at almost all times. The newspaper with all its stories and advertising to buy can easily take up an hour a day filling us if we so choose. Our children can often be on 2-3 or more sports teams at the same time. The TV and Internet are just a click away.

Examine your life in a day as a cup. The thing about being a cup is that you have a choice of what is poured into you. What do you choose to fill yourself with in the first hours of your waking- readying your family for the day, the newspaper, noise, quiet and prayer etc? How much of your day will you fill your cup with TV, Internet and music? How much will you be present to your loved ones or take time for yourself?

As a people it seems to me that in so many ways we have become powerless with the most powerful gift we have been given- our freedom to choose. We aren't choosing what goes in the cup; we are chosen for. Society is so much determining what we are filled with and we just go with the flow. But we don't want to just go with the flow and go where we do not want to go.

Our choice is the determining factor of what is poured into our cup. Many things vie to fill us. What is the quality of what you pour into your cup each day? Quantity is a given in our lives but should we choose less quantity and how much quality is there in our quantity? Do we put reading the newspaper/watching the news above daily scripture reading? There is the old saying, "Garbage in, garbage out." In relation to that saying and our lives as a cup, I would like to say, "Seeking and loving God/others in, seeking and loving God/others out."

You choose what is poured into the cup of your life. You choose quality, quantity, garbage or Good News. Don't let anyone or anything else do the choosing for you! May your cup runneth over with God.

Word of Eternal Life

"You have the words of eternal life." John 6:68

Jesus' words are much more than just coldly mouthed verbal statements that have little relevance or power for the hearer. Rather, Jesus words effect what they say. If believed, the power of his words makes believers out of unbelievers. They turn sinners into saints. Jesus not only offers us forgiveness of sins and eternal life through his words but we experience that same forgiveness and eternal life as we place our trust in those words. What Jesus says, he gives.

Jesus gives words of challenge as well as words of comfort and hope. Words of challenge... Whoever wants to follow me must take us his cross daily and follow in my path. Love your enemies and pray for your persecutors. How many times must I forgive- 70x7 times? Blessed are the merciful, mercy shall be theirs. Blessed are you when they insult you and persecute you and utter every kind of slander against you because of me. Anyone who looks lustfully at a woman has already committed adultery in his heart. Etc.

Words of comfort and hope... Whoever eats my flesh and drinks my blood will live forever. I have loved you with an everlasting love. Come to me all you who are weary and find life burdensome, and I will refresh you. How blessed are the poor in spirit, the reign of God is theirs. Nor do I condemn you, go and sin no more. Father, forgive them for they know not what they do. Jesus began to wash his disciple's feet and dry them. Father, I pray that they may be one as you, Father, are in me and I in you.

Who do you go to for words of eternal life? Too busy? You are not going to worry about "forever?" Out loud and to yourself, say and pray his words of life, over and over. Seek, memorize and paste in front of you his words of challenge, comfort and hope. He does what he says he will do.

Disciples and Discipline

Jesus said to those Jews who believed in him, "If you remain in my word, you will truly be my disciples, and you will know the truth, and the truth will set you free." John 8:31

At a weekday Mass God gave me a particular joy. I had a smile on my face because the makeup of the congregation was different than normal. Besides the faithful elders, there were children and teenagers who chose to go to Mass that day. For me, there is not anything much more beautiful when a young person believes and loves the Lord. After Mass, a young mother came up to me and told me her young son commented on how there was only one young disciple by me at Mass. This little one, of course, was referring to my altar server that day. The mom tried to teach that that person was the altar server but this little boy again called my altar server "the young disciple."

There is much food for thought in the young boy's image of the altar server as a disciple. The word "disciple" means "learner." In the young boy's view, the altar server was a disciple who was serving on the altar. What if each of us took on that same paradigm? Let us try on the metaphor that we are all disciples who serve at the altar during each Mass. We come before our Teacher to learn what salvation is all about. Salvation is a mystery of indescribable joy and we keep coming back to the altar to plunge deeper into the mystery. We want to learn, learn, and learn about the wonder of God's saving love for each of us. Inherent in all of this is discipline which, is derived from the same root as the word disciple. It takes day after day discipline to keep putting Jesus, prayer and growth first.

Jesus told us that if we remain in his word we would be his disciples. There is no doubt that if we call ourselves Christian we should be reading the bible each day. Also, we can look at the Mass as the way disciples remain in God's word. Basically, the first half of the Mass is listening to God's word. We hear about all of God's wonderful deeds for us and, namely, about how Jesus died for our sins that we might have eternal life. We plunge deeper into understanding the sacred mysteries offered to us. Then, in the second half of the Mass we physically receive The Word of God, Jesus, into our bodies in the Eucharist. So, in the Mass, we always hear the words of God from scripture but these words of God always lead us to the Word of God, Jesus. The words of God from scripture prepare, enliven and enflame our hearts to have a living encounter with The Word of God, Jesus, in the

Eucharist. The awesome beauty of the Mass is that we receive into our very bodies the One to which all the words of scripture; angels and saints, human beings and creation speak! We always end up receiving the Real Presence of Jesus. God grants us our greatest desire-to see Jesus face to face!

I know in my life I can often complicate things. There is so much information always coming at us I am surprised we do not have more nervous breakdowns. We are bombarded by information overload. And, maybe many of us feel the need to take it all in and understand it. Obviously, this is impossible. Might I suggest going simple. In relation to being a disciple who serves at the altar each Mass, just try to pick one thing Jesus is trying to get to you with. He might offer peace or healing, show you your sin, teach you a new way of relating, tell you to slow down or simplify your life, nudge you to ask forgiveness or reach out with a note, phone call or flower, put your priorities straight etc. Whatever it might be, just open yourself to Jesus in church and pick one thing. Then, disciple, put into practice what you have learned.

St. Patrick - Keeper of the Covenant

"God also said to Abraham: "On your part, you and your descendants must keep my covenant throughout the ages." Genesis 17:9

Each March 17th we celebrate the life of St. Patrick, bishop of Ireland. He was a keeper of the covenant. At age 16 he was kidnapped to Ireland and made a slave for 6 years. He escaped at 22 and returned to his homeland Britain. He followed God into the priesthood and, when an opportunity to serve as a missionary in Ireland came before him, he offered his life to do so. Pope Celestine sent Patrick back to the pagan and often-hostile land of Ireland. By the time of his death, a native clergy was in place and Christianity had touched most all of the Irish.

It is inspiring to think about St. Patrick and how he kept the covenant. He came back! He came back to the place where he was made a slave. He came back to the land where he experienced oppression, hostility and rejection. He came back to pagan Ireland to love it and bring it God.

St. Patrick kept the covenant. A covenant is a total giving in God's love of all that you are for the whole of your life. The covenant does not break, wear out, or die. It is about being faithful through thick and thin, in good times and in bad, for better or worse, forever.

Simply put, St. Patrick imitated the covenantal love of Christ proven on the cross. The cross is the absolute truth that Christ will be with each of us always, offering his saving love unto heaven. This offer will not be revoked, changed, lessened, break down, wear out or die! It stands forever sealed in his blood!

Jesus keeps coming back to us! He keeps coming back to us who have, at times, offered him only oppression, slavery, hostility and rejection. He keeps coming back to us only to love us and bring us to God and heaven. He keeps coming back to us in the Eucharist and says, "My child, I love you forever! Nothing will ever make me change my mind about my infinite love for you. Receive me."

Be a keeper of the covenant just like St. Patrick and Jesus.

Eat Dinner Together

"I love you, O Lord, my fortress" Psalm 18:3

It would be interesting to know how much time the average person spends each day thinking about, preparing and eating food. Food is a focal point in our lives and I think we do well to remember how it brings us together physically and spiritually.

There seems to be a real correlation between the breakdown of families and the breakdown of having meals together, particularly dinner. Statistics show the negative impact of families who do not eat dinner together. Children who do not eat dinner regularly with family are more sexually active, are more likely to take drugs/alcohol, do more poorly in school, etc. then children who regularly eat dinner with their families.

It is obvious that we need food to keep functioning physically. Often less apparent but surely extremely important, we need food for our souls. Dinner is a prime opportunity to come together as a family to be fed both physically and spiritually. As we come to dinner to eat our temporal food we must remember to engage in eternal feeding. In the end the most important feeding is the feeding of our souls by being present to each other with God's love and care. When the eternal feeding of the souls gets disregarded and thrown out we see how family members suffer from the lack of connection with God's love.

The physical food that we hunger for at dinnertime should remind us of the eternal food of God we long for in our souls. Dinner is a time to feed each other with love, presence and care. It is a time to exchange the stories of joy and struggle during the day. It is the time for a family to really get to know each other. If a family does not know each other how can it love each other? And if a family is really not loving each other then what it going to do besides fall apart?

A fortress is a stronghold that offers protection from the enemy. Our families need strongholds in order to stay together. Spiritually, the enemy is the devil and he wants to tear our families to shreds. He wants to divide and destroy families. He wants to take away any eternal feeding of knowing and loving each other in the family. We all know the incessant assaults on family life. Turn off the TV's, phones, sports, meeting and craziness and make dinner the priority. Get to know and love one another over dinner. Be present to one another and let all members expose their hearts at that meal. Dinner can be a fortress against the devil who is assaulting family life. Make dinner time sacred!

Fear or God?

"Joseph, son of David, do not be afraid to take Mary your wife into your home." Mt. 1:19

Isn't it amazing how we can give the greatest power to the people we know the least in our lives? Someone, who we hardly know from Adam, can make a negative comment about us and it can send us into a tailspin for weeks. If we look at it logically, it is amazing and puzzling how we let other people determine who we are.

As Christians we celebrate St. Joseph, husband of Mary. Joseph is caught in quite a predicament which was surely fear-producing. Mary was pregnant outside their betrothal which was punishable by death. Joseph, a just man unwilling to expose her to the law, decided to quietly divorce her to save her from a possible sentence of death. Then, God's angel intervened and said, "Do not be afraid" because what is happening is the work of God. In response to the angel's message, Joseph chooses God over fear.

I am afraid that we often choose fear over God (no pun intended). A big fear that drives us is what other people think. It is a foolish activity to let what other people think determine who you are. I can remember two comments I received within in two weeks of each other as a priest a few years ago. One person told me that I was a horrible pastor. (bummer!) Another person came up to me after a Mass and said, I just want to shake your hand so that when you become the Pope I will be able to say that I shook his hands before he became the Pope. (nice!) Who should I believe? God.

There is a huge correlation between living a life of fear and not praying. If we do not pray then what is determining us? If we let other people determine us we are being foolish. One moment they are cheering us and the next they may well be jeering us. Why would we ever let other people's weak, changing or conditional opinions determine us? Let God determine you. His opinion never changes.

Do you fear man or God? Let us be inspired by Joseph who chose to fear God over man. We see in Joseph how God's perfect love casts out all fear. Sadly, so many choose to fear and please man who cannot save and disregard Jesus who can save.

Brothers and sisters in God's love, do not fear the one who can kill the body but not touch the soul. Do not fear man but fear and please the one who has power over the soul.

The Lamb of God Become the Eucharist

The Mass is a sacrifice, meal and thanksgiving. Let us focus on the sacrifice of the Mass as Jesus goes to Jerusalem to die for us.

"They have pierced my hands and my feet" Psalm 22:18

Animal sacrifice- In ancient Israel, animal sacrifice meant many things. It recognized God's rule over all creation by giving back to God what was always His. It was the praise and thanksgiving of man to God. God gave creation to man. Man gave thanks to God for all that God had given to him-which was everything! Animal sacrifice was a way of solemnly sealing an oath/agreement/covenant before God. Also, it could be an act of sorrow for sin. The person offered an animal in place of his sins to avoid punishment and death.

The Lamb- In Exodus 12:1-23(this is important to read-the Mass has its foundation here!), God establishes the Passover Ritual. The context is that God, through the leadership of Moses and Aaron, is going to free the Israelites from the slavery of the Egyptians. The night before their Exodus out of Egypt, each Israelite family was to take a lamb, kill it, and sprinkle its blood on the doorpost. Also, that night, they were to eat the lamb. If there was no blood on the doorpost, The Lord would strike down the firstborn of the family and flock. If they obeyed the prescription of the Lord, the family's firstborn would be spared. This is the Passover! God would pass-over the houses with his sentence of death where the blood of the lamb was on the doorposts. The Passover, then, celebrates how the sacrificial lamb died in place of the firstborn of the Israelites.

The Lamb of God- We came to find out, however, that animal sacrifices were not good or powerful enough to forgive our sin. That is where Jesus, the New Testament, the New Passover and the New Covenant come into play. We could not get back to God on our own. We needed God to get back to God. So, God sent his son to save us from our sins (John 3:16) Jesus, based on the Old Testament Passover Ritual, prescribes a New Passover and Covenant. He says, "No more animal sacrifices for forgiveness of sins. It will be my sacrifice which will be good for forgiveness of sins for all people and all time. I will give my body and blood for you. Take, eat and drink. This is how you will Passover from sin and death to life." The Lamb of God becomes the Eucharist.

But, why call Jesus a lamb? Lambs are not smart, strong, and powerful. We call Jesus a lamb because it fits in with the divine pattern of our salvation. Jesus builds on the old idea of animal sacrifice for sins to teach about the total sufficiency of his sacrifice as the Lamb of God on the cross.

Sacrifice- The purpose of our lives is to sacrifice for others. Sacrifice is a need of the human heart. We surrender our lives to Jesus in the Eucharist in order to be transformed and changed. We receive Jesus on Sundays in order to sacrifice our lives for others all week long. If the Eucharist does not compel us to sacrifice, our worship is empty. How is that for a challenge!

"If our behavior doesn't match our religion doctrine, one of them has to go." Which one have you and I sent away? The Eucharist or our behavior?

Foot Washer

"Mary took a liter of costly perfumed oil made from genuine aromatic nard and anointed the feet of Jesus" John 12:3

Mary is lowly and takes the form of a slave to wash Jesus' feet. It was the slave who washed people's feet when they entered the house. We remember Jesus who took the form of a slave when he rose from table at the Last Supper to wash his disciple's feet. The washing of the feet symbolizes how he will give his life on the cross to wash away our sins. Read and pray about the humility of Jesus in Philippians 2:6-11; "Though he was in the form of God, Jesus did not regard equality with God something to be grasped. Rather, he emptied himself, taking the form of a slave…"

Feet can be an embarrassing body part. They are often dirty and smelly. But we see how lowly Mary and lowly Jesus embrace the often embarrassing, smelly and dirty body part. And in their embrace of the feet, they are embracing the totality of the person. They wash the person, including all that is embarrassing, smelly, dirty and ugly etc., in the unconditional embrace of God's love. Like them, we are called to be foot-washers who wash every person in front us with the total embrace of God's love.

If you were asked if you were more of a foot-washer or the one who gets their feet washed, what would your answer be? In other words, how readily are we willing to bow down before others and wash them in God's unconditional love? Do we look at our relationships with others and life in general and ask, "What are you going to give me? What are you doing for me?" Or, are our questions more like, "What can I give you? What can I do to wash you in God's unconditional love?"

I know of a family in which member held a lot of bitterness and anger towards each other. One brave family member called the whole family together for a meeting. He did not say much at the meeting but go a basin of warm water, a towel and he washed all their feet.

In Vain?

"Though I thought I toiled in vain" Isaiah 49:3

There are different ways we can question the purpose of our lives works. Many people suffer the fact that their loved ones have left the faith, church, and God. The years of Christian education and example seem to be a big waste. What about when we are really trying to follow God and we lose or job, health, comfort? How about when relationships come crashing down or when bad things happen to innocent people? What about divorce? Life can seem to be lived in vain if we only consider the earthly plain. Without the hope of resurrection, in the final analysis the sum of life is that we are going to toil, suffer and die.

As the author of the book of Hebrews tells us, Jesus is fully able to relate with our feelings of toiling in vain. Jesus, Our High Priest, was tempted in every way like us but did not sin. As we look at life through his eyes, he must have been tempted many times to question the worth of what he was doing. Many people were rejecting the Good News of forgiveness, healing and salvation. In some ways, Jesus' life, then, could be viewed as a waste.

But, Jesus did not put his faith in results, respect, and affirmation from the people. He put his faith in God. His food was to do what the Father wanted him to do. He sought that out in prayer and lived it out in his life- regardless of the consequences. Any meaning Jesus was going to offer us would come from the author of all meaning. It was through his relationship with the Father that Jesus knew his life would not be lived in vain. In contrast, the meaning that the Father poured out in Jesus' heart led to the most meaningful life Jesus could lead. Likewise, you and I are called to live the most meaningful life we can by opening our heart to the way of God in prayer. We seek to faithfully follow God regardless of results and feelings of vain living.

There will be results if we bring God's meaning to the world. Some will accept and some will decline. When someone accepts, we will see the results. However, whether someone accepts our rejects is not our concern. Our concern is to always bring the meaning and let God worry about the rest. We do what God wants and let him take care of it from there.

One time reporters were asking Mother Theresa why she was so successful, "Mother Theresa, you are known for your incredible work in the hearts and minds of people the world over. What do you attribute your success to?" Her reply, "I have never seen the word success in the bible. I have seen the word faithfulness but not success." That is our call: to be faithful. To be faithful to the unpopular way of Jesus, regardless of results and feelings of vain living.

A plaque on Mother Theresa's desk read, "Faithfulness, not success." Amen.

The Power of the Tongue

"The Lord God has given me a well-trained tongue" Isaiah 50:4

"Death and life are found in the power of the tongue."(Proverbs 18:21) We should never underestimate the power of our words. The words we speak and how we speak them have the power to destroy life in another person or build it up. The words we fail to say can rob people of life that they might very well need to go on. Consider the power of words and how much they affect you. There is a reason the tongue is the most coordinated muscle in the body. It has the power for great good and great damage.

We all know that "Thou shall not kill". But killing means more than just physically taking the life of another. Have we considered how we can kill life in others through our words? Think about the spiritual/emotional/personal killings that can go on in just one day with our words. Analyze the killing words that popular TV, radio, media inundates our world with. Think about how we treat each other with our words in this society. If people keep getting killed with words of death they are going to soon wonder why life is worth living. The assault and killing through words in our world is immense and catastrophic. Why do I say that? Because even if one person takes their life because killing words have drowned out the truth of God's love, then that is a catastrophe.

I was leaving the hospital after anointing a parishioner in critical care. Two college age kids were sitting on the steps I was ascending to my car. I said, "Hello" and one of the kids said, "Fr. John". I was surprised this person knew me but not too surprised because you meet lots of people as a priest. Through our conversation I found out that this person had tried to take their own life. I wondered about how much killing/assaults had occurred in this person's life verses all the occurrences of hearing the truth of God's love and forgiveness.

Considering all the words of death that are dealt each day, we have work to do. We not only need to eradicate any words that kill/assault from our vocabulary but, like St. Paul says, we need to say the good things that others need to hear. Remember, life and death are found in the power of the tongue. And that life includes a more important life than physical life- the life of the soul which is eternal.

It is always good to be concrete when talking about the good we are called to do. Let us look at three ways we can bring the power of God's eternal life to others through our words. <u>Words of service-</u> A wonderful priest I know was always asking others, "How can I serve you?" Wonderful! My friend asking me, "How can I lighten your load?" Wonderful! Children saying, "Yes, mom. Yes, dad.", when they are asked by their parents to do something around the house. Great! <u>Words of affirmation-</u> Build up others in the goodness, gifts, and virtues that God has given them. Tell them how important and valued they are. Remind others constantly that they are loved, blessed, and forgiven by God. <u>Words of forgiveness-</u> Examine your relationships with others and be quick to ask forgiveness as soon as you see the need. If you are not sure you have hurt someone, go to that person and make sure there is nothing between you.

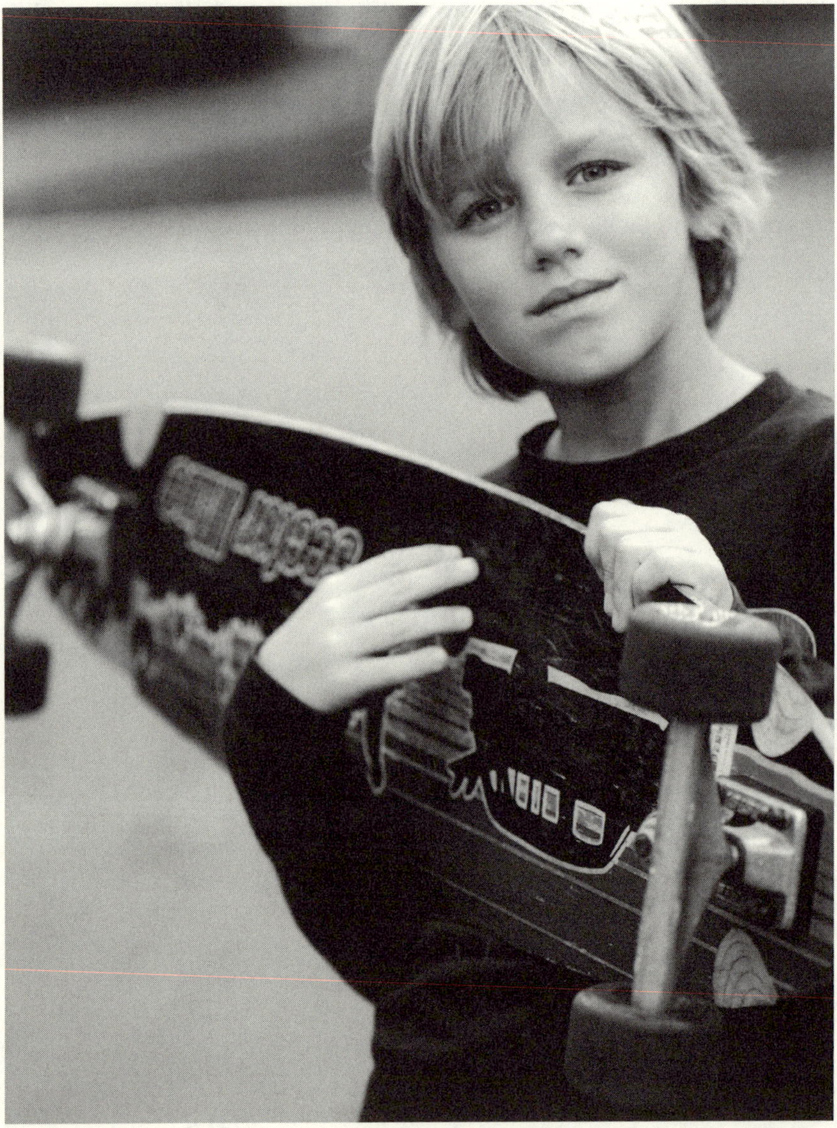

Who You Are

"This day shall be a memorial feast for you, which all generations shall celebrate with pilgrimage to the Lord, as a perpetual institution" Exodus 12:14

Our lives are in comprehensible without Christ. Christ reveals us to ourselves. He set up the perpetual institution of the Eucharist to show us who we are. We find the meaning of our lives in the Eucharist.

In the movie <u>Good Will Hunting</u>, a psychiatrist asks a young man the following three questions, 1) Where did you come from? 2) Where are you going 3) How are you going to get there? The deepest meaning of our lives is found in the answers to these questions. Go deep with these questions! Spend time, thought and prayer with them. Reprioritize and live your life according to the answers of these questions.

We came from God. He created us. God is Trinity- Father, Son and Holy Spirit. God the Father, Son and Holy Spirit is a perfect union of loving relationships. God has always been and will always be. God has no beginning and end. The Father, Son and Holy Spirit have always been living united in total love. And just think, we are invited to live in that same love forever! That is where we are going to- we are going home to heaven. How are we going to get there? God sends us Jesus and the Holy Spirit to perfect us in his love.

The Eucharist tells us where we came from, where we are going and how we are going to get there. We came from love and we are going to love as we are perfected by love on our pilgrimage home. Jesus commands us to remember all of this. Find out who you are in the Eucharist.

The Really Real

"He was pierced for our offenses, crushed for our sins" Isaiah 52:13-53:12

We want what is real and lasting and what is really real is Jesus Christ and his love for us. If we get real and cry out to Jesus for help, he will become real for us. So, let us do so!

We follow Christ so that reality will become really real to us. We want the really real to become really real to us. The cross is The Sign that reality has become really real for us. Jesus is what is really real. His infinite love and goodness to us is what is really real. He hangs on the cross in total self-sacrifice and cries out to God, "Father, forgive them." In utter compassion Jesus begs, "Come to me. I thirst for you. I want all your suffering and sin. Lay it at the foot of my cross. You give me your sin and I will give you my mercy, compassion and goodness which last forever. This is the exchange I desire. This is the trade-off I offer. Come to me. I fully absorb all your suffering into my body and, in return, I will raise you up in my goodness and love today- and forever. Come to me for I give my flesh and blood for you."

Each year during Holy Week, we celebrate Good Friday. But why do we call Good Friday called "Good"? How could there be anything "good" about a horrible and excruciating crucifixion of the God/man? The goodness comes from the power and glory that is shown through the cross. Suffering, sin and death is defeated by the cross of Jesus Christ. Heaven gates are opened wide for all who will believe in God. God's goodness is most evident in the cross. That is why this day of crucifixion is called "Good" Friday.

On "Good" Friday every promise of mercy, forgiveness, love, joy, peace, Eucharist, communion, loving union, and everlasting life in heaven is fulfilled in Jesus on the cross. But "Good" Friday is not just for "Good" Friday. The goodness that Jesus showed on "Good" Friday is the goodness that he wants us to enjoy all the time. Each moment of our lives he reaches us to us with infinite goodness. Goodness is reality which lasts forever.

St. Theresa of Avila said, "The cross is love." Take a crucifix into your hands. His arms are open for you. Open your heart to his open arms. Let him pour the infinite goodness of his love into your heart. Pray, "Jesus, fill me with your love. I invite you fully into my life. Pour out the infinite goodness of the cross into my heart and into the hearts of all your children. I want to know you, for real. Thank you, Lord Jesus. I love you."

Cling to the cross of Christ with all your heart, soul, mind and strength, and never let go. Live with the really real. The cross is love.

No Shame

"The Scripture says, 'No one who believes in him shall be put to shame'. Romans 10:11

Shame, how much do we do it? I chuckled as I pondered the above verse about how God will never let us be put to shame. I wanted to say that it is "a shame to shame" without shaming anyone who might be reading this reflection. But we need to call each other on how we might knowingly or unknowingly shame each other. Dare we ask others closest to us, i.e. our family and friends, if we play the shame game? Maybe we shame to create power or position over another or maybe we shame because it has a root in our life. Regardless, shaming is not part of the redeemed life God has offered us.

People can be so fickle. One minute they can be praising you and the next they can be calling you a loser, or a various assortment of some not so complimentary names. One time I was at a college football game and several people were real mad at the quarterback because he got sacked. Four plays later he threw a beautiful touchdown strike and these same people were high-giving each other and going crazy with excitement. This is the milieu of human relations we find ourselves in.

I have prayed 1,000's of times and never been put to shame by God. Yes, I might have felt ashamed of something stupid or clumsy I did, but Jesus was always there to lift me up in forgiveness. Other human beings might try to shame us but Jesus cannot shame us. Jesus is not fickle! No one who believe in him shall be put to shame.

Status

"Thus says the Lord, your redeemer" Isaiah 48:17

Upon coming out of the water at his own baptism, our redeemer heard these words, 'You are my beloved Son with whom I am well pleased'." Jesus' status in this world was with God the Father. God's love was the source, motivation and fulfillment of his life.

Our baptism should always be a reminder of our status in God. Webster's dictionary tells us that status means state or position. Our state and position is that we belong to God but have been cut off from a pure love relationship with him because of sin. Jesus came to redeem us from our sin and restore us to perfect union with God. As we continue to choose to accept the gift of our redemption, we understand more fully that God's love is the source, motivation and fulfillment of our lives.

Perhaps you have seen a professional athlete or someone else making the sign of the cross. Each time Catholics enter the church; they dip their hand in the holy water font and make the sign of cross to remember our redemption. While making the sign of the cross from the forehead to the chest and then each shoulder, the words, "In the name of the Father and of the Son and of the Holy Spirit" are prayed. This action always brings us back to our state and position in the world.

The whole idea of redemption is bringing back a slave or someone to their original status that was somehow taken from them. That is what our redeemer does for us slaves. He brings us back to our place of original status of loving union with God and all creation. We turned our back on God but through Jesus and Holy Spirit he eternally extends his hand out to lift us up to our original status as daughters and sons of the Father.

How has Jesus and the Holy Spirit brought you back to your original status? Think of the ways. That is what remembering our baptism is all about.

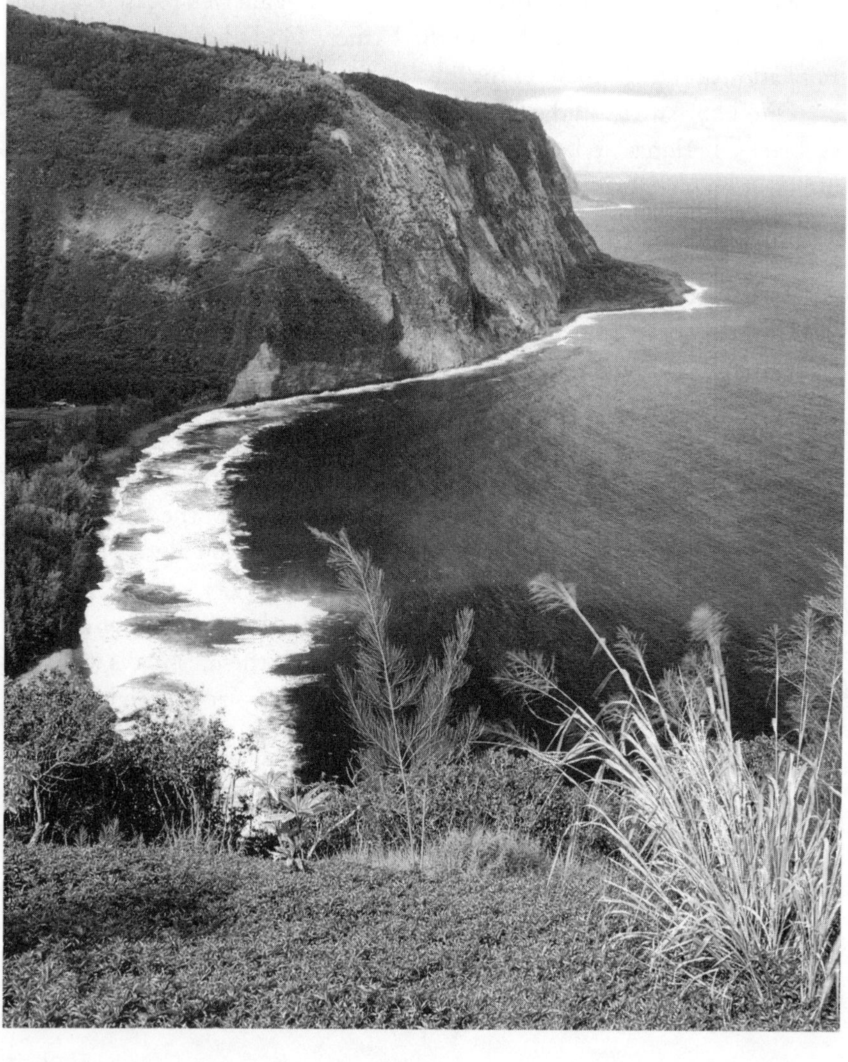

Behind the Veil

"On this mountain he will destroy the veil that veils all peoples." Isaiah 25:7

Take some time to ponder the next few sentences… You are loved relentlessly and tenderly. You are loved eternally. Think about the total experience of God and his love in heaven. The same way that God will be loving you forever in heaven is the same way he is loving you right now.

So many times, however, is seems that we struggle to see that love as if it was hidden behind a veil. Remember, it is OK to struggle. I struggle often. Some say that John wrote so much about love in his gospel because he struggled so much to know God's love in his heart. Keep struggling to see behind the veil. Jesus says seek and you will find. If you seek, how will you ever find? He will pull back the veil for you in prayer and quiet. If you do not seek love, how will you find it?

Moreover, we do not live for ourselves. We seek what is behind the veil in order to share that with others. The meaning of our existence is to share what we see on the other side of the veil. Only Jesus can pull back the veil so we beg him, day by day, to pull back the veil so we can see a little more.

Be a beggar. Keep tapping Jesus on the shoulder to see more. The most radical beggars find the most radical love. Then share it.

Our Possessions Possess Us

"The man went away sad, for he had many possessions." Mark 10:22

What possessions does God want us to have?

Think about the following example. A young couple gets married and they are just starting out to build their home, life and family together. They do not a have a large financial nest egg and yet they feel the need to buy the new car, TV or refrigerator that they should have as a newly married couple in our society. Is the TV, media or their neighbors/friends lifestyles that tells them the "should" have certain possessions? Have they prayed together and asked Jesus what they "need" to have a peaceful and Godly family life?

How much does this statement ring true for you? "We do not possess our possessions. Our possessions possess us." We buy more, and we have to care for more, and worry about it more, and spend more time on it, and it is a material thing that cannot love us. And the buying frenzy grows and the momentum gains.

Be counter-cultural. Don't keep up with the Joneses. Simplify. Own as few things as possible. The less "things" you have, the more you can have time for love and relationships. It has been my experience that "things" often take us away from the love we all long for.

Submission - To be Sent Under a Mission

"John the Baptist appeared, preaching in the desert of Judea and saying, 'Repent, for the kingdom of heaven is at hand!" Matthew 3:1

Psychologists tell us that we human beings rebel against the words "no", don't" and "can't". If you think about it, what is your first reaction generally when someone tells you can't do something? I usually think, "Oh, yes I can. And who do you think you are telling me what I can or can't do?" There is a rebellion in us that has a difficult time submitting to authority.

The lived experience of the church and the scriptures command us to be submissive to God and his will for us. God's design comes to us in a myriad of ways. It surely comes to us through the church, bible, community life, parents, teachers, children, and nature and on and on. God is constantly coming to us and offering us a more profound experience of life. He promises if we submit to him we will come to the fullness of life. However, it is not easy for us fiercely independent human beings to submit to an authority outside ourselves.

The word "submission" comes from the Latin and it means, "to be sent under a mission." In our pledge of allegiance we say, "One nation, under God." Yes, we are sent into life to be under the mission of God.

Today, John the Baptist tells us to repent. We are to turn from arrogance and live in submission to Jesus. We are sent to live under Jesus and look up to him so that he can lead us to the fullness of God's love. We have countless people and experiences in our lives that call us to be submissive to God. Are you submissive to God and his leading? If not, now is the time to submit and live life to the full. More submission to Jesus means more life. Hence, be submissive and live!

Let us pray with John the Baptist, "Lord, may you increase and I decrease."

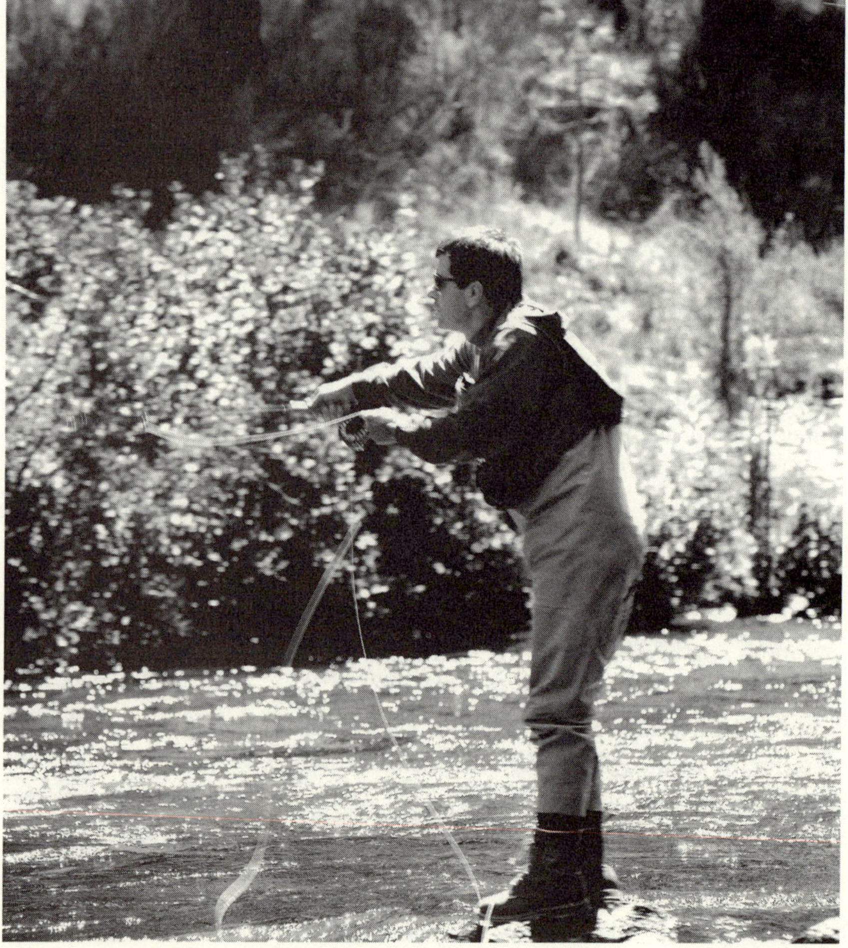

No Strings Attached

"Without cost you have received; without cost you are to give" Matthew 9:8

Today in our verse from Matthew, Jesus is giving instructions to his twelve disciples. He is telling them to bring the Kingdom of God with all its healing and power to those who do not know about it, i.e. the lost sheep of the house of Israel. They are not to count the cost of bringing the Kingdom to others. Because they have been freely given the fullness of the Kingdom their responsibility is to fully and freely give the Kingdom to others.

Like the first twelve disciples, our way of life is to be the same. We are charged to freely share the fullness of the Kingdom of God to anyone and everyone who will give us the chance. There can be no strings attached. We can't be in it for fame, status, rewards, glory, affirmation, gain etc. We are just to give it away because it is given to us.

To me, it is unbelievable and imaginable how Jesus came to earth to offer us endless life and we crucified him in return. He gave totally and freely without counting the cost. It is this amazing love that Jesus calls us to live. We are to love without expecting any return. For myself, I know that the majority of the time I want payback for how I have given.

Think about how Jesus gave you eternal life some 2,000 years before you were born. He freely gave everything that is his to you without demanding anything in return. Think about your parents or other people who gave to you without expecting anything in return. What about soldiers who have given their lives for our freedom? Reflect on those people who have loved you with no strings attached. Then, thank them for how they have freely given you the Kingdom of God.

Silent No More

"Tell his glory among the nations" Psalm 96:3

Each December 7th, we celebrate the feast of St. Ambrose, bishop and doctor of the church. His life speaks to how amazingly, mysteriously and uniquely God works through the life of a sinner to show forth his glory. A talented political leader in Milan, the clergy and people of the town elected him bishop before he was even baptized! The life of Ambrose shows how God wants to uniquely work through each of us to show his glory to the nations. Exciting! - How has he used you to show forth his glory?

Is the very loud minority running the silent majority in this country? Is it just a handful of non-believers and their lawyers who have gotten prayer and God out of our schools? The bible tells us to pray ceaselessly and the courts are telling our country to cease praying. If God is not allowed in then where is the illumination of the incarnation going to transform our sinful nation? We see all the death and despair that has entered our world since we kicked God and his glory out.

The whole purpose of our life is to glorify God. How will people know about God unless we all are able to tell the amazing, mysterious and unique way he has personally worked in our lives. We focus so much on the current news through the paper and watching/listening to endless hours of news but the news you and I should be most familiar with is how God's glory has been poured out into our lives. How has he raised you from hopelessness to hope, from sin to forgiveness, from death to eternal life?

St. Ambrose said, "We shall be called to account not only for every idle word, but also for every idle silence." Be silent no more. Glorify God with your words.

Your Word, O Lord

"May it be done to me according to your word" Luke 1:38

Your life is not about you. It is about Him in you doing what you can't do.

Each December 8th, we celebrate the Feast of The Immaculate Conception of the Blessed Virgin Mary. God chose Mary to give birth to his Son Jesus for our salvation. She was given the singular grace of being born without original sin because God needed a sinless vessel to bring the sinless savior into the world. The angel Gabriel comes to Mary and tells her that she will conceive and bear a son whom she is to name Jesus. After struggling to understand her new mission, Mary responds, "May it be done to me according to your word."

What a curve ball, huh? Did Mary have any idea that she would be God's own mother? A faithful Jewish girl, she must have had visions of making a home and family with her husband Joseph just like her other friends intended to do in Nazareth- you know, the white-picket fence with a dog and two-car garage (well, maybe not exactly like that!). Then, God radically breaks into her life with the word that she is to give birth to the savior. All creation hangs on her response.

Mary's life shouts, "Your life is not about you. It is about him in you doing what you can't do." She had other plans but God's word comes to Mary and asks her to bear Jesus to the world. Notice how it is not Mary's word to God but God's word to Mary that brought the savior of the world. She wasn't leading; she was listening.

God has a radical word for you and me. He wants us to bring the savior into the world. How? Who knows exactly? But we look to Mary as the way to do things. Her "yes" to God's word brought Jesus into the world. So will ours. She listened and let herself be led by God. Her life was a lot different than she ever imagined but she lived it according to God.

Are we listening or telling God what to do? Is it our word to God or his word to us? The world doesn't want you or me- it wants Jesus. We will give them Jesus if we say "Yes" to God's word. Will we give them Jesus? So many people hang on our response to this question.

Your life is not about you. It is about him in you doing what you can't do.

God is Good - All the Time

"The Lord is good to all" Psalm 145:9

God is good- all the time. All the time- God is good. God has chosen you and me to pour out his infinite goodness into our hearts. (All that goodness in little ole me? It makes me think that my body would explode into millions of pieces if I really took in infinite goodness) No matter the "bad" in our lives, God's goodness is always greater than the bad. God's mercy is always much greater than any sin we could commit. If we are sincere and sorrowful, he will forgive the worst sin imaginable. His love is greater than any broken relationship we might face. His help, comfort and hope are greater than any illness. He reigns over death and all who have given their lives to him will be raised from death to celebrate his goodness forever. God is good- all the time. All the time- God is good.

You might be thinking that I am living in an ivory tower by saying that God's goodness is always greater than the bad. It seems that we are constantly exposed to the bad in our lives and the bad can be really bad. We see the war, violence, abuse and brokenness on TV all the time. And why is it that a child should die from cancer or AIDS? What about the innocent teenager who was shot and killed in a drive-by? What about the car wreck that claimed the lives of a most loving, faith-filled family? In all this bad, we need to keep coming back to that fact that God's love is greater than the greatest suffering and he will lift us up in the goodness of his love today and forever if we follow him as Lord and Savior of our lives. The challenge is to see the good in the bad, to invite the goodness of God in the bad and to proclaim and live the good in the bad.

We can focus on the good or the bad. What do you focus on? I think we need a lot more meetings, small groups, church service, conversations, family meals and interactions, etc. that focus on the infinite goodness of God. We need help to deal with all the bad and the help is the good. We give so much glory to the bad and it drowns our hope and life. How about we make it our lives aim to focus on the Good News and be lifted out of the mire?

God is good- all the time. All the time- God is good. God is infinitely good to you all the time. Let him be.

Hosting Jesus

"Elijah has already come, and they did not recognize him." Matthew 17:11

The Jews held that, before the Messiah came, Elijah would return to be his herald and forerunner. He would make the world fit for the Messiah to return to. The conception was that Elijah would be a great and feared reformer who would destroy evil and set things right through the use of his awesome power.

In today's verse Jesus is referring to John the Baptist as Elijah. He tells his disciples that the people did not recognize John the Baptist as his forerunner. Jesus goes on to say that the people will not recognize him. Might we be lumped in this group who fail to recognize?

Think of what makes an excellent host/hostess. Overall, their job is to make sure the customer is fully satisfied. They offer top-notch service. They are "all" ears and eyes to make sure those whom they serve are happy. If they have any question in terms of what the guests want or need, they ask it and follow through. A good host/hostess through words, body language, attitude and action communicates the best service possible.

Jesus wants to be the guest in the home of our hearts. What kind of host are we? Do we recognize his coming? Are we "all" ears and eyes to him? Do we ask clarifying questions when we don't understand his desires? Are we good at following through with his radical demands? Do we give our whole heart, soul, mind and strength to make sure Jesus is happy and fully satisfied?

Called to be a Prophet

"Take as an example of hardship and patience, brothers and sisters, the prophets who spoke in the name of the Lord." James 5:10

We run from pain, suffering and death in our society. We try to deny, delay and distract ourselves from our mortality. The bible and the church call us to deal squarely with reality. St. Benedict reminds us to keep death before us so that we might truly know how to live. St. Francis says that it is in dying that we are born to eternal life. One who follows Christ is called to directly deal with death. Obviously, this is in radical contradiction to what society is preaching.

As with the area of suffering and death, what a Christian speaks for will often be in direct confrontation with what society is espousing. The Christian is a prophet. The Christian is a prophet who calls people back to God and his ways. Whether the word is popular or unpopular, the prophet hopes in God and declares his word faithfully.

As I think about the call to be a prophet, it is challenging. There will always be intense opposition to God in our world. How intensely will that opposition oppose me? Consider the prophets in the bible. Most were put to death. Will someone oppose me to that point?

What kind of prophet am I? Do I live and teach forgiveness and not revenge? Do I speak up for the right for all human beings to live from conception to natural death? Do I oppose gossip, slander, dirty jokes, porn, racism, prejudice, unhealthy addictions etc. in others and myself? Do I challenge laziness, infidelity, non-commitment, and narcissism? Do I challenge people to look at our own sin and death and see the need for our Savior? The list goes on and on.

The prophet, i.e. you and me, will be opposed and suffer. How much are we willing to speak up for the eternal life Jesus has offered us? What price are we willing to pay?

Hypocrisy, Belief and the Church

"Everyone who believes in him may have eternal life." John 3:15

Some people might say that it is just a bunch of hypocrites that go to church. That is exactly right! We go to church because we are hypocrites who want to become less hypocritical. Looked at in another way, it would be hypocritical to go to church if we were perfect. Why go to church if you do not need savior?

Further, how believable are we in the sometimes hypocritical lives we lead. In other words, do people see a good, redeeming and merciful God saving us. That is the point. Our forever good and merciful Jesus saves all sinners who call upon his name.

Be challenged by this statement, "The single leading cause of atheism in our world today is Christians who profess Jesus with their lips in church and walk out the door and deny him by their lifestyles." That is what an unbelieving world simply finds unbelievable.

Be a believable hypocrite!

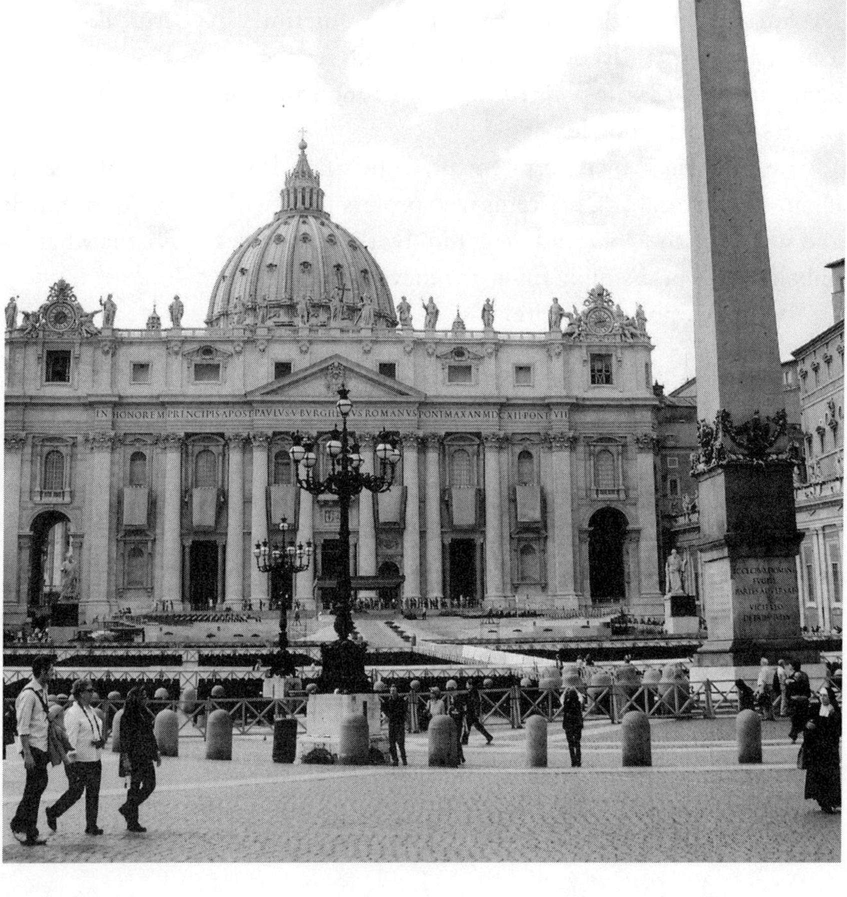

Just Five Words

"When Jesus had come into the temple" Matthew 21:23

Jesus- Faithful and True. Healer of our Souls. Prince of Peace. Emmanuel- God with us. The King of Kings and Lord of Lords. The Lamb of God who takes away all the sins of the world. Author and perfector of our faith. The Way, the Truth and the Life. Our Hope. Friend, brother, condemned, crucified, buried, risen Savior. Eternal life. Jesus.

Had come into- "Though He was in the form of God Jesus did not deem equality with God something to be grasped at. Rather, he emptied himself and took the form of a slave, being born in the likeness of you and me" (Philippians 2:6ff) He walked and talked and slept and felt and was like us in every way except sin. He became a flesh and blood human being just like you and me in order to prove God's love to us. He proved God's love to us by dying for us while we were still sinners. When Jesus walked into our lives, Eternal Life walked in. It is the illumination of the incarnation that will lead to our total transformation and the decimation and elimination of sin in our lives.

Temple- The heart of life. The center of worship. Where believers came to learn about God and give him thanks and offerings. Where people offered animal sacrifices and waited to see if their offerings were accepted and sins forgiven. Their offerings did not work and so Jesus comes to offer himself as the Lamb of God who takes away the sins of the world. It works! And now Jesus says I will make your heart my temple. I will be in the heart of all your joys and tribulations. I, Eternal Life, will walk with you wherever you go.

"Jesus, had come into, temple"- Just 5 words from the bible. 5 words. Words of Eternal Life. And we can spend so much time reading <u>anything</u> else.

Read the scriptures. Pray the scriptures. Memorize the scriptures. Come to personally know the Word of God, Jesus and LIVE!

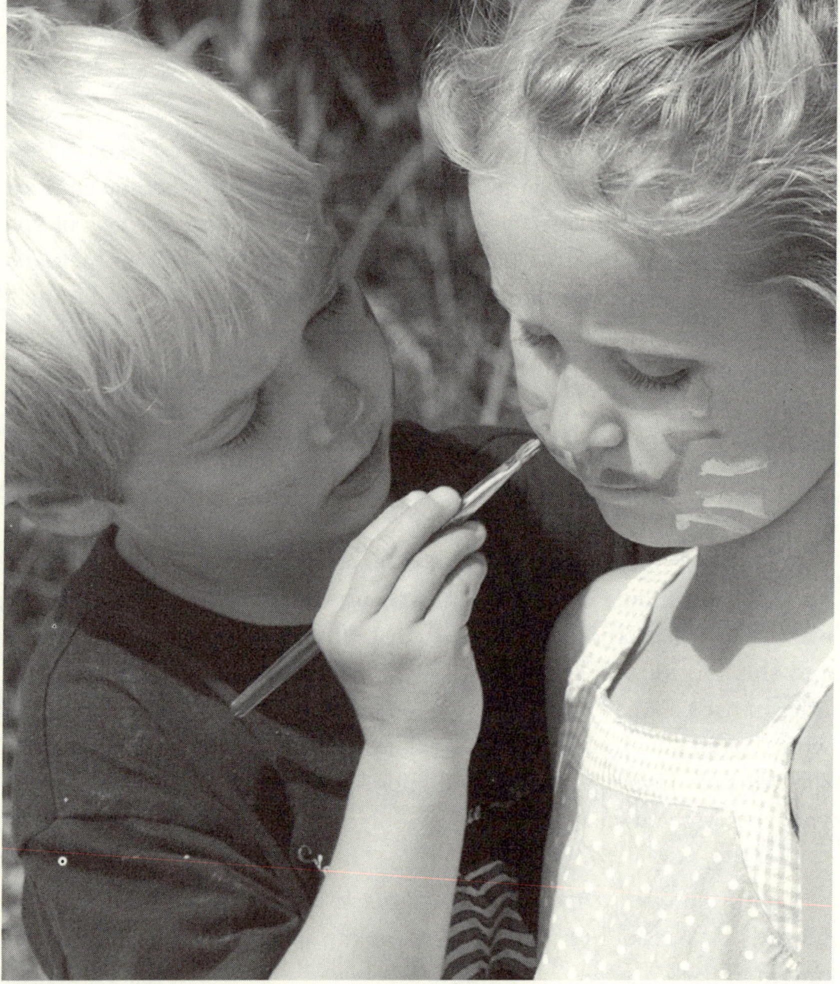

Share Your Heart

"Nor shall there be found in their mouths a deceitful tongue" Zephaniah 3:13

Growing up I guarded my heart fiercely. I protected myself and would not enter into friendships. Why? Because if you enter into a friendship and share your heart with the person there is always the possibility that they can walk on your heart. I don't know about you, but I do not like the pain of my heart being walked on. I still struggle to reveal myself in friendships because I fear that I will be somehow dishonored or disrespected.

The result of not sharing and relating on the level of what is really going on in the heart is and empty and lonely life. I lived this life, which is the exact opposite of what God has created us for. The truth of our lives is that God wants us to be in personal, meaningful and eternal relationships with him and each other. I have often been deceptive with my heart and tongue in the way I have lived life. I simply did not want to be vulnerable and have someone using what I shared against me.

One time a family was pondering with me why one of their members committed suicide. Someone suggested that the person stated they did not want to be a burden to the family. Being a "burden" to others is a thought that comes straight from hell. Society repeatedly teaches and insinuates that if you can't produce you are just extra baggage of burden. God, in direct contrast, teaches that we are total gift to each other- in good times and bad, in sickness and health, in life and death.

A deceitful tongue can be seen as a tongue that doesn't share the truth of the life behind that tongue. We live in a world that doesn't share hearts- especially men. Make it a priority to share your heart with your spouse, family, friends, and God. Seek a safe time and person to share your victories, joys, dreams, hopes, disappointments, suffering etc. Do not be deceived into thinking your life is a burden or somehow unworthy to be shared. God wants you to share the truth of your heart at least with some other people. Find that place and share your heart.

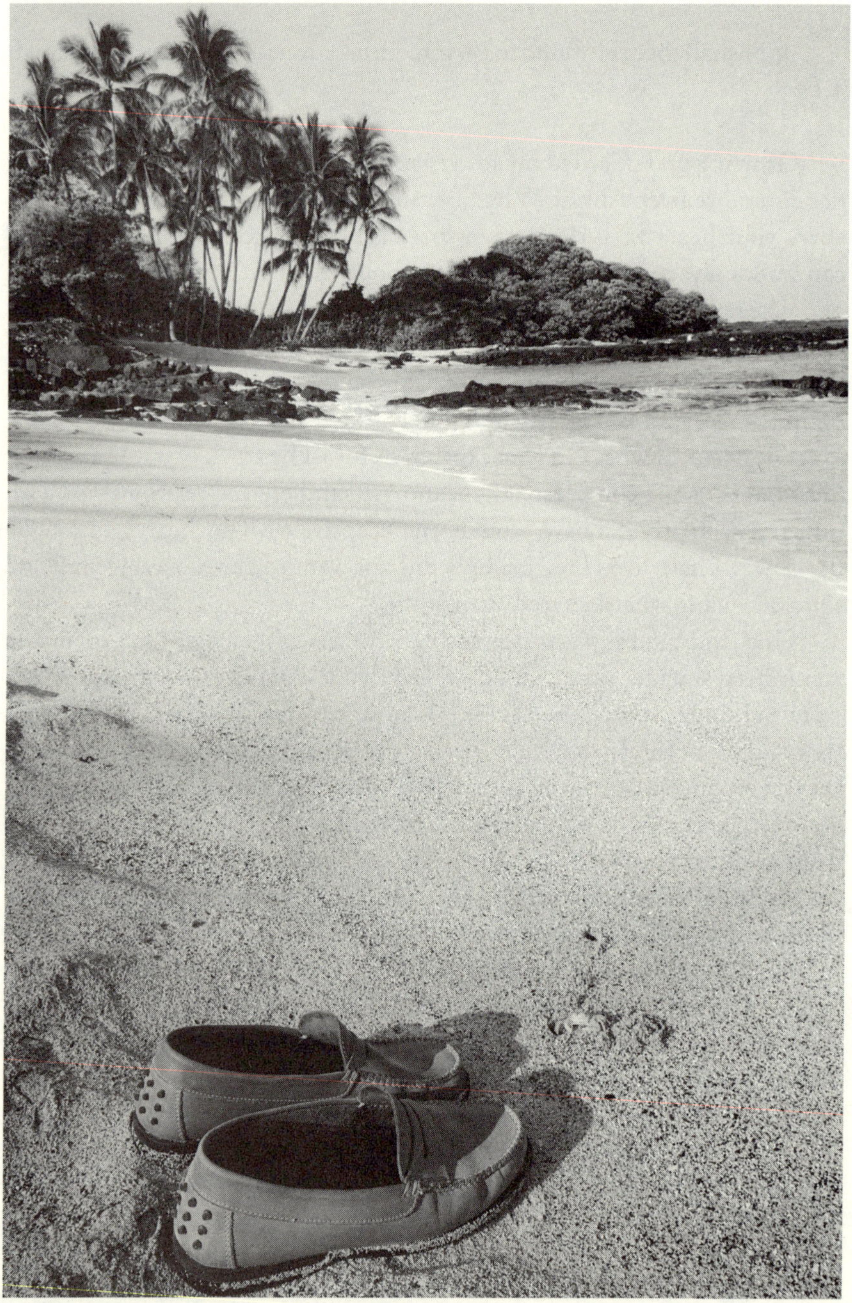

Be Least

"I tell you, among those born of women, no one is greater than John; yet the least in the Kingdom of God is greater than he." Luke 7:28

Can you imagine the scene? I think about it every time right before we receive Jesus in Eucharist at Mass when we say, 'Lamb of God, you take away the sins of the world: have mercy on us. Lamb of God, you take away the sins of the world: have mercy on us. Lamb of God, you take away the sins of the world: grant us peace.' John the Baptist is baptizing people in the Jordan River and Jesus comes along. John, the great and popular leader, sees Jesus and says, 'Behold, the Lamb of God." John, a prominent figure in the history of salvation as the forerunner of Jesus, introduces the world to the Lamb of God. Imagine the exhilaration and joy that John and others felt at the Messiah's coming. The hope of every human heart walked onto the place where John was baptizing. And John introduced us to our hope in life. John would be forever an inspiration for us because he loved and followed the Lamb of God into martyrdom. His love for Jesus was greater than his love for his own physical life. Yet, Jesus says that the least in the Kingdom of God is greater than John.

Jesus says there is no one born of women greater than John. So John is greater than Abraham, David, all the great prophets, and Paul etc. But Jesus goes on to say that you and me, i.e. the least, are greater than them all? Wow. It is so important to be least. That is a teaching that is in direct opposition to the culture's teaching to be number one.

Think of all the great ones- Francis, Mother Theresa, the martyrs. They served the rest. They were the least. It was their way of life- the way of Christ.

You are in a room with one other person. Be number two- be the least. You are in a room with two other people. Be number 3- be the least. You are in a room with three other people. Be number four- be the least. And so on, and so on...

An Angel of the Lord

"The angel of the Lord appeared" Matthew 1:20

As a priest I try to take one day off each week. I enjoy that time just to slow down a little bit and relax. I usually try to make it a leisurely day by playing tennis, running unrushed errands and enjoy not feeling "pulled" in many directions. One day off, one of my errands was to switch my wireless provider and phone. Have you ever done that? What an ordeal. I had to worry about the previous contract, "porting" my number to the new service, my credit history etc.... Well, after about 2 frustrating hours I was walking back into the store that I was switching to. I was not happy about spending the past 2 hours of wasting my precious free time on my day off. As I opened the store door I heard a car honking. I turned around and a high school kid yelled, "Fr. John, you are loved!" How cool is that? She was my angel that day and brought me back home to what life is all about- living in God's love. I reflected on the two different realities- a silly cell phone or being loved by the King of Kings. Angels keep us focused on what is really important.

"The angel of the Lord appeared"

I visited someone in the hospital who lost his wife this past year after 39 years of being happily married. He is facing some serious medical issues. He said his family and, in particular, one friend has been right there for him. He said this friend teaches him the fidelity of God. God, once again, sends an angel.

"The angel of the Lord appeared"

An angel of the Lord is a messenger who keeps us protected in the truth and hope of God. In the sense that we can bring infinite truth and hope to others, let us each consider ourselves as angels. As angels of the Lord, we can carry countless messages of God's truth and hope to all we meet. Pray about how you are to be an angel to other people in your life. Ask God to give you the most meaningful words of truth and hope to share. Be an angel of the Lord.

Present to Presence

"The virgin shall conceive, and bear a son, and shall name him Emmanuel" Isaiah 7:14

I knew a mother of 5 children from ages 5-20 that was a shining example of how to be present to others. For instance, it was not uncommon for her to stop right in the middle of making dinner to give her total attention to whoever was at the door. She always tried to make the person in front of her feel like the most important person in the world by being present to them- even if dinner had to wait.

On the other hand, I knew a man who never seemed to be present in conversation. It always seemed like he was somewhere else in his thoughts. His lack of presence did not make me feel too important.

In Isaiah 7:14, we read Isaiah's prophecy that the virgin will give to us a son who will be called Emmanuel, meaning, "God with us." The prophecy has been totally fulfilled because Jesus died and rose from the dead and will be totally present to each of us forever! Jesus knows everything about us- he has got every hair on our head counted (For those who are hair challenged- that doesn't mean he knows or loves you less!) He has searched us through and through and wants to lift us up to the fullness of life in his love.

Everybody else's love pales compared to infinite, ever-present love of Jesus. So why, then, do we let days go by without being present to his presence? Let us learn the details of Jesus' life. That is when he will teach us to be present to ourselves and others. Learn to be present as Jesus is present. I know I really struggle with this. Let us help each other to remember that the greatest gift we can give each other is total, loving presence.

Don't Compare

"Do not be afraid, Mary, for you have found favor with God" Luke 1:29

The angel announces to Mary she has found favor with God. She is highly favored among women because God has chosen her to conceive and give birth to Jesus. Jesus will be the Savior for all people and of his kingdom there will be no end. A fair question to ask in all of this is, "Does that mean that God loves Mary more than any other mother because he chose her over every other woman to be the mother of Jesus?"

I know I can get into trouble when I start comparing myself to other people as a way of defining my love-ability. There will always be someone who seems more favored by God. There will always be someone who is brighter, faster, funnier, better at reaching out, more humble, or whatever etc.… If I think I have to be the best and brightest to win the favor of God's love, I will be frustrated to no end.

Does God love Mary more than you and me? No. God is not fickle. He loves each of us indiscriminately and totally. While Mary was chosen as a key figure in salvation history that doesn't mean God has chosen her over us to know his love. God chooses all. He equally wants all people to be with him forever.

Do not compare, lest you be eternally let down because you can never measure up. There will always be someone who is better looking, smarter and more talented. Be your beautiful self and live fully the person God made you to be.

Sacrifice

"After Samuel's father had sacrificed the young bull" 1 Samuel 1:25

I have a picture in my office of my dad when he was about my age. I ask people who they think it is and half of them say me and the other half say dad. One of the things I think of when I see that picture is sacrifice. Dad worked 40 years as a children's dentist to feed, cloth, raise, insure, and educate eight boys. Being a dentist is one of the most stressful jobs and I thank dad for his sacrifice for my brothers and me.

One year there was a woman in our RCIA (a eight month process of classes and formation whereby an adult converts to the Catholic faith) who drove two hours each way weekly in order to come to class. She missed only one class and was serious about wanting to live her faith. It took time, money, effort and dedication for her conversion. Needless to say, we are all blessed by her sacrifice.

We recall Samuel's father sacrifices a bull to God for his son. Let us think about our own sacrifices to God. What return shall we make to God who has given us every breath and heartbeat? St. Maria Goretti was murdered because she would not sacrifice her virginity to the man who tried to take it from her. How much more is my sacrifice to God than an hour on Sunday's?

We are made for sacrifice. It is in the heart of our DNA. We want to give every ounce of our being away to pour out our lives in loving others. In other words, we want to be just like Jesus! We find our deepest happiness in giving our lives away for the good of all people.

Jesus only wants one thing from us – everything!

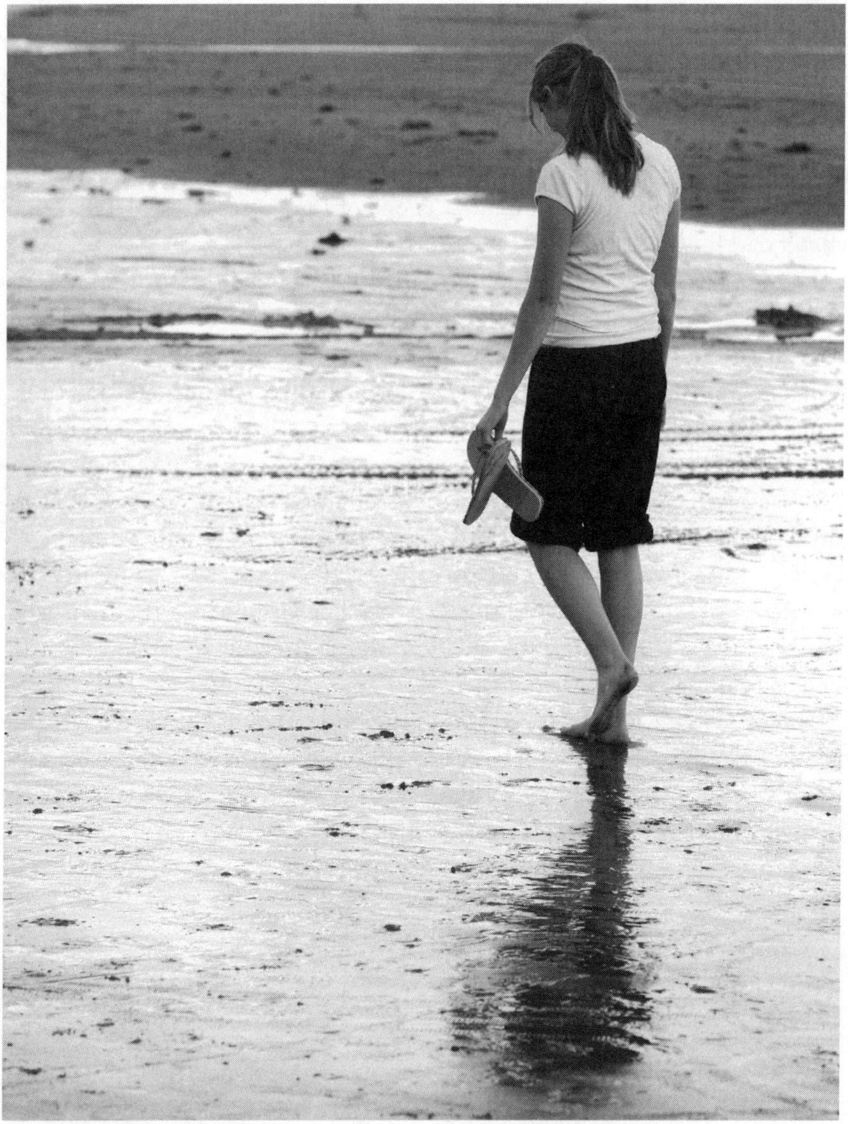

Arise, My Beloved and Beautiful One, and Come

"My lover speaks; he says to me, 'Arise, my beloved, my dove, my beautiful one, and come.'" Song of Songs 2:10

The book of the Song of Songs, meaning the greatest of songs, is about the mutual love of the Lord and his people. The Lord is the lover and we are the beloved. The Lord woo's us to himself where he can captivate and inebriate us with his presence. The lover seeks to share everything with the beloved. His constant beckoning is, "Arise, my beautiful and beloved one, come."

Many people do not have the hope, will, energy or desire to arise and face the day. I know I have my days and times I do not want to "arise" to. Maybe the work or pressure is just too much or the suffering is too heavy. Maybe joy, purpose and meaning have flown away. In faith we must remember that our Lord and lover is constantly wooing us, "Arise, my beloved and beautiful one, come."

There are many, many voices out there that say, "Arise and come to me and I will give you love and peace." Which ones have we followed? Money, sex, power? There is only one voice that doesn't lie and break its promises. It is the Lord and he delivers. He is love and he inebriates us with it when we are truly in his presence. So, that is the key- to be truly in his presence.

Seek his presence. Search the bible and see how the Lord is wooing you. See the Lord pouring out his love for you in every page and verse of the scriptures. Be captivated and inebriated in his everlasting love for you. The Lord is the Lover and you are the beloved. Be who you are- beloved.

Listen to the eternal song of the Lord to you, "Arise, my beloved, my dove, my beautiful one, and come."

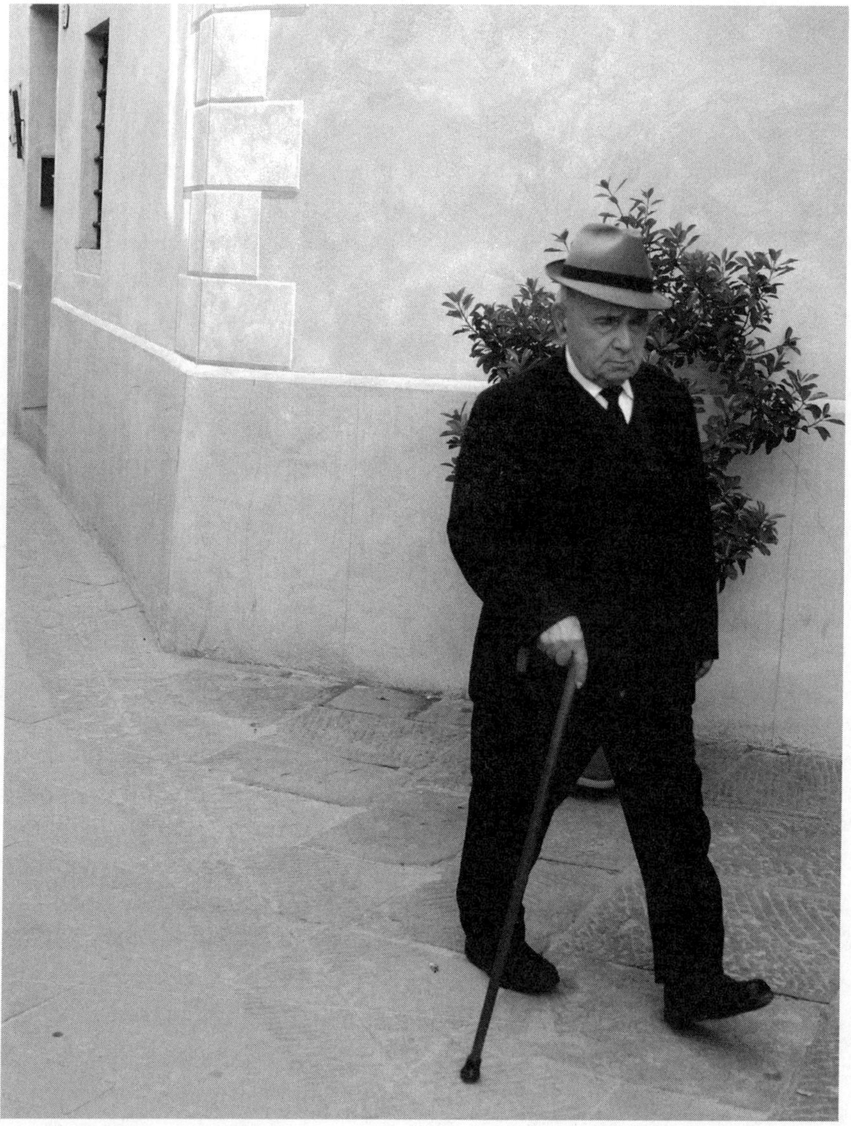

Good News Messengers

"Thus says the Lord God: Lo, I am sending a messenger to prepare the way before me." Malachi 3:1

Good News! God becomes flesh and dwells among us. In the first chapter of John it is translated that the word "pitched" his tent among us. He is right in the middle of us. He is alive, active and seeks to transform us into the holiness of God.

Do we see how Jesus is actively reaching out to us and the world offering his loving salvation? We are all called to be messengers that prepare his way but if we can't see and don't talk about the way that Jesus is reaching out to us day to day then how convincing of a messenger are we going to be? If Jesus, who is life itself, is right in the middle of us and we can't talk about him then whose heart can we prepare to accept him?

I continually challenge people to share how they had seen the Risen Jesus in their life. The whole point is that if Jesus is active, alive, in the middle of us, seeking to rule our hearts in perfect love etc., then why aren't we able to speak of this Good News? The Good News is that Jesus has come to save sinners like you and me that we might live in his love forever. And the meaning of our lives is that we are to be Good News messengers. We have so much "news" going on each day through the TV, newspaper, Internet, magazines that has nothing to do with the "Good News." We gobble it up and become depressed. Wouldn't it be wonderful if the five o'clock news started and was full of stories of how people came to experience the reality and love of Christ that day? What people really, really want is the "Good News" that Jesus has pitched his tent among us, in the middle of our family's home, relationships, work, school, games and sin, to save us.

The dismissal at the end of Mass in Latin is, "Ite, missa est" which means, "Go, you are sent." Yes, you and I are sent forward in the power of the Word and the Eucharist. We are empowered by the all-powerful one to unceasingly proclaim Jesus to a fallen world. We are "Good News" messengers who keep talking about how Jesus is in the middle of our lives to forgive us and lift us up to life everlasting.

Go now, you are sent to prepare hearts for Jesus.

Run to God

"The dawn from on high shall break upon us" Luke 1:79

The dawn of everlasting light shines in our world but how might we have blocked its transforming power from our hearts?

One time I made a hospital visit to anoint a sick person. There were a few other people in the room visiting, one who was very unsettled. As soon as we moved to a prayerful time of anointing and Eucharist, this person literally bolted from the room. The everlasting light was coming and the person went running. Running away from his light and not to his light puts our soul in grave jeopardy. The "one fleeing the light" came back to the room right before I left. I looked at this person right in the eyes and said, "Don't run from God. Don't run from God."

The dawn from on high is the everlasting light of God's love that seeks out sinners. It is a piercing light that looks into every corner of who we are and asks us to surrender all of our sinfulness to God so that we might live in peace. It can be a quite painful and arduous journey to move from a life of sin to love but that is what we desire. The journey to God's way of love cannot happen without the piercing, convicting and transforming dawn from on high.

Don't run from God. Don't run from light. Wake up each day with a plan of how you are going to run to him. Run to him in prayer. Run to him and find him in your family. Run to him in your service. Run to him in the poor. Run to his fullness in the Eucharist. Run to him in suffering. Run to his everlasting light in the sacrament of reconciliation.

Run to God. Run to the dawn from on high. Make that the image of your life. It is the most loving thing you can do for yourself and the world.

Naming

"God looked at everything he made and he found it very good." Gen. 1:31

When God finished creating us, he gasped in delight and found us very good (Genesis 1:31). This is called the Original Blessing. But this blessing was greatly clouded through sin so Jesus had to come to give God's true view of us. And that view is once again revealed at Jesus' baptism. Upon coming out of the water, God the Gather says to Jesus, "You are my Beloved Son, on you my favor rests." And that is how God names us. We are God's beloved daughters and sons on whom his favor rests! He gasps in delight for us and h finds us very good.

How have others named you in your life? I remember my friend telling me how his fourth grade teacher told him he was stupid because he did not do well in school. Later in life, my friend learned that he was a visual learner, not a verbal leaner. So, he learned to learn visually. The happy ending of the story is that he is now a very successful psychologist. What names have others given you that you have taken on? Some possibilities are: bright, loving, funny, creative, giving, stupid, loser, jerk, etc.. Spend some time writing those down. I know that I can call myself dumb.

OK. Once you have your list, let us exam any negative name under the microscope of the following sentence. "All that matters is what Jesus Christ thinks about you." So, if that is all that matters – find out what Jesus Christ thinks about you. In his infinite love for you, he names you in infinite loving ways. Seek his names for you the scriptures, prayer, the community of believers and any way it will come to you. Know how Jesus names you – it is all that matters!.

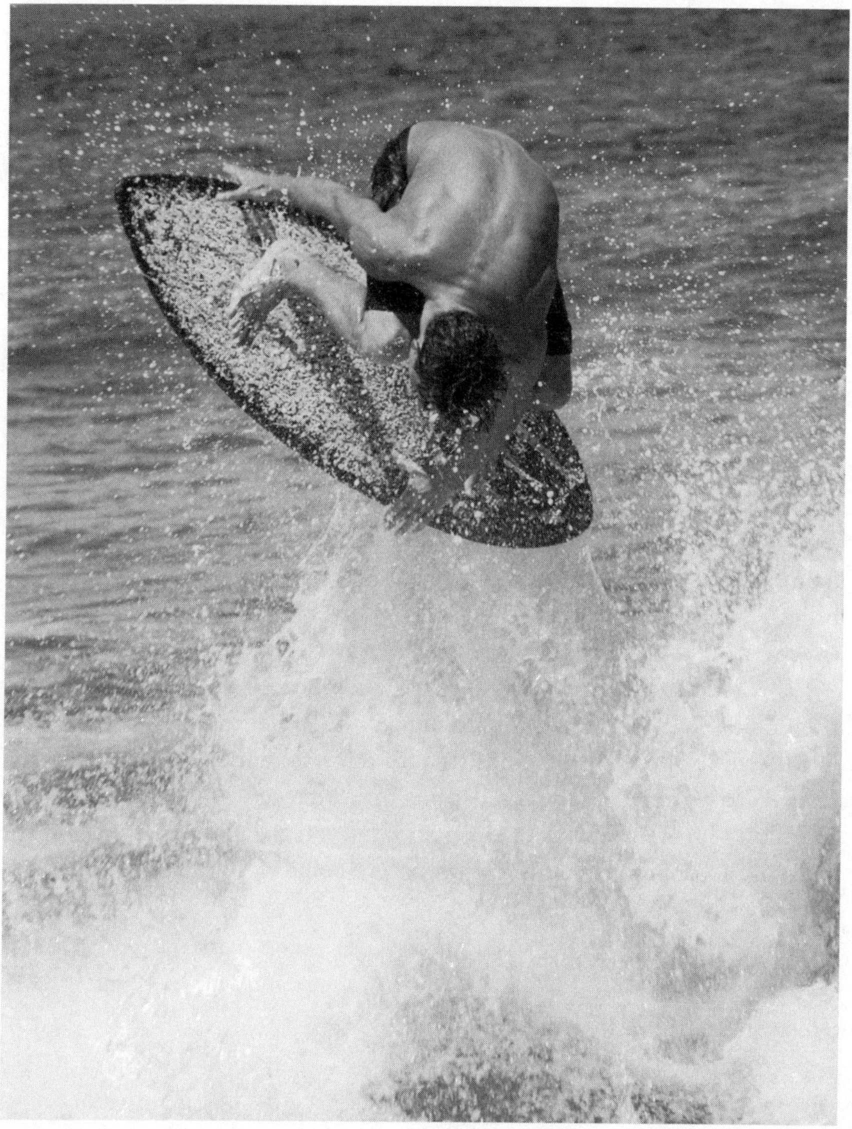

Outside the Box

"For a child is born to us, a son is given us" Isaiah 9:3

One time I went to a basketball tournament. When the final game ended at 11:30pm I headed back to my car in the 38 degree night wind. It took about ten minutes to get to my car and when I arrived it was not there. Someone had stolen it-or so I thought. I looked to find my car for about 20 minutes to no avail. I remembered parking my car on a specific street facing west. Should I call the cops? I was worried, tired, cold, and mostly frustrated. Then I thought I should think outside of "the box." I thought I parked my car facing west. I was in a rush to get to the game after work. Maybe there were a lot more possibilities to solve my problem. Well, I looked around for about five minutes on the same street I had parked. Maybe I did not park my car facing west. Maybe it was facing east. And, sure enough, I found it facing east. I figured I passed it three or four times on my original search because I was so focused on finding my car in one place – facing west. I laughed and thanked God I finally got our of my rut of thinking inside "the box."

I think God wants us all to Think outside of "the box" when we look for Jesus.

Watch for Jesus with the eyes of your heart. Do not focus on just one place. Do not get stuck in the rut of limited thinking. Think outside "the box." The possibilities are endless. The child is with you now. The child is with the next person you encounter. The child is everywhere. The child wants us to pick him up with our hearts.

Think outside "the box." Look outside "the box." Pick Jesus up with the eyes of your heart. Meeting Jesus in your life is the most non-neutral experience you will ever know. I pray that the whole of your life will be filled with the non-neutrality of Jesus. May you see Jesus born in the "box" of the stable and everywhere outside the "box" of the stable and most especially may you see Jesus born in your heart.

Be Holy

"He who remains in Zion and he who is left in Jerusalem will be called Holy" Isaiah 4:3

God desires us to be "holy." Holiness is His will for us. In the liturgy, with all believers, we cry out to Jesus, "Holy, Holy, Holy." With his whole being, Jesus cries out to us, "<u>Be</u> Holy, Holy, Holy."

The word "holy" means "different". Jesus was much different than what many people thought he would be. Instead of conquering evil domination by brute force, he hung on a cross. He ushered in the Kingdom of God through non-violence. He could have retaliated when injured but his whole life shouted, "Father, forgive them for they know not what they do." Jesus was "different, different, different" and he invites us to be "different, different, different."

Reflect on how you are different because Jesus is in your life. Know the differences he has made and be thankful for them. Each day there are so many people around you that do not know the difference of love and forgiveness in their lives. Be ever ready to share the love, forgiveness and eternal difference Jesus has made in your life.

There is nothing as beautiful as when a believer believes and becomes holy as Jesus is holy.

Let us Pray: Jesus, I want to be like you. I want to live as you lived. Fill and fire me with your Holy Spirit that I may be Holy as you are Holy. Amen.

PIG - Peace in God

"Jesus came and stood in their midst and said to them, "Peace be with you." John 20:19

A father and his son were talking about what they liked the most for breakfast. The father said he liked bacon and the son shared that his favorite was eggs. The son asked the father why he liked bacon the best and the father said, "In order to be able to even enjoy the great taste of bacon I realized what had to happen. The pig had to sacrifice his life for me. I am very aware how the pig had to give up everything so that I could enjoy the gift of bacon. I look at it as a total investment for me. The pig gives his life in order that I can have my favorite breakfast food. The chicken, on the other hand, does not give up his life. The total sacrifice and investment is not there. It just lays the egg and moves on with its day."

At this point I bet you are getting the connection. Jesus is totally invested in you. For you to enjoy what God wants for you, Jesus had to sacrifice his life. Jesus came to give us the best – uncontained, unrestrained, undiscriminating, overflowing, relentless love, life, goodness, beauty, joy, peace, etc. – by dying for you and me. And the whole of our existence is about becoming fully aware of that reality.

As we become more fully aware of Jesus' total sacrifice and just what he has invested in us, peace flows through us and fills us and calms us. God is in control. Everything has a purpose. Through grace and the Holy Spirit we are being lead to a land where peace will reign forever.

How did I come up with an acronym for PIG? Well, you know that as a priest I want to be the best teacher that I can be. As a teacher, I want people to remember the things of God and go deeper and deeper and providing acronyms is one way of trying to be a good teacher. So, as I taught about the total investment and sacrifice of the pig reminding us of the ultimate sacrifice of Jesus, a member of my flock told me that I needed to come up with an acronym for PIG. It took about five seconds and I thought, "Peace in God." Yep, when we know Jesus' sacrifice for us that we might enjoy eternal life, we will have peace. Peace in God.

Forever, Jesus stands in front of you and says, "Peace be with you."

May you become fully aware of what Jesus is eternally offering you. He put his life on it!

I wish you PIG. I wish you Peace in God.

Prayers

MY FLESH

My Child,

I ache for you. I seek you all through the night and all the day long. Since the time you were conceived in your mother's womb, I have looked upon you with infinite love and affection. There has never been one moment in your life where I have not loved you freely, totally and eternally. There will never be a moment where I will not love you infinitely. Do you know my infinite love is present and personal for you with every breath you take? Believe, please believe. Open your heart to me. Give me your sufferings and tears. When you suffer and cry, so do I. I suffer with you. I love you. I long for you. I cry for your love.

How badly do I want your love and friendship? How much do I long for you? I gave you my body. I gave you my body and they crucified it. They took my flesh and whipped it. The whips had metal hooks and they ripped my flesh from my bones. The pain was excruciating but I did it for you. They destroyed my flesh but they did not destroy my love for you. My love for you is forever and ever. Yes, the bread I give is my flesh for the life of the world. Yes, the bread I give is my flesh for you. Believe. Believe in me. Believe in my love for you in the Eucharist.

I love you,
Jesus

KNOW AND MAKE KNOWN

Know you are valued, and value.
Know you are forgiven, and forgive.
Know you are loved, and love.
Know you are fed, and feed.
Know you are clothed, and clothe.
Know you are taught, and teach.
Know you are given to, and give.
Know you are cared for, and care.

Know you are reverenced, and reverence.
Know you are blessed, and bless.
Know you are called, and call.
Know you are chosen, and choose.
Know you are redeemed, and redeem.
Know you are healed, and heal.
Know you are prized, and prize.
Know you are embraced, and embrace.
Know you are honored, and honor.
Know you are on a journey to heaven and share that good news with others.
Know that you belong to God.
Know God and make Him known.

We are called to be Anawim like Mary the Mother of God. "Anawim" is Hebrew for, "little ones who rejoice in their dependence on the Lord." Yes, we are "little ones" who rejoice in our *utter dependence* on the Lord who invites us to share in His Kingdom and Reign. Wow! Holy Mary, Mother of God and our Mother, teaches us to be Anawim. (Read Luke 1:45-55) She shows us the way.

ANAWIM

>   Be Anawim
>   It will set you free
>   Be Anawim like Mary Our Mother
>   Bow before the King of ALL
>   Full of love, kindness and goodness
>   For all his "little ones"
>   Be filled with the One who made the stars,
>   Wind and sea and all they hold
>   Be filled to the overflowing
>   Be Anawim